Dmitry Furmanov

CHAPAYEV

University Press of the Pacific
Honolulu, Hawaii

Chapayev

by
Dmitry Furmanov

ISBN: 0-89875-388-0

Copyright © 2001 by University Press of the Pacific

Reprinted from the original edition

University Press of the Pacific
Honolulu, Hawaii
http://www.universitypressofthepacific.com

All rights reserved, including the right to reproduce this book, or portions thereof, in any form.

In order to make original editions of historical works available to scholars at an economical price, this facsimile of the original edition is reproduced from the best available copy and has been digitally enhanced to improve legibility, but the text remains unaltered to retain historical authenticity.

FURMANOV'S *CHAPAYEV*

This book is a novel about the gifted and popular Civil War hero and commander Vasily Ivanovich Chapayev (1887-1919), about the role of the Party in educating the people in the communist spirit.

The time is 1919, when the young Soviet republic fought foreign invaders and the whiteguards Backed by the Entente, Kolchak launched a major offensive on the Eastern Front which ended in total disaster. The book depicts the valiant record of the 25th Division, headed by Chapayev, in these battles.

Just before the Kolchak offensive, the Chapayev Division was reinforced by a detachment of weavers from the town of Ivanovo-Voznesensk, who had volunteered for active service in answer to Lenin's call for an all-out effort against Kolchak. The first chapter of the book gives a description of the departure of this detachment for the Eastern Front. Among the workers was Furmanov himself, who is introduced to the reader as Fyodor Klichkov. A workers' detachment leaving for the front to join peasant regiments—this fact reveals one of the most essential traits of the socialist revolution: the leading part played by the revolutionary proletariat in its alliance with the peasant masses. Throughout his novel Furmanov stresses the importance of the role played by Ivanovo-Voznesensk weavers, in their "green helmets with red stars," in the war record of the Chapayev Division, in directing its guerrilla enthusiasm along an uncompromisingly straight revolutionary road.

Chapayev's outstanding talents of military leader and organizer blossomed out in the rigorous conditions of the front

Chapayev was a people's hero More fully than any one else, Furmanov wrote, did he embody the raw and heroic mass of his comrades-in-arms.

Neither love of fame nor an adventurous spirit motivated Chapayev in his revolutionary struggle, but a conscious hatred for the enemies of the working people. In naïve and artless words he describes his life to Klichkov: his hungry and joyless childhood, the humiliations suffered by a soldier in the tsarist army, his attempt to seek the truth in books and among "sensible people"—the ordinary, "colourless" life story of a man who is driven by all the circumstances, the privations and events of his personal life towards active protest. The Revolution awakened in Chapayev a sense of human dignity, taught him to value himself, his life, so precious for his people. "I don't want to give up my life in vain, brother," says Chapayev, who is ever ready to sacrifice himself for his beloved country in a just cause.

Furmanov glorifies not the devil-may-care guerrilla in Chapayev but his sterling courage, born of an awareness of the great goals of the fight waged by his people.

Such are the words with which Furmanov paints Chapayev's portrait as a commander: "It was indeed heroism to have fused this division into a single unit with one burning desire, to have made it believe in its invincibility, and to have taught it to bear the hardships and privations of the march with patience, and even with contempt. He had given the division its commanders; he had selected and tempered them, and he had instilled into them his own impetuous will; he had rallied them round him and concentrated their thoughts on one aim—victory."

Furmanov is not afraid to "belittle" Chapayev by shearing him of the usual attributes of a book hero. The novel lays emphasis on Chapayev's common outward appearance; at times he is presented to the reader in surroundings far from "heroic," in everyday scenes. To quote Furmanov himself, his hero is portrayed with a soberly realistic brush, without leaving out "any human rubbish." This does not detract from the attractiveness and heroic essence of the great soldier. It is a wonderful and noble portrait that is shown to the reader

Depicting his hero during the seething everyday activities at the front, Furmanov shows Chapayev in situations which best reveal his qualities of military leader. A pair of compasses in his hand, he studies the scene of a future battle and works on the plan of a new offensive. Now the battle is at its height, and Chapayev, riding at full gallop, shouts out brief and pointed orders in his imperious manner, catches the replies of his commanders, and flies from flank to flank And when the firing became heavier than ever, Chapayev inspired his men by his very presence, by an encouraging word, instilling confidence in victory in one and all.

But we see Chapayev not only studying his map or in the thick of battle. Between battles, with equal enthusiasm he takes up such peaceful affairs as aid to the local Soviets, to the starving and needy, to peasants who come to him with complaints.

Chapayev's range of activity is boundless. He is never an indifferent onlooker when the vital interests of the people are at stake

An insatiable thirst for knowledge is strongly pronounced in Chapayev. No matter how intense the life at the front might be, he seizes every opportunity of learning from his commissar, of resolving his doubts and questions; he does his best to improve his reading and writing, and picks up everything he can in his quest for knowledge.

Chapayev's portrait embodies the best traits of the Russian character His speech at times approaches the poetic spoken language of folklore. "His soul is full of song," wrote Furmanov in his diary.

However, Furmanov nowhere attempts to idealize his hero, does not gloss over his weaknesses—arbitrariness, hot-headedness, lack of self-discipline. The contradictions in Chapayev's character are not depicted as a haphazard combination of positive and negative traits but as genuine life-like contradictions typical of a representative of the peasant masses, whose world-view undergoes a profound change, the new ousting the survivals of the capitalist past.

Furmanov portrays his hero in dynamic development Chapayev is not a static figure. As the narrative proceeds, Furmanov reveals new aspects in him, new attitudes and qualities of his nature.

This principle of gradual portrayal determines the general construction of the novel. Furmanov showed how, in the fight for the motherland, together with his division, Chapayev's character matured.

Chapayev's commissar, Klichkov, who is a symbol of Party leadership in the book, played a most important part in moulding his political views. The commander's ideological growth is bound up with his increasing trust in his commissar. This creative co-operation between the Party and the people, typified in that between Chapayev and Klichkov, was and remains a source of the triumphs and invincibility of the Soviet state.

Without false heroics, stylistic trickery, or formalistic twists, Furmanov tells in a simple and straightforward manner of the remarkable courage of Soviet people defending their socialist motherland and fulfilling their revolutionary duty in a modest but selfless manner.

Furmanov's simplicity and ease of form stem from his clear and profound understanding of historical processes, his knowledge of the life he depicts and his striving to write for the broad masses of the working people.

Dmitry Furmanov, the commissar of the Chapayev Division, wrote his novel drawing largely on his diaries, personal observations, reminiscences of his contemporaries, and historical archives. But the documentary truth of *Chapayev* did not restrict the ideological and artistic merits of the novel: Furmanov created a work of immense capacity, far-reaching generalizations, a book about the revolutionary people—creator of their own history and their own heroes.

Chapayev, written while Soviet literature was yet in its infancy, has become a heroic epic of the socialist revolution

L. POLYAK

CONTENTS

	Page
Preface	5
I. THE WORKERS' DETACHMENT	11
II. THE STEPPE	28
III. URALSK	46
IV. ALEXANDROV-GAI	59
V. CHAPAYEV	71
VI. THE BATTLE OF SLOMIKHINSKAYA	92
VII. ON THE ROAD	130
VIII. AGAINST KOLCHAK	158
IX. BEFORE BATTLE	173
X. ON THE MARCH TO BUGURUSLAN	188
XI. ON THE MARCH TO BELEBEI	228
XII. FORWARD	272
XIII. UFA	300
XIV. THE RELIEF OF URALSK	324
XV. FINALE	335

I

THE WORKERS' DETACHMENT

There was a jam at the railway station. The platform was black with people, and it was all the Red Army cordon could do to hold back the excited, rumbling crowd. At midnight, the workers' detachment Frunze had mustered was to set out against Kolchak. From all the Ivanovo-Voznesensk cotton-mills and plants, the workers had come down to see off their mates, their brothers, fathers and sons.

The new "soldiers" were funny somehow—they were so clumsy, so naïve. Many had stepped into a soldier's uniform for the first time. Their great-coats did not sit well, but bulged out everywhere like dough puffed up in a kneading-trough. But what of that? It didn't keep the lads from being brave fellows, all the same. One had pulled in his belt till he had no more waist than a wasp;

the poor chap could hardly breathe, but he was strutting jauntily along, his hob-nailed heels ringing. Another was importantly holding forth to his neighbour with the devil-may-care air of an old soldier, his hand placed carelessly on the hilt of his clumsily-belted sword. A third, with a cartridge-belt draped snake-like across his chest, a revolver hung on his left hip and a couple of hand grenades on his right, was tearing from one end of the platform to the other in his warlike outfit, showing off before his friends, relatives and acquaintances.

The black, mighty crowd of workers gazed at them and talked about them with love, pride and frank admiration.

"They'll learn, mate, they'll learn—when they get to the front, they'll find out what it's all about damn quick."

"Right you are. The front's not a game of knuckle-bones!"

And all of them fidgeted and laughed and stretched their necks.

"You'd never know Terenty there. Back in the pickling shop he used to be smeared up black as a kettle, and now look at him—quite the dandy."

"He's a swell, all right—got a real general's sword —look at the way it's dragging on the ground."

"Terenty!" someone laughed. "You'd better tuck that sword in your pocket—the Cossacks'll take it away from you!" The crowd greeted this with a burst of boisterous guffaws.

"Your ma'll take it to chop up cabbage!"

"You'll stumble on it and break it, Terenty!"

"You'll cut your dainty finger—you half-baked general!"

"Oh, my!" "Ha, ha!" "Ho, ho, ho!"

Terenty Bochkin, a friendly and good-natured lad of about twenty-eight, red-headed and freckled, glanced round at these jokes, and with a sheepish grin hauled his sword back in place.

"I'll—I'll show you!" he threatened the crowd, in his confusion not quite knowing how to defend himself against the gale of jokes and gibes.

"What'll you show us, Terenty? What'll you show us, eh?" roared the irrepressible wits.

"Here's some sun-flower seeds to chew on, soldier boy."

"They must have taken that coat of yours off a calf!"

"Ha, ha, ha!" "Ho, ho, ho!"

Terenty stalked off towards the carriages, grinning self-consciously, and disappeared within the grey, seething mass of Red Army men.

Every time some awkward young chap was noticed he at once became the butt for a volley of biting jokes spread thick with spicy sarcasm. And then, sober, serious talk would again prevail. A nervous alarm, solemn and tense, quivered in the air. The mood changed rapidly, and the talk jumped from one thing to another in the crowd.

The crowd hummed with talk. "If it comes to it, we'll drag the devil right out of hell. Everybody was whining —no boots, no uniforms, nothing to shoot with—and now, take a look!" The speaker jerked a thumb at the carriages to show that it was the Red Army men he was talking about. "We must have outfitted a thousand."

"How many, d'you say?"

"A whole thousand, there must be, and more are being got together and we've got everything ready for them. You can find anything if you want to bad enough —no time for scratching your belly now, mate. We're in for plenty now."

"Things have come to a pretty pass, all right," echoed a hoarse bass.

"Of course they have. That Kolchak fellow's pushing for all he's worth. And now trouble's brewing in the Urals."

"Ah, me," sighed a little old man in a short fur-trimmed jacket; he was puckered up like a dried mushroom, and his face was blue with the cold.

"That's right. How're things going to turn out with us now? They *have* got pretty bad," quavered a cheerless, aggrieved little voice.

Someone answered him sternly: "Who can say what's coming? Things don't turn out by themselves—you've got to make them turn out. This is a beginning—this thousand soldier lads—this is a great thing, mate, a great thing! The papers say there's too few workers in the army, they're needed there. The workingman's got more sense than anybody. Take our Pavlushka Lopar for instance—that chap's made of iron, you might say, and got a head on him—they won't cook *his* goose, you can bet."

"Don't we know it!"

"Yes, they're not like the peasants. Look at Marfa Kozhanaya, there. She's no dried herring for you. I expect she could make some men look like babes."

Marfa, a weaver, heard her name mentioned, and turning quickly, came up to the speakers. Broad in the shoulders and wide in her slightly pock-marked face, she had wide-open blue eyes, and looked considerably younger than her age—thirty-five. She was wearing a new uniform—pants, boots, tunic and all; her hair was cropped, and a cap was perched on the very back of her head.

"Why're you jerking my rope?" she demanded.

"Why should we jerk your rope—you'll come yourself. I was saying that our Kozhanaya was no woman, but an unbroken mare."

"So I'm a mare, am I?"

"Well, what are you, then?" And then, suddenly dropping his bantering tone: "I say you'll make a fine soldier—that's what I say."

"Fine soldier or not, I've got to go."

"Of course you've got to." He was silent a moment, and then added. "Well, and what about things at home?"

"What d'you mean, 'at home'?"

"I mean your own affairs."

"Affairs, affairs—" Marfa made a helpless gesture. "I put the kids in a children's home—what else could I do with them?"

"That's right—what could you do with them?" He drew a deep breath, and said in a sympathetic husky voice, "Well, we'll look after them, Marfa, don't you worry. We'll look after them, all right. That's our job now—to work for you. The time may come, and then we, too—eh?"

"You're right, there," nodded Marfa. "It's sure to turn out that way—do you think one detachment'll be enough? It's bound to be that way."

"The lads there are getting a bit anxious." The speaker nodded towards the carriages.

"Why not?" answered Marfa. "All they want is to get away as soon as they can—they're all tired of waiting. They keep saying the same thing. 'Let's get going —what're we waiting for?'—Hey, Andreyev," Marfa shouted to someone passing. "What do they say there about starting?"

A Petrograd turner, but recently arrived in Ivanovo, twenty-three years old, with the darkest of darkblue eyes in a pale face, slender and agile, wearing a worn, brown army great-coat, and with a Red Army helmet on his head—that was Andreyev. He marched up to Marfa, as though making a report, clicked his heels, saluted, and with his serious fine eyes boring into Marfa's, declaimed without the least hint of a smile:

15

"I have the honour to inform your Excellency that the train will leave in forty minutes!"

Marfa jerked him by the sleeve. "Are you going to say good-bye, or not? The fellows are waiting—there ought to be some kind of farewell speeches, I suppose. Where's Klichkov? What's he gone and done with himself?"

Andreyev again saluted, and answered distinctly in the same unruffled tone, "He's rinsing his belly with tea, your Excellency!"

Marfa slapped his hand. "Cut it, you devil—have you gone plumb crazy? A fine general you've found."

He at once dropped his pose, and said in his own clear, ringing voice:

"Marfa darling! You won't be speechifying yourself, eh?"

Marfa didn't answer him, but raising herself on tiptoe looked over the heads of the crowd:

"That must be them coming there."

Those standing near also raised themselves on tiptoe and stretched their necks in the direction in which Marfa was looking. Three people were walking along, closely ringed about by the crowd. Lopar stood out distinctly—tall and slim, with long black hair and shining eyes. He walked along passing out a hello to this one and that, so gangling and clumsy that he seemed to be falling over his own feet.

Beside him was Yelena Kunitsina, a weaver of twenty-two, whom everybody loved for her simple, sensible talk and clear mind, and for her beautiful, strong voice which the weavers had heard so often at meetings. She had not yet put on a Red Army helmet, but had a kerchief tied round her head; instead of a soldier's great-coat she was wearing a thin little black coat—and this, mind you, in the January frost. A quiet joy was imprinted on her pale, serious face.

Beside Yelena, was Fyodor Klichkov. He was not a

weaver, not a worker at all. Not long ago he had come back from Moscow, got stuck here, begun to feel at home, and was running around giving lessons, living like a bird on what he could pick up. He had once been a student. During the Revolution, he had quickly discovered that he was a good organizer, and at meetings would talk enthusiastically, interestingly, and with great feeling, though not always with the same good sense. The workers were on close terms with Klichkov; they liked him and looked on him as one of themselves.

At sight of Lopar, Kunitsina and Klichkov, the crowd on the platform surged forward and a loud whisper ran through it:

"I expect the speeches'll begin now."

"The train'll soon be leaving."

"It's about time to be saying good-bye—time to go home to bed."

"We'll kiss them good-bye now—and it'll be all over."

"There goes the bell!"

"That's the first, isn't it?"

"The first."

"They'll pull out at twelve."

"They've timed it to midnight exactly."

Greasy short overcoats; sorry fur coats with bald collars and short sleeves out at the elbow; short black jackets of cloth or leather. A stylish crowd!

The platform was narrow, and there wasn't room for many. The cleverer ones were hanging on to the fence or had clambered on to the window-sills; many had hoisted themselves on to the station shed, and were hanging their heads over the edge staring down at the crowd; or, twisting themselves in knots, they clung to any projection handy. Others, clinging to the cornices, had occupied the passages; still others had perched themselves on the carriage roofs and on the steps and ladders. A nice jam! Everybody was trying to squeeze forward nearer to the box where the speaking would be done. There was squealing, grunting, scolding, cursing.

And now Klichkov appeared on the box—his great-coat was old and shabby, a relic of 1914. His bare hands were freezing, and he kept sticking them into his pockets or in the breast of his great-coat, only to pull them out again to blow on his stiff red fists. Today, Fyodor was paler than usual; the last two nights he had slept but little and that badly. The days had been one mad rush; he had worked a lot and was worn out. His voice, always so clear and rich, was hoarse and muffled, and sounded hollow as if from a cave.

Klichkov was to talk first; he was to say good-bye to the weavers on behalf of the detachment. It was cold. The crowd was half-frozen—have to hurry—no long speeches. His eyes ran over the crowd, and there was no end to the black mass—the edge of it was somewhere beyond the gas-lit square. It seemed to him that somewhere beyond the thousands he could see before him crushed together and disappearing into the thick darkness, there were other thousands behind them, and still others, and so on without end. At this last moment, he suddenly realized with a sharp pang how dear this black crowd was to him, and how hard it was to part with them. Would he ever see them again? Would he ever come back? How many of those leaving now would come home again? Would he ever come back here and talk to them as he had talked so often these years?

Overcome by these mournful thoughts at parting, with no time to think out his short speech, and not knowing just what he would say, Klichkov shouted unusually loudly, louder, somehow, than ever before:

"Comrade workers! Only a few minutes are left for us to be together—the last bell will ring, and we'll be leaving. On behalf of the soldiers of the Red detachment—farewell! Remember us, your mates, and remember where we have gone and why. Be ready to follow us at the first call. Keep in touch with us—send messengers, and send what you can of your kopeks to help us soldiers. Comrades, at the front, there's little to eat—it's harder there than it is here. Don't forget that! Also, don't forget that many of us have left our families fatherless and unprovided for—we have left children to go hungry —don't forget them. It'll be hard for us in the trenches; it'll be tough on the marches and in the fighting, but it'll be a hundred times harder for us if on top of it all we hear that our families are dying, helpless, forgotten by everybody. Now, just one more thing before we go—work! work hard! You're weavers and should know that the more cloth you turn out in Ivanovo, the warmer it'll be in the snowy steppes around Orenburg and Uralsk and wherever else your cloth goes to. Work, and always remember that victory doesn't depend just on our bayonets; it depends on your labour, too. Shall we ever see each other again? Let's all hope for the best. But if we aren't to meet, there's no use crying about it. The Revolution doesn't count individual victims. Farewell, dear comrades, in the name of the soldiers of the Red detachment—farewell!"

And as the wintry storm sets the snow-covered steppe to wailing, a deep-throated groan arose in the crowd:

"Good-bye, comrades!" "Good luck!" "We won't forget you!"

The cries died away, and a mournful silence set in. It lasted a moment, and then a whisper suddenly rustled through the crowd:

"Yelena—Yelena is going to talk—Kunitsina—"

Yelena appeared on the box. Her beautiful light-brown eyes were deep, absolutely black. With a quick movement she passed her hand over her cheek and temple, pushing some strands of hair under her kerchief, and with both hands smoothed it down tight on her head. Then she said, not loudly, but almost to herself:

"Comrades!" The dumb, waiting crowd stretched forward towards her. "I want to tell you before we leave, comrades, that we're going to be the front, and you what they call the rear, but that means that one without the other we can't hold out at all. We've got to help each other out—that's the main job now; if we know that behind our backs everything is quiet and going well, why, nothing's going to be hard for us, comrades. But if everything goes to pot here—then where'll the war be? We workers didn't go through what we did these last two years for nothing, did we?—or was it all for nothing? I say 'no,' comrades, it was all to the good. Here, for instance, we women are going—there's twenty-six of us. We understand what the whole country's going through. We're needed, and so we're going. We've got to go—that's all there is to it! These women—mothers, wives, daughters, sisters, sweethearts and girl-friends—they all ask me to say good-bye to you. Farewell, comrades —keep your spirits up, and we will too!"

She was answered by a thousand-tongued shout of heart-felt gladness and gratitude—passionate vows in reply to her brave and sensible speech.

"Ah, Yelena, you ought to be a statesman! There's a woman for you—a regular machine!"

An old weaver in yellow jacket, greasy cap and felt boots, squeezed his way out of the crowd and climbed on to the box. The old man's shrunken face was creased with deep, dark furrows; his lips mumbled in an indistinct whisper. Waves of boundless joy welled up in his wet, but clear eyes, and across his illumined face.

"Yes, I'm going to answer—We want to say something too—" He faltered a moment, and suddenly bared his grizzled head. "When we got you together, we knew what for. You'll see everything, go through everything

—maybe you won't come back to us at all. And we, your fathers—never mind how hard it is—we say, all the same—go! Since you've got to go—go! No use hanging around here. Only don't fall down on your job. That's the main thing—your job! When things are the very worst, think of us and it'll be easier. We give you our word, too—we won't lose sight of your kids, we won't forget your womenfolk. We may not be able to do much, but still we'll help them! Of course we'll help them— that's what war means. How else...."

The old man made a staid, sweeping gesture with his hands, and added in a sad voice:

"Anyway, there's no other way out."

He stood for a moment, trying to collect his thoughts, and not succeeding, waved his hand, quickly stuck his cap on his grey, baldish head, and—when he was about to climb down—shouted in a sharp, ringing voice:

"Good-bye, mates—maybe for ever—"

His old voice quivered with tears, and a tearful tremor cut like a galvanic current through the crowd.

"It may be—anything can happen. Who can say in war-time—war's that way—"

And tears gushed from his eyes into the dark furrows of his cheeks. With the dirty sleeve of his old jacket, he smeared the tears over his face. Many in the crowd were weeping. Others shouted to the weaver as he climbed down:

"That's true, Dad. That's right, that's right, old fellow."

The old man got down. The box remained empty. The second bell rang out over the crowd, thin and shrill. Klichkov jumped up on the box for the last time:

"Well, farewell! Once more farewell, comrades! Hurrah for our meeting again! Hurrah for a happy meeting!"

"Hurrah! Hurrah! Hurrah!"

As soon as the crowd had quieted a little, the command rang out: "Detachment—to your places!"

There was a feverish flurry of hats, caps and Red Army helmets, and the clicking of farewell kisses. There floated over the crowd the mingled hum of hurried partings, staid advice, sorrowful entreaties and vain attempts at comforting. A mother's quivering head lay on the shoulder of a gloomy Red Army man; her grey face was wet with tears. Mother and son—two halves of one being—one moaned and sobbed and wept monotonously, the other was cold, serious, firm and lost in thought.

The detachment were in the carriages now. The crowd pushed closer—from the windows of the carriages it looked like a solid faceless mass—shifting, rumbling, restless, like an enormous, shaggy, bear-like animal with a thousand paws and thousand eyes.

The third bell.... Whistles trilled like so many nightingales; the engine hooted like an owl, then snorted hoarsely, let out a puff of acrid smoke and began to breathe heavily; the wheels screeched on the frozen rails and crunched as they began to turn; the carriages groaned, moved and began to slide away.

The Red Army men yelled from the windows, and the yelling crowd flowed along beside the train. Then the carriages were swallowed up in the gloom, and only far away something rumbled and clanked, making its way deeper and deeper into the black night. Downcast and dejected, the weavers left the station; tearfully and sorrowfully, they went back to their homes through the cold of the January midnight.

It took the detachment a long time to get from Ivanovo-Voznesensk to Samara—a full two weeks—but that was record going in those days. They didn't tire much on the road—it was good to see new places, and the strange surroundings stimulated them, the changing impressions kept them strung to a high pitch. The sharp newness of everything they saw washed away the grey monotony of riding and the boredom of long waits on the sidings of little out-of-the-way stations.

At every stop there was lively work for the troop train. The whole long journey was punctuated with meetings, conferences, impromptu lectures, and wordy talks with anyone who wanted to listen. This detachment of Bolshevik weavers, sensible and self-disciplined fellows, ploughed a deep and unexpected impression in the minds of the people along the whole route. In those days, countless irregular bands of "guerrillas" scoured the stations, large and small, the small towns, the villages, and tiny God-forsaken hamlets. No one organized them and no one kept track of them. They consisted of all kinds of detachments and semi-detachments, all kinds of "local formations"—erratic, obscure people, wandering without rhyme or reason from end to end of boundless Russia. All this enormous, non-paying, roistering and lawless mob was sponging off the country. The way was wide open to rioting because there was no one to curb it: in the outlying places, the Soviet power had not yet been consolidated into a vigorous force.

A person felt keenly in those days that it was not enough to have but one pair of sharp eyes, only two alert and sensitive ears, two hands ready for work, one head on his shoulders and a lonely heart in his breast. In those inhuman days it was hard to be a human being.

The best people in the Soviet Land were going off to the front. Others worried along in the unceasing, consuming worry of the rear. How could they look after everything, take heed of everything and do everything that should be done? What went on in those riotous days in the thickets of remote provinces, in the impassable forests of the peasant hinterland—that is something that no one will ever know. Men's distress filled their grey lakes of eyes to overflowing. The irresponsible, mad, and unrestrained trampled the young shoots of Soviet life on the gallop, and, reckless and drunken, whirled away.

There was no old, and there was no new. Where was a defenceless person to seek refuge? And who had sown this fiery whirlwind? Ah, the Bolsheviks? So it was their drunken freebooters that gave peace to none? So it was they who were the cause of the people's terrible misfortunes?

There were people who did not realize that the new government was just beginning to weave a tough rope to curb the unbridled marauders. The peasant hinterland spewed out all their accumulated woe and rankling anger against the Bolsheviks:

"Robbers! Ravishers! Barbarians!"

And now suddenly, the peasants and the small-town dwellers, saw in this detachment, this thousand Bolshevik weavers, good people, to put it simply; people who calmly and attentively heard them out, quietly answered all questions, explained everything in plain and simple words, never rummaged through the granaries of their own free will, or ripped open the cellar doors, took nothing, or if they did, paid for it. The peasants marvelled at this. It was something new; it was something strange; it was welcome. It sometimes happened that when the troop trains were held up for days at some little station, the inhabitants would creep out of their remote hamlets and villages to "listen to wise people."

The agitation was carried on in a way that left nothing to be desired—it opened wide the door to the titanic work which the lads from Ivanovo-Voznesensk performed later in the Civil War. And where only weren't they to be seen—on the Chinese border, in the Siberian forests, in the Orenburg Steppe, on the Polish frontier, in the Sivash at Perekop. Where only were they not, those Red weavers! Where only did they not drench the fields of battle with their blood! That was why they were so cherished, and so hunted down; so loved, and so hated. That is why the memory of them is like a song over the boundless plains of the Soviet Land.

Now they were going to the front in freezing cold goods waggons in the biting January frost. They were studying, working and thinking, thinking, thinking. Because they knew that they must be prepared for everything. They must know how to wage war not only with their bayonets, but also with a sensible, fresh word and a good head—with knowledge and the ability to understand everything instantly and explain it to another in the right way. In the goods waggons there was a continual hum of books being read aloud; studies slowly got under way; noisy arguments filled the air like a flock of jackdaws; and then suddenly a song would burst out in the pure, frosty air—light, ringing, bird-like:

> *Young smiths we are—our hearts will never die,*
> *We're forging happiness for men,*
> *So raise your sledge, and brandish it on high*
> *And smite upon the anvil once again!*

And from the creaking goods waggons, crawling tortoise-like along, militant songs rang out over the plains, above the rusty song of the wheels, spreading far and wide the thunder of victory. How they sang! How they sang, those weavers! The years of underground struggle had not been for nothing! That was why, later on at the front, there was no regiment which so cherished these songs of struggle and sang them the way the Ivanovo-Voznesensk Regiment did—with such simplicity and such ardent feeling, such infinite love. These songs fired the other regiments with pride and enthusiasm. Ah, what a song can do to a man's heart!

The closer they came to Samara, the cheaper they bought bread at the stations—bread and food in general.

In hungry Ivanovo-Voznesensk, where not a pound of bread was issued for months at a time, they had got used to looking on a crust of bread as a great treasure. And here the workers suddenly discovered that there was plenty of bread, that the trouble was not in the lack of bread, but in something else. They began bitterly to bewail the general confusion, the fact that the ties between the industrial working-class centres and the grain-producing areas were weak. It was as if they were taking their revenge in this abundance of bread for the years of hunger—they were hurrying to make up for the poods they hadn't eaten. One would think that they should have expected, as they moved into the heart of the Samara granary, that they would find more of everything and that everything would be cheaper. But no, they didn't believe this—hunger had cured them of such gullibility. At some little station where the bread seemed particularly cheap and especially white, they would buy whole poods. How could they let such a rare opportunity go by? And then the next day, they would arrive at another place and see that here the bread was whiter and cheaper still; they would grin in confusion and whisper together shamefacedly, not knowing what to do with their stores which were already getting stale.

As soon as they arrived in Samara and stopped somewhere on about the "fifteenth" siding, at the end of nowhere, where there were only piles of rusty rails and the skeletons of broken-down waggons, they spilled out on the tracks, huddled together, and raised a hubbub, hurrying their commanders to find out as soon as possible what was to be done with them. When and where were they to be sent, and what for? Were they to set out right away or would they be kept in the city for a day or two?

Only Frunze could give an answer to all these questions. Frunze was already in command of the Fourth

Army. He had left Ivanovo-Voznesensk a few days before the detachment itself, and was now in Uralsk. He had left a note for Fyodor Klichkov at the local Revolutionary Military Council, saying that Klichkov, Lopar, Terenty Bochkin and Andreyev were to press on to Uralsk at once, and the detachment was to follow them.

Frunze's note contained a warm, cordial greeting to his fellow townsmen. It briefly explained the situation, pointing out that they had hard work cut out for them. Klichkov read the note to the detachment, and they listened to the hearty words of their beloved commander with enthusiasm. Someone proposed that they send off a telegram of greeting to him.

"That's it—send off a telegram!"

"And thank him!" someone shouted.

"'Thanks' isn't the right word," other voices interrupted. "You want to say that we've got here and we're ready for action—wherever we're needed—that's what."

"Right! Tell him all of us to a man are ready for action!"

"Come on, fellows, let's make up a telegram! Hurrah for Frunze! Hurrah!"

Hats, caps and Red Army helmets flew up in the air like a flock of frightened jackdaws.

The warm tone of Frunze's note threw Fyodor into a fever of excitement. He waved it over his head absurdly, and shouted in reckless ecstasy: "Comrades! Comrades! Here it is—this little note. It was written by the *commander of the army*, and don't you just feel it was written by a man in every way equal with us? Don't you just feel—from his comradely manner, from his simple tone —that with us there is really only one step from private to commander-in-chief? Not even a step, comrades; the two make one whole. The two are one—the commander and the Red Army man! That's why our army is so strong—because of our unity, our solidarity—that's where our strength lies. So, 'Hurrah for our army! Hurrah for our victory!' "

Again the Red Army men threw their hats high in wild enthusiasm, and shouted "Hurrah!" Their vows, joy, and pride, and readiness to fight were like stones torn from the ocean bed during a storm and hurled upon the shore.

Now, events began to follow one another like fleet-footed hares. The detachment received its muster-orders. The commander was called to Army Headquarters and told to see to it that the detachment was ready to march. The four people designated in the note received a reminder in the Revolutionary Council: "Leave for Uralsk at once!"

They began to bustle, to hurry, and hardly had time to say good-bye to the soldiers in the detachment. Then, too, they believed that soon they would see each other in Uralsk.

Two three-horse sleighs dashed away from the Headquarters of the Revolutionary Military Council: in the first sat Fyodor and Andreyev, in the second—Lopar and Terenty Bochkin. The horses plunged forward; the driver's whistle pierced the air; the whip uncoiled snake-like and cracked; the light sleighs disappeared like birds in a cloud of powdery snow.

II

THE STEPPE

The mornings are cold in the steppe. The drivers were bundled up tight in their shaggy sheepskin coats. Their heads were concealed from their dozing passengers by their rough collars.

"Frozen, Lopar?" asked Bochkin leaning over, himself chilled through.

"To the marrow!" Lopar replied horsely in doleful tones. "Will there soon be a stop, do you think?"

"Don't know—we'll have to ask our friend here— Hey, old man!" He poked a thumb into the yellowish sheep carcass. "Will we soon be getting somewhere?"

"Chilly?"

"It's cold, friend. I asked if there'd soon be a village."

"Seven versts, it ought to be, or maybe all of twelve," the driver joked, not turning his head.

"Talk sense—how far?"

"Why, that far!" the driver snickered.

"What did you say the name of the village was?"

"Ivanteyevka."

"Is it very far from Ivanteyevka to Pugachov?"

"Why, nothing'll be left." And the peasant squinted his eye in a severely business-like way, and stuck his frozen finger well up his nose. He was silent a moment and then announced: "Practically nothing'll be left, you might say—to Tavolozhka, eighteen, and then from Tavolozhka, twenty-two—just make it by dinner-time!"

"You from Nikolayevka yourself?" began Bochkin, trying to feel the fellow out.

"From there—where else would I be from?" An injured note could be detected in the peasant's tone. "Why the devil such empty talk?" he seemed to be asking; if he took passengers in Nikolayevka, it meant he himself was from there.

"Well, why not, Uncle? You might be from Ivanteyevka," Bochkin tried to object.

"Not likely—Ivanteyevka, humph!" and the peasant clucked somewhat derisively and hastily shook the reins without need.

Among the peasants the following custom had sprung up: some Ivan what's-his-name of Ivanteyevka, for example, would take someone to Nikolayevka, while what's his-name Ivanovich of Nikolayevka had already received orders to take someone to Ivanteyevka. Accordingly, Ivanovich wouldn't take his fare, so as not to make an extra trip, but would turn him over to the home-bound Ivan, and the latter, with his tired horses, would crawl along with his passenger God knows how long. Then later, Ivanovich would do the same good turn for Ivan. This was very convenient for the peasants, but hell for the passengers—driving at a slow walk, it took four or five hours to cover some little twenty-verst stage. And this in spite of whatever extraordinary paragraphs there might be in the order: "Most urgent!" "First priority!" "Special appointment!"

All these terrible words had little effect on the drivers —they grinned in their frozen beards, slowly and good-naturedly pulled the icicles out of their shaggy moustaches and soothed their anxious fares:

"You're a little too spry—have patience, you'll get to your grave soon enough."

Terenty had heard about this custom among the coachmen, and recalling it now, understood why the peasant had clucked so contentedly and slily.

"I know what it is, friend. You're taking us in a swap for someone else."

"Who said I wasn't!" exclaimed the driver, coming to life. "Everybody knows swapping is easier."

"Easier, yes, but who for?"

"Easier for everybody!" retorted the driver, trying to dispel Terenty's suspicions.

"It's easier for you, I know. No one'll deny that," Bochkin agreed. "But that system is the deuce for us— you can't make any time with tired horses, you just have to drag along the whole day."

"So my nags are tired, are they?" demanded the driver, suddenly taking offence. Jerking his sheepskin around him with his powerful shoulders, he slapped the reins with a great air, and with a whoop, put the horses into such a mad gallop that the snow whirled up, stinging the riders' faces. "Eh, you devils! Gee-up, there! Not far now-w-w! Get on-n-n with you, my beauties!"

The driver was unrecognizable. He was burning up the wild snowy steppe like a race-course. When his resentment had cooled, he checked his heated horses, turned his head within his high collar and remarked gruffly:

"There's 'tired' for you!"

"That's the spirit, friend!" his passengers encouraged him.

"That's how it is," the peasant agreed, and added with dignity, "and if the nags are worn out sometimes, there's good cause for it—there's a power of driving—have to do your own business, have to fulfil orders. The devil himself would get tired, let alone a horse."

"Do you often get these orders?" Lopar wanted to know.

"A power of orders," the driver echoed. "So many people gadding back and forth, just try to keep them all in horses. And why those devils are doing all this rushing about, I can't understand. Back and forth! Back and forth! And they all want horses. Just try not giving someone horses and he tries to get at you with his fists!"

"That so?" asked Lopar doubtfully.

"What else? Who're you going to complain to?"

"You peasants are good at fibbing," Lopar said seriously to the driver.

"Well, you try lying better yourself!" retorted the peasant, half offended and turning heavily on his seat.

"What the devil!" exclaimed Lopar, flaring up. "Some beggar thinks up a tall story and then begins to believe it himself. Believes it, that's all, and what can you do with him?"

"Huh! Tall story!" muttered the driver sulkily, displeased that the talk had suddenly taken such a sharp and hostile turn.

"Did anyone ever hit you?" demanded Lopar

"Oh, didn't they! One—you remind me of him—jabbed me with his sword, the son-of-a-bitch. Good thing my sheepskin was thick or he would have let my guts out."

"Was the fool drunk?"

"Maybe he was, seeing how he carried on."

"Well, you can't ask much from a drunk," Lopar let fall.

"I'm not asking anything."

Terenty wanted to find out how the Soviets were getting along here—whether they were strong, whether they were working well. He interrupted the driver's evasive speech and began to ask him other questions, but here again nothing hitched—he found the same holding back, the same equivocal answers, as though the peasant was afraid of something.

"Let it be...." "You have to put up with everything...." "What can we do...." Terenty only got scraps of words, instead of a fair, straightforward answer.

"Can't get a straight word out of you—speak plainer," angrily exclaimed Lopar, losing patience.

"Awful slow at catching on, young fellow. You think a little, maybe you'll catch on."

"Wait a minute!" Terenty stopped Lopar, fearing that he would ruin the conversation. "I'm asking about your Soviet here—is it good or nothing extra? Has it got down to business?"

"Why shouldn't it get down to business—only Gorshkov doesn't hand out the orders fair—"

"Not fair?" Lopar pounced on the one word he could understand like a cat on a mouse.

"'Course not? You can be sure he tries to pass over his father-in-law every time—he lays it on folks like me when it's not our turn at all."

"You should complain," advised Terenty. "Go to the Soviet—tell them how it is. Show them. They'll soon give the rascal a good drubbing."

"Oh, yes, they'll give someone a drubbing," the peasant muttered in a doleful voice, and hopelessly slapped the horse's rump with the reins. "Only watch out or it'll be you gets the drubbing, and you'll fetch up somewhere you'd rather not."

"What nonsense are you talking?" Lopar again flared up.

"Not nonsense but just what always happens," said the driver sadly, and his head sagged over like a dead bird's.

"Have there ever been any such cases?" asked Terenty, directly and sternly, in the tone of a cross-examiner.

"That's just it."

"Well, and then what?"

"Why, nothing at all," and the peasant barely moved his frost-covered lips. "That was the last of him —'lived and died before his time, leaving naught but this sad rhyme.'"

"But why did you keep quiet?" snapped Lopar.

"Why, we kept quiet so that there wouldn't be any noise," the sly peasant explained unruffled. "If you're quiet, things pass by themselves."

"Enough of joking!" Lopar cut him off. "Or else—" Then, as though recollecting himself, he added good-naturedly, "By the way, is this hauling passengers such a loss to you, Uncle? There are posters hanging at the Soviets everywhere, 'If you travel—pay your way! If you take anything at all, pay for it all!' You've read them? Seen them yourself?"

"I've seen them—let them hang."

Lopar spat in despair, buried himself deep in his sweaty collar, and fell silent. He was used to talking in town, to workers, openly, in an entirely different manner. The obscure, evasive, sly answers irritated him beyond measure. The rest of the way to Ivanteyevka he didn't say a word, but for a long time Terenty Bochkin went on fishing out, like precious pearls, little isolated facts, scattered thoughts and opinions, which the cunning muzhik let fall in the flood of his false and obscure peasant talk.

In Fyodor and Andreyev's sleigh an entirely different conversation was in progress.

"You yourself were in his detachment, Grisha?" Fyodor asked the young fellow who was driving.

"It was with him that I hurt my leg," said Grisha, poking his finger at the seat where his leg should have been. "All summer they kept chasing all over the steppe—they were hunting us, and we were trying to dodge them. The Czechs are mere babes, but you can't trick the Cossacks—they grew up here themselves—what else can you expect of them?"

Grisha had thrown open his collar and was sitting on the seat sideways, so that Fyodor could plainly see his face, burned brick-red by the sun—brave, open, simple. He had a trick of lowering his upper lip firmly on the lower, squeezing it tight and covering it after some animated remark. He had a broad, flat nose, deep grey eyes, and a low forehead with oily creases in it—a face like any other face, nothing at all remarkable! But at the same time it gave one a feeling of sound strength—deep-rooted and genuine. Grisha was only twenty-two years old, but to judge by his face, one would say he was all of thirty-five. The hard life of a farm-labourer and the suffering he had gone through when his left leg was torn off in battle had left their indelible stamp.

"Well, and he himself—is he young?" inquired Fyodor continuing the conversation.

"Yes, he's still young—can't be thirty yet."

"From these parts, is he? A Cossack?"

"Not at all. There's a village—Vyazovka—not far from Pugachov—he must have lived there. Other people say he used to live in Balakov before he came here—who knows?"

"What's he like?" greedily catechized Fyodor, and it was apparent by his agitated face that the conversation had taken complete hold of him, and he was afraid to miss a single word.

"Why, what'll I say? In one word—he's a hero!" said Grisha as though thinking it over to himself. "We're sitting in a cart, say, and the fellows glimpse him a long way off. 'Chapayev's coming! Chapayev's coming!' We see him maybe ten times a day, and still want to see him oftener. That's the kind of a man he is, friend! And we climb down off the cart and stare at him like he was some wonder. And he walks along, twisting his moustaches on this side and that—he was terribly fond of his moustaches and was always smoothing them. 'Are you sitting there?' he'd ask. 'Yes, Comrade Chapayev.' 'Well, go on sitting.' And he'd go on. He didn't have to say anything else; it made you glad somehow from top to toe. Yes, a real man if there ever was one!"

"And he's a hero? a real hero?" Fyodor probed.

"No doubt of that," and Grisha jerked his head meaningfully. "Look at the way he hurried to the Ivashchenko Factory, for instance. How he did want to save the workers! But he failed—didn't get there in time."

"Too late?" Andreyev winced.

"Too late," Grisha repeated with a sigh. "He was only a bit late, at that, but how many workers were butchered because of it. Ugh-h!" Grisha let his hand fall gently and bowed his heavy head.

Overcome by sad thoughts, both were silent for at least a minute. Then Grisha said, more quietly than usual: "Some say one thing, some say another, but at the very least there must've been two thousand of them. They were laid out in rows between the factory buildings—the whole yard was filled up. There were women there, and kids, yes, and some old women—they shot them all, no difference who. That's what they did, the swine."

One could hear him grit his teeth as he jerked the slack reins.

"Did you see it yourself?" Fyodor questioned him.

"How could I keep from seeing it. It was too fierce for words. Nothing but blood and flesh on the muddy ground. The bastards mowed them all down with their machine-guns—made no difference who."

"Well, and what about Chapayev?"

"What could he do? He was wild—his eyes were glaring, and he was trembling like a horse after a gallop. He whanged his sabre on a stone with all his might. 'There'll be a lot of blood let for this blood,' he yelled. 'We'll never forget, and we'll have our revenge!'"

"And did he get revenge?" asked Andreyev seriously.

"That he did!" Grisha answered. "He scoured the steppe like a man gone mad; told us not to take one Cossack prisoner. 'Kill all the bastards,' he said, 'I won't ever forget the Ivashchenko Factory.'"

Again they fell silent. Then Klichkov went on questioning Grisha, who was only too glad to answer.

"Well, Grisha, and what kind of people did he have with him—his soldiers—where were they from?"

"Why, people from these parts—who else would it be? Farm-hands like me, and poor peasants—then there were barge haulers—they joined up even before we did."

"Was it a regiment you had, or what?"

"Yes, we had a regiment when we were at Pugachov, but later it was mostly called a partisan detachment. Chapayev himself didn't like to call it a regiment. 'A detachment,' he'd say, 'that's more like it.'"

"Well, yes—a detachment. But the wounded in your detachment—and your dead—how did you manage with them?"

"We managed," drawled Grisha thoughtfully, collecting his thoughts. "We managed all kinds of ways. Any wounded we didn't gather up, the Cossacks would finish off—you can depend on it, they wouldn't leave a one. Whoever we picked up, we hid in the villages—our people are everywhere around here. Some of the wounded were here in Tavolozhka. But not only here—everywhere."

"How did you look after them?"

"Their wounds were looked after here, too, only there wasn't any medicine at all; whatever some granny would think up was their medicine. If a man was hauled to town, he was more or less all right, but here in the villages—oh, my, how they were nursed. What could an ignorant peasant woman know about bandaging a leg when all that was left of it was some ragged ends flapping about and some smashed bones scrunching like a kid's rattle? What kind of a nurse is an ignorant woman in such a case?"

"Were there such cases?" asked Fyodor with a catch in his voice.

"Why not? Anything can happen in war-time."

"That's right!" Andreyev suddenly blurted out. He had been sitting silent, his head buried deep in the collar of his sheepskin coat, as though angry with someone, or displeased about something. "What you say is true," he repeated emphatically, and gave Grisha a friendly slap on his sheepskin.

"Of course." And the latter waved his hand cheerfully. "We had to put up with all kinds of things."

"Grisha," Fyodor interrupted, "you got your food from the villages, too?"

"From the villages," Grisha answered with great dignity, apparently very well pleased that they were so interested in him. "We lugged very little along with us—how could we, what would we do with it? Everybody here lived off the villages—if they came, they took; if we came, we did. It was give and no take for the villages whoever came."

"Yes, it must have been pretty bad," sighed Klichkov.

"It was past all telling bad for all, but was it easy for us?" Grisha caught him up, as though he was afraid they wouldn't understand him properly.

"No, no, of course it wasn't easy," Fyodor hastened to reassure him.

"That's more like it," said Grisha. "There were good times and bad. Anything might happen. Sometimes they'd begrudge us bread, or oats for the nags, or didn't want to change nags when ours were plumb wearied out. We couldn't dilly-dally—we had to take, so they had to give—no words wasted. I've no doubt it was the same with us as it was with them. Why should we boast that everything was always pretty? Sometimes it was ugly. We might be hungry for days at a time, and tired out with the march, and we couldn't get a crust of bread anywhere—can you expect anything pretty? Give us a bite to eat, we'd say right off, and he'd show us the door. What could we do—smile and go? Well, some we arrested, and some we smacked their mugs for them, if their bellies were too fat—we had no time to talk about the weather."

"You beat them up?" asked Klichkov, catching his breath.

"We did!" Grisha answered firmly and simply. "Everybody did—that's war."

"Fine lad, Grisha," Andreyev again interposed gaily. He liked this plain, unvarnished, rough truth.

"Sometimes I caught it too," said Grisha, turning around. "One day, Chapayev himself poked me one. What can you do if it's got to be that way?"

"What? Chapayev? What for?" Fyodor was all attention at the mention again of this magic name.

"Well, I was standing sentry," Grisha explained, "at some station or other just a little way beyond Pugachov —forget what they call it. I kept standing until I began to get awful tired. Of all the damn jobs, I thought, this standing sentry is just about the worst. I was bored something terrible. Well, there were some birches right next to the station, and I saw there were a lot of daws sitting there, trees fairly black with them, and all of them making an awful racket: caw-w-w, caw-w, caw-w. I thought, I'll let go once, then you'll hold your noise. First I thought it to myself, joking like, and then I began to think of firing in earnest. Who'll see me here, I thought, and anyhow lots of people keep shooting there all the time. I took aim into the thick of them and let fly: bang! bang! bang! I shot off the whole five without stopping to think. The two or three I hit came tumbling down, their wings catching on the twigs and fluttering before they died. But the rest! They flew up in clouds and began to cuss something dreadful. How did I know that Chapayev, himself, was sitting there with the commandant? And now he came out—black as a thunder cloud.

" 'Was it you that shot?'

" 'No,' I said, 'I didn't shoot—it wasn't me!'

" 'Who scared the daws, you booby?'

" 'Must have flown up themselves.'

" 'Show me your gun!' and he makes a grab for my rifle. And there's my rifle in his hand—and it's empty!

" 'What!' he starts to shout, 'Where'll you get cartridges, you son-of-a-bitch? What'll you shoot Cossacks with, you blockhead? More afraid of the daws than of the Cossacks, are you? You damn fool!' And how he did ram that rifle butt into my ribs!

"I kept quiet. What could I say to him? Then I called to mind what I should have done but it was too late. When he tried to take my rifle, I should have jerked it back—don't come close, or I'll shoot; you can't touch anyone's rifle when he's on sentry-go. He would have tried one thing and then another, but it would have been no use. I'd have pointed the bayonet at his belly. That's what he liked—he'd have forgiven me right off."

"That's what he liked?" Fyodor asked inquisitively, screwing up his eyes.

"Oh, didn't he though! The more spunk you showed, the kinder he got. He did love a chap with grit, no matter what it cost him. 'Stout fellow,' he'd say, 'since you've got a stout heart.' But it would take a long time to tell you everything about him. Well, there's Ivanteyevka."

Grisha brightened up. He sat himself squarely on the seat, as befitted a driver, loudly slapped the middle horse with the reins, clicked his tongue, whistled, and kept fidgeting all the rest of the way to the village. He only turned round once. "Want me to take you to the Soviet?"

"Yes, yes! To the Soviet, Grisha."

"Or else I could take you to Parfyonich—he'd tell you all about Chapayev."

"Who's Parfyonich?"

"One of our fellows—he was in the detachment before me. His arm was blown clean off, and so he came back."

"Lives here?"

"Yes. But his farm's ruined—the Cossacks destroyed everything he had. They pulled down his hut and burned the sheds—left the man naked, you might say. He's been trying to put things to rights but hasn't been able to do much."

"Point out his place when we pass it," Fyodor told him, just in case.

"All right."

They drove into Ivanteyevka, a big village with broad streets, the silvery snow well trodden down. Winter turns a little village into a bear's den: it cuts it off, buries it up with snow and smothers it. A big village, on the other hand, is only made more beautiful by winter.

Grisha whipped up the horses, and for swagger, sailed along at a smart trot. He jerked his thumb at one of the huts—it was Parfyonich's. He also pointed at another and, turning quickly, grinned; without a word, he threw back his head, making a motion as though downing a glass of vodka. His passengers were evidently to understand that they made home-brew there. They drove up to the Soviet. It was situated, as was usually the case, in the main square, in the house of the former village administration.

They crawled out of the sleighs, stepping uncertainly on their numb feet; pulled off their sheepskins, all covered with snow and frost; and took up their baskets and bundles in their hands and under their arms (pitiful possessions they were—not more than half a pood apiece). Then they went up the steps to the office of the Soviet.

It was the usual kind of office—spacious, awkward, uninviting, dirty and dull. It was still early. In the city at such an hour one wouldn't find anyone in the offices, but here—what a crowd had collected! What could they have wanted, coming here at such an early hour? Making themselves comfortable along the greasy brown wall, they rolled cigarettes of shag, stinking up the already unbearably sour air; others squeezed to the windows and scratched various nonsense on the frosted panes; they slapped their hands to keep them warm, and exchanged dull, chance phrases. It was obvious that the majority, if not all, had crowded in here for no fixed purpose—nowhere to go, nothing to do, so they had gathered here.

Seeing people enter, they turned in their direction, looked them over, and made remarks about the cold, about the evident fatigue of the new-comers, as well as about where they might be going and why, and the difficulties of travel in general. They talked about the shortage of oats and barley, said there was sure to be a snow-storm today, and that one mustn't go anywhere under any circumstances.

"Hullo, Comrades!" said Lopar, who had been held up outside for some reason, and now came in last.

"Hullo!" mumbled several voices.

"We'd like to see the chairman."

"He's in there." They pointed to a room behind a partition.

During the whole journey Lopar had acted as spokesman for the four travellers. It was he that carried on negotiations, got horses, found out where they could get something to eat, spend the night, etc.

Andreyev had not taken off his sheepskin coat. Unceremoniously shoving aside a peasant sitting on the window-sill, he lit up, silently offering the peasant a smoke, too. Terenty had already pushed his way into the crowd and was talking to everybody, asking how many people lived in the village, how things were going, how the Soviet was functioning, and whether they were satisfied with Soviet government—in a word, he had got down to business without delay.

Fyodor's imagination had been captured by Grisha's stories. The legendary figure of Chapayev, the ataman of the steppe, was continually before him. "He is a real hero—a hero from the masses," Fyodor thought to himself, "a hero from the camp of the freemen, like Yemelyan Pugachov, Stepan Razin and Yermak. They did brave deeds in their time, but he, Chapayev, is living at a different time, and his deeds are different, too. From Grisha's stories one might think that the most striking thing about Chapayev is his boldness and a reckless display of courage. He is more a hero than a fighter, more of a passionate lover of adventure than a conscious revolutionary. Unrest and a driving thirst for changing impressions, developed to the extreme, were, probably, predominant in him. Still, what a unique personality against this background of peasant uprisings; what an original, vivid, picturesque figure!"

Fyodor found out from the peasants how to get to Parfyonich's, and when Lopar, after his talk with the chairman of the Soviet, took the rest off to have tea, Fyodor did not go with them. He explained that he wanted to see Parfyonich, and started out to find the address he had been given.

In an hour and a half they left Ivanteyevka. Fyodor sat gloomy and silent. He had not found Parfyonich at home—he had gone to Pugachov the day before. Andreyev asked Fyodor a question or two, trying to draw him into conversation, but desisted seeing that nothing came of it. Terenty and Lopar just sat there, and getting bored after a while, took it into their heads to sing. Their duet was something to be remembered. Lopar did not sing at all; he only croaked tunelessly, while Terenty squealed in a wild falsetto. The resulting ear-splitting din was frightful. When he could stand it no longer, Andreyev shouted to them from his place in the front sleigh to stop howling. Apparently agreeing with him, the singers left off. They all dozed the rest of the way to Tavolozhka, and arriving there, made no stop but ordered fresh horses and pushed on towards Pugachov.

Driving out of Tavolozhka the peasant drivers had looked askance at the dense clouds moving like black smoke across the darkened sky. The wind sprang up in sharp, fitful blasts, blowing from no set quarter but from all sides at once, as though attacking an unseen enemy. It hurled itself upon him like a watch-dog on a chain; it sank its fangs into him, and frenziedly tore his flesh, but every time was hurled back with a mighty kick. Again it attacked and again recoiled, whining, barking and howling convulsively. Dizzy whirlwinds of snow tore along the ground, spinning and gyrating; the road was choked tight with powdery snow. The twilight of the blizzard closed in on them, quickly becoming denser. The furious wind struck out from all sides more and more persistently, and with ever greater strength and violence. The sky became darker and darker; the snow was sucked up more and more steeply and swiftly in a mad vortex of needles, pellets of ice and chunks of snow which were hurled right in their faces.

The passengers buried themselves deep in their sheepskin coats like moles in their burrows. The drivers peered out warily. The head wind took their breath away. The biting frost seared their faces. They rode on and on, and the further they went the more furious and unfettered raged the mad blizzard in the steppe. When the road went along the bottom of a gully where sparse bushes stretched along the high bank, it was a little quieter, but as soon as they climbed out on to the plain, the storm again ran riot like an uproarious host at a drunken orgy: "Everything's mine, and what I break is my own business!" The steppe was drunk with storm, riotous and threatening.

It was still some dozen versts to Pugachov; they met caravans of swaying camels on the way, and here and there lonely riders—probably a good number of them never got to their homes: they were frozen to death outright, or lay out the night in the snow, to be dug out in the morning and somehow brought back to life.

"We haven't had such a storm for many years," the steppe dwellers said. "God must have sent it to punish us for our bad praying—for forgetting His holy shrines."

That was what they said, but it was obvious that these were but empty words, only a phrase in common circulation—the thing to say. The peasants said it more out of Christian politeness, but themselves didn't believe a word of it.

Quite a lot of people had been driven into the railway station by the storm. When our passengers rode up and rolled out of the sleighs like so many snowballs, they were not content with sending Lopar on alone as scout, but one of them went to the station authorities, and another to the commandant, while good-natured Terenty was sent along the snow-covered tracks to hunt out any trains that might be intending to set out for Uralsk. This "division of labour" arose from the fact that during their journey to Samara the fellows had seen a hundred convincing demonstrations of the skilful way in which the railway bosses in charge of sending off trains deceived people, deliberately or otherwise. If they said that a train was leaving in an hour, one might be sure that it wouldn't budge until the next day, but if they said that the train would leave "only in the morning," then one had to be prepared to see it pull out under one's nose.

After some hunting they finally found a little waggon in which, as it happened, a group of political workers were preparing to travel to Uralsk. A little discussion and explanation, and they piled in with their few belongings. But they had their fill of worry before they finally got to Uralsk. This side of Yershov, the track was snowed under—everyone climbed down and cleared away the snowdrifts. Then they exchanged abuse with the commandants, managed by hook or by crook to get wood, and thawed out their coffin of a waggon. The train crawled along slowly with sickening monotony. They had just got a little way beyond Yershov when something went wrong with the engine—again confusion; again they had to climb down, and again there was a long nerve-racking wait. Next they began to have trouble with axle-boxes and that meant more halts and more fuss and trouble while repairs were made; always some new anxiety. It took them all of two days to cover the trifling distance from Pugachov to Uralsk.

III

URALSK

Once in Uralsk they phoned the commandant from the station. He sent two sledges, and the lads got in with their scant belongings, and rode to the Central Hotel. It was terribly cold at the hotel, and the rooms were damp and dirty and bare—nothing to sit on, nowhere to lie down, and one didn't know where to place one's things. However, they adjusted themselves somehow or other, looked round and took possession of a room, all four of them together so as not to be separated.

They were so cold that they drained two samovars of tea without stopping, and then went out to wander about the town to kill time. Already at the station they had learned that Frunze had left that morning to be closer to the front in order to direct the offensive that had just been launched. At that time, the nearest positions were only twenty versts from Uralsk, and it was an urgent matter to drive the enemy as far away as possible. These first engagements, by the way, were not particularly successful for the Red forces; they did not succeed in pushing back the Cossacks until later, when a broader and more cautious plan had been worked out for a general offensive on several sectors simultaneously—not only from Uralsk but also from Alexandrov-Gai against the Cossack village of Slomikhinskaya, and from the latter to cut the highway linking Uralsk with Guryev through Lbishchensk, the road along which the Red forces advancing from the North were to drive the Cossacks.

But of this later—everything in its place. We shall have occasion more than once to return to the arduous road from Uralsk to Guryev.

Our friends each had his own favourite occupation, one might even say speciality. Terenty Bochkin, for example, had a passion for letter-writing, and almost all his letters were devoted, for the most part, to matters of a household nature—he would be sure to find out what was to be had, and where, and at what price; he would remember all this, write it out and make comparisons.

Klichkov, for his part, kept an accurate diary. Whatever the situation, whatever the conditions, he contrived to write down what seemed to him most important. If not in his note-book, then on sheets of paper; at times, while on the march, making use of a fence as a support, he would be sure to write everything down. His friends usually laughed at him, not seeing any sense or use in this.

"What're you spoiling good paper for, Fyodor?" Andreyev would ask. "Why do you have to write down every trifle? Do you think you can write down what everyone did or said? And if you want to write, you've got to write *everything*, understand? No sense in writing only part, it'll even do harm—you'll only give people the wrong idea."

"No, you're wrong, Andreyev," Fyodor would explain. "I'll see a bit here, another will see a bit there, then a dozen more will see other things—fit them together and you get a pattern that'll give a true picture of history."

"You're probably thinking up rubbish of various kinds —what sort of history will that be?" retorted the doubting Andreyev.

"I know what I'm about," Fyodor insisted, experiencing acute embarrassment at this unceremonious and persistent badgering.

"What do you know? You don't know anything," Andreyev brought him up short. "You're wasting your time on trifles."

Klichkov did not like discussions on this topic, and knowing how hard it was to convince Andreyev, kept silent—some questions he did not answer at all, and the conversation was dropped.

In his diary, Klichkov usually wrote things which never got into the papers at all, or if they did, were given a most wretched write-up. Actually, he didn't know himself what he was writing for—there seemed to be some inner compulsion for which there was no clear explanation.

As for Andreyev, he had a different speciality—to find out everything concerning the labour front. He was drawn to this just as Terenty was drawn to his letter-writing or Klichkov to his diary. It may have been unconsciously, by a sort of instinct, but whenever Andreyev began to talk to someone new, and in a new locality, he began to ask questions of a quite particular sort: were there any factories, and had they been built a long time; were they working well; had they been shut down long and why; how many workers were there and what were they like; were they class-conscious or not; in what way, how and when had they shown themselves; etc., etc.

In all this, one saw a worker who was drawn to his native environment, to questions, needs and cares of peculiar interest to himself. He was also interested in the general situation, for the most part in the resources of the district, and the population, its composition and degree of reliability. These questions, it must be added, interested all four in an almost equal measure.

Lopar was a specialist in military matters—he at once found out what military units were stationed nearby; which regiments were better, and which worse; what was being done in the way of political work among the Red Army men; whether there were many Communists, and how they were working; what was the general situation at the front, etc., etc.

These specialities had made themselves felt to a certain extent on the road, but even more later, when all four were drawn into real work. For some of them—Andreyev for example—the field of observation was narrowed (workers' centres were scarce); for others, like Lopar, it was broadened; but for all of them one thing was obvious from the very first day: military matters and military interests began to engross them more and more completely, pushing any other life, any other interests, into the background until they finally engulfed them completely.

They walked all over town from one end to the other. Their surroundings were new and amazing—something quite peculiar. Everywhere there were grey soldiers' great-coats, rifles, bayonets, cannon, military vehicles—it was a genuine armed camp. Red Army men marched through the streets in columns, or hurried about singly, cavalry galloped by, guns rolled slowly along, and caravans of loaded camels swayed majestically past on their way to the positions. Everywhere there was unceasing firing, unnecessary and unrestrained, which only abated somewhat at night: some were "cleaning their barrels," others shooting "game," while still others claimed their guns "had gone off accidentally." One military expert, who had counted up how many such random shots were fired on an average per second and per minute, figured it out that every day from two to three million cartridges were wasted in this stupid shooting. It is hard to say whether this calculation was correct or not, but the firing was truly shameless. At that time there was as yet no conscious, iron discipline in this steppe army; there were no cadres of politically conscious Bolsheviks in the regiments capable of at once transforming them. That came later, but at the beginning of 1919, it was almost exclusively peasant regiments that fought around Uralsk, and fought well—fought bravely—heroically. There were either no Communists at all, or there were very few, and half of these were "fakes."

These regiments had been taken in by shady agitators who alleged that the Communists were rapists and gendarmes, that they had come from the towns to set up their "communes" by main force.

It was often said in these regiments that the Bolsheviks were comrades and brothers, while the Communists were bitter enemies. Two days after his arrival, Klichkov even had to give a public lecture on the absurd question: "What is the difference between Bolsheviks and Communists?"

There was, by the way, nothing surprising in this, for the question of Bolsheviks and Communists had run the rounds of almost the whole country; it was debated with particular heat in the outlying regions—the Caucasus, the Ukraine, the Urals, and Turkestan; it even penetrated into Georgia.

One may judge how complicated the situation in the regiments was then if only from the fact that the able and tactful Lindov, noblest of revolutionaries, was killed, together with a whole group of Bolsheviks, by his own "Red Army men."

A few days later, when the Ivanovo-Voznesensk detachment arrived in Uralsk, wearing the characteristic Red Army helmets with the enormous red stars, and assumed guard over the town, fire was opened on them from behind corners. The shooting was done by Red Army men from the "free" peasant regiments whose reckless "freedom" was being clipped and taken away by the weavers.

However, in a very short time, when the peasant regiments saw what the weavers could do in battle—how bravely and stubbornly they fought—their prejudice against them immediately evaporated, and new, friendly relations grew up among them.

In Uralsk itself there were few Communists—some had been killed in battle, others carried away by the Cossacks; part had been intimidated and dispersed even earlier, part had remained active. The work was mostly carried on by Bolsheviks who had arrived from other places. The central figure among them was a miner called "Fugas,"* a fine character, a beloved comrade, and a tried fighter. In contrast to him, and always competing with him and mentioned along with him, was a certain Pulemyotkin,** a wretched little intellectual, a political humbug and poseur. He also claimed to be a Communist, but he was one of those people whose personal qualities arouse thorough and acute dislike. He showed himself to be a vain boaster, an empty twaddler, and a phrase-monger, always trying to attract attention and win cheap popularity. The four new-comers quickly took the measure of the "groupings" around Pulemyotkin and "Fugas," and took the side of the latter; in a few days they became close friends.

When, tired out with walking, they had returned to their unheated little cubby-hole, and Terenty had half finished his regular letter, in which he reported that fried sour cabbage and bread cost five rubles, and black cav-

* *Fugas*—The Russian word for a land-mine.—*Tr.*
** *Pulemyot*—The Russian word for a machine-gun.—*Tr.*

are twenty-three rubles a pound, an orderly came from Headquarters to inform them that Frunze had returned. The lads were on their feet at once and off, at full speed. At Headquarters everything seemed strange and unusual. They were not even admitted at once but someone went to announce their arrival. To whom? Why, to Mikhail Vasilyevich whom they knew so intimately, with whom they had worked in such close contact, whom they were used to regard as a comrade, as one of themselves. Was this all a dream? Hell, no! No dream at all: in front of them stood a sentry with fixed bayonet. He didn't look at all friendly at the young men who had arrived and who had attempted so unceremoniously and conceitedly to push their way in to the Commander.

They shuffled their feet for a minute or so in the corridor, feeling awkward and trying not to look at one another.

"Come in!" someone called.

They went in. The meeting was of the simplest and heartiest possible, and most sincerely comradely. They felt that before them was the same plain, accessible comrade whom they had always been so fond of. They gradually recovered a little, but here again there was something new. Some military experts were sitting around Frunze, not any of your small fry, but real pike—former colonels and generals. All of them were trying to show their approval of everything he said; all of them were exaggeratedly respectful, hanging on his every word. The lads understood the word "discipline"; they realized that very likely it couldn't be otherwise, but themselves couldn't get into the swing of it—they almost called the Commander "Misha" and talked to him in the tone they would have used if they were somewhere together in a Party committee. The colonels listened and looked on them in bewilderment; they smiled uncomfortably and held themselves even more painfully on the alert, for fear that in the company of these new-comers they might make a slip and themselves be guilty of insubordination. So there were two camps till the end of their talk—in one, the military experts, and in the other, the young workers.

Frunze told them about the situation at the front, what could be expected, and what measures had best be taken in the immediate future. The lads attempted to look wise as they vainly tried to remember everything, to understand and to get a clearer picture of things. Nothing came of it. In the first place, they didn't know the maps and so the names of Cossack villages and strong points were to them but empty sounds; in the second place, they had only a general idea of such conceptions as "strategy," "tactics," "manoeuvrability" and the like, and did not realize their real significance.

Soon the experts went away leaving the friends together. The conversation took on an entirely different tone; plans were laid forth openly and in detail. Fyodor looked sideways at Frunze in amazement—where had he got such a clear understanding of military matters, how was it he had such a real grip of everything and was never at a loss no matter what the question might be. He was absolutely at home here: he understood everything, foresaw everything, took everything into account—what the devil! Was it so long ago that he had been a helpless muff of a civilian? Even in those days when Frunze had just become a commander, certain peculiarities stood out clearly in him. These characteristic features were the ease, quickness, depth and clearness of his understanding; his ability to make a timely and thorough analysis and to take everything into account; his confident approach to the solving of a problem; and his belief, his unbounded belief in success—not empty, but well-founded belief.

They sat together and chatted about their native Ivanovo-Voznesensk, mutual friends and their recent work together. It was after midnight when they broke up, and in the morning Frunze left hurriedly for Samara. He said that he would send them their appointments from there, but in the meantime they would have to work here in Uralsk in the local Party Committee. This chance Party work kept them busy for eight days until all four were assigned work in the Army.

Among themselves they talked about Frunze:

"Mikhail Vasilyevich has changed a lot."

"That's only to be expected—there's an awful lot of work."

"The old fellow has got yellow and his face is thin."

"Enough to make you worse than yellow—the troops here are a raving mob—do you think there won't be any trouble with them? They say he's ordered them to stop firing, and more than once, and what's come of it—just listen!"

They glued their ears to the window. In the streets could be heard the bang and rattle of crazy firing.

"Damn this anarchy!" Andreyev angrily exclaimed. He was silent a moment and then boomed confidently: "We've got the better of worse things than that—we'll put things right."

The twenty-third of February holiday was approaching—the Red Army anniversary. Things had begun to stir long before, as is usual in such cases, but the real organizational work for the celebration was conceived and carried out during the last three or four days. The meticulous Lopar had discovered the day after their arrival that the Party organization was deplorably weak, that there was no one, in fact, to take charge of organizing the celebration, and that it might all fizzle out if someone didn't actively intervene—if the whole matter were not concentrated in reliable hands. The Revolutionary Council informed Lopar that the Party Committee was in charge of everything, but when he went to the Party Committee he was referred to some non-existent committee and sent back to the Revolutionary Council. On Lopar's insistence, a meeting was speedily called and workers' representatives invited to attend, but still no one appeared from the Revolutionary Council. Lopar decided to act at his own risk and declared the meeting valid and competent; in a few words, he informed the meeting about the coming celebration and of the impossibility of any further delay in its organization; he proposed that an effective executive organ should be elected.

Lopar was elected chairman of this committee and Andreyev, secretary. The work got under way. The town was divided into sections, places were selected where indoor meetings and outdoor mass meetings would be held, and where lectures would be given on the occasion; it was decided who would speak and where, and how to make the best use of the theatre, the cinema and the bands in the town. The trade unions were got in touch with and asked to send men and women volunteers; some were put to build speakers' stands, others got out leaflets, placards and the next number of *Yaitskaya Pravda*. The women workers were in charge of the children, for whom better food as well as matinees in theatres and cinema houses were to be arranged that day.

In three days all was ready. Early on the morning of February the twenty-third, columns of workers from the various trade unions began to arrive at the central square from all directions. They lined up in front of the speaker's stand, leaving a space in the middle for the military units which were somewhat better dressed and cleaned up for the occasion. The square was full of people. Speeches, speeches and more speeches. The workers and soldiers accorded the best reception, the warmest and most sincere, to the short, plain, sensible speech made by "Fugas." After "Fugas," Pulemyotkin, as usual, jumped on to the platform, and began to froth and foam, chewing over platitudes about the "hydra of counter-revolution" which everyone knew and was tired of hearing about. There was no limit to how much he could rattle if he were not shut up. Ten minutes went by—then twenty—then thirty—and Pulemyotkin was still going strong. They had already jerked him twice by the coat-tail but it didn't help. Everybody was tired to death. The day was frosty and the Red Army men had long ago begun shifting from one foot to the other. Everybody was freezing. It was not to be tolerated any longer. Lopar, standing behind Pulemyotkin, said distinctly and impressively: "If you don't stop this very minute, I'll shout 'Hurrah!' D'you understand?"

Pulemyotkin glanced quickly around, his watery eyes glaring angrily, but seeing the determined expression on Lopar's face, realized that he wasn't joking. He hurriedly finished his speech, climbed down from the stand, and was lost in the crowd. The speeches were what speeches always are. Similar speeches were made all over Soviet Russia that day. The evening celebration was also like all evening celebrations. Probably they were the same everywhere—with lectures, shows, films.

From the square they marched through the town carrying red flags and singing revolutionary songs. They came to the grave of the fallen fighters—here also there was a speaker's stand. Speeches were made by "Fugas" and Lopar. Pulemyotkin, all ready to make another speech, was held back in time and not given the floor. When Lopar spoke about the comrades sleeping in the common grave, and explained for what cause they had perished and that their memory should be held sacred, his impassioned words, fresh and forceful, were followed by a long, deep, concentrated silence. Then suddenly a shot was fired. This solitary, and it may be, quite accidental shot, acted as a signal. All the units in the vicinity began happily firing into the sky. A deafening, crazy fusillade began—nothing like a ceremonial salute. In such confusion, any whiteguard could easily have picked off the Bolsheviks standing on the platform; it would have passed unnoticed and undiscovered in the general delirium. They were ashamed to leave the platform, and so they continued to stand there until the Red Army men had shot off all their cartridges. Lopar stood pale as a ghost—in those few minutes he experienced the terror of the grave. Never afterwards, even in the hottest fighting, did he experience that undefined, raking trepidation which set his whole helpless body a-tremble. There is nothing worse than to feel helpless and in the power of blind chance.

In Uralsk, Red Army Day was celebrated, one might say, satisfactorily, but how it was observed throughout the region, who knows! They hadn't got around to sending proper instructions—only a general reminder as to what was to be done. Bochkin and Fyodor Klichkov had gone to the front the day before; they had taken along what political literature they could—the jubilee number of *Yaitskaya Pravda*, appeals and leaflets. They didn't return until late at night. They woke up their friends, and with great excitement began to tell the bewildered, half-awake Andreyev and Lopar what a fine reception they had been given at the "front-line" (they pronounced the words with incredible pride), how grateful the soldiers had been for the presents and for being remembered, how they had listened to the speeches and asked them to come again. Their sleepy friends responded sluggishly to this enthusiastic recital. Andreyev, only half-awake, cursed and declared that he was tired to death of these "fish-stories." It was clear that the conversation wouldn't hitch. Soon, not finding any listeners, the storytellers had to break off, in spite of their burning desire to tell everything down to the minutest detail about their wonderful trip to the real "front-line." And so ended Red Army Day for our friends.

After dinner one evening a few days later, when all four were together, a telegram arrived—Lopar and Bochkin were to leave for Brigade Headquarters next morning! The time had come for them to part! This put all of them in that peculiar frame of mind that goes with leave-taking; they were filled with unexpected thoughts and feelings. There was nothing surprising in the fact that two of them were to set out in the morning, and the other two perhaps soon after them. This was what they had been expecting. Still, all four reacted in an unusual way. Lopar and Terenty suddenly began to display an unwonted belligerence, as though the battle-field was all they had known up to now. Andreyev was more sombre than usual, while Fyodor, seemingly concentrated on something, kept silent, listening with a smile to the excited and rapturous talk of his departing comrades.

In the morning, Terenty and Lopar were put in their sleigh. Andreyev and Klichkov said good-bye to them, kissed them at parting, and two of the friends rode away. And now another telegram arrived—Andreyev was to stay where he was and work here in the division as commissar; Fyodor Klichkov was to go to Alexandrov-Gai to put in order the political work in the army group being organized there, and which Chapayev had been appointed to command. When Fyodor read this, his heart jumped in his breast—at first he couldn't believe it. He read the telegram a second and a third time—there could be no doubt: it was Chapayev! The blood pounded in his temples, and raced through his veins.

"With such a hero—shoulder to shoulder with Chapayev—how wonderfully it has all come out—it's really unbelievable—here I was dreaming about Chapayev like some legendary figure, and all of a sudden it turns out we're to be together, side by side, without any ceremony, like me and Andreyev here. Maybe we'll get along well and even get to be close friends. Devil take it! It *is* strange the way everything has turned out!"

From this moment, Fyodor was obsessed with one thought only, one burning desire—to see Chapayev as quickly as possible. No matter what he began to talk about, it all came back to Chapayev. From the telegram one could gather that at present Chapayev was not in Alexandrov-Gai, but was only getting ready to go there, but just the same, just the same—he must hurry to Alexandrov-Gai immediately! Fyodor didn't wait for the next day; he was ready to go in three hours. His parting with Andreyev was that of two friends, simple and moving. Fyodor left, and Andreyev remained in Uralsk alone.

IV

ALEXANDROV-GAI

Fyodor had been assured that the train would get him to Algai (short for Alexandrov-Gai) almost the next day. Then it turned out that he would have to change in Yershov, Urbakh and Krasny Kut. Three changes—no joking matter! Whoever had occasion to travel in 1919 will realize that to change trains three times was a wearisome and no easy matter. Fyodor calculated that the journey would take him a week and a half. So after thinking it over, he got off the train at Dergachi and set off on posthorses—it was a hundred and fifty versts to Alexandrov-Gai as the crow flies.

Again steppe, open spaces, blue horizons, endless sheets of snow. Here and there the snow had melted and the naked earth was thrust up in black hillocks. Since there was no wind, and the sun shone warm, spring would soon be singing and dancing in. Here in the steppe the villages were few—twenty-five or thirty versts from one to the other. They lived in plenty, and each held aloof from the rest of the world; here few brides were given in marriage outside their own village—no need for that—there was plenty of young men for all. Each village was something of a small republic—it felt independent, that it had no need of anyone or anything, and was greatly inclined to be self-sufficient. These big villages which one passes through on the way to Algai played an enormous role in the history of the Civil War in the Ural steppes. Such were Osinov-Gai, Orlov-Gai and Kurilovo. They not only contributed individual volunteers—they gave whole Red regiments. True, many kulaks also left these villages to join up with the Whites, but there can be no doubt that the preponderance was always on the side of the Reds. When the Cossacks broke into Kurilovo in 1918, and acting on information given by the local kulaks began to hunt out the workers of the local Soviet, the whole huge mass of the rural working population rose up as one man, and armed with whatever came to hand, killed most of the Cossacks and drove out the remnants. They decided there and then to organize their own regiment—the Kurilovo Regiment they called it.

It was under pretty much the same circumstances that the other local regiments were formed. These included the Domashkin, Pugachov, Stepan Razin, Novouzensk, Malouzensk and Krasny Kut regiments. In the beginning they were organized to guard and defend their native villages, and soldiers and commanders were all from the same place (at first there were no commissars). The ties between them, it goes without saying, were incomparably strong—these people had known one another for many years—they were often old friends and many were kin. In the Kurilovo Regiment, for example, there was a father and five sons. There were also cases where once close friends parted—one ran away with the Whites while the other became a Red Army man in the village regiment. There were even more striking cases when a family broke up—part going over to the Whites, part staying with the Reds.

All these local regiments, formed for the defence of their villages, were soon forced by the course of events to quit their native places and go deep into the Ural steppes, from there against Kolchak, after Kolchak again into the steppes, and from the steppes to the Polish front, against the Polish landowners.

Among the most meritorious and gallant regiments, was the Moslem Regiment, comprising people of fourteen nationalities. The majority were Kirghiz, a people who up to that time had been pitilessly and shamelessly exploited by the blood-sucking well-to-do Cossacks for whom they had an inveterate and savage hatred.

These volunteer regiments performed truly heroic deeds. Without shells or cartridges, with inferior weapons and not enough of them, badly clothed, and almost barefoot, they firmly held their ground, fought stubbornly and bravely, and many times beat down the Ural Cossacks when these rose against Soviet government. In fighting qualities they stood on a high level from first to last; as for political consciousness, they did not mature at once; they did not grasp and clearly understand the causes or the enormous scale of the social struggle then developing. Bad discipline, their own peculiar idea of "freedom," a long struggle for the principle of elective command, a vague and inaccurate understanding of tasks and directives issuing from the centre—all these features long distinguished these valiant volunteer, peasant regiments from those of Central Russia.

Alexandrov-Gai was but little different from the other "gai's"—Orlov-Gai and Osinov-Gai and the like, or probably from any of the other steppe villages, all of which were very much alike. It was large and rambling —muddy in the central part, and impassable at the edges. At that time, Alexandrov-Gai was an exceptionally lively point; here were Brigade Headquarters, the Political Department, various commands, and military units. There was a brisk traffic in all directions—to Shilnaya Balka, to Bai-Turgan and Port Arthur, and to Uralsk. Contact was maintained with military units and with the operative centres. There was an endless stream of vehicles; people were coming and going; restless cavalrymen were hurrying away to some place or other; whole baggage trains crawled by in peasant carts or swayed past on haughty camels; there was loading and unloading, hauling in and hauling away—the village fairly boiled with life in a way probably unequalled before or since. Every evening the local "intelligentsia" promenaded in the square and along the main street as though it were a fair, and as might have been expected, the Red Army men missed no opportunities—a full half of the Algai women-folk had by then succumbed to their charms.

From time to time, the Political Department of the brigade organized meetings both for the Red Army men and for mixed audiences. These meetings, for the most part, were limited to stereotyped reports on current events. It was of course more difficult to draw the local population into the political work than the Red Army men—the latter were glad to go to the meetings; they listened to the speeches attentively, and asked to have the meetings called more often; they wanted the reports to be more comprehensive and detailed. This was a commendable desire, but it was not always possible to satisfy it, and that not only for want of political workers— considering the time and the place, there were perhaps enough of them. Often, meetings and open-air rallies could not be called because of the military situation—

there were Cossacks all around. They might suddenly make a raid, catch a mass of unarmed soldiers at a meeting and do no end of mischief.

At that time, Nikolai Nikolayevich Yozhikov, a Petrograd worker, was the head of the Political Department. He was quite young, only twenty-two, but mature, intelligent and earnest. He was at the same time the Brigade Commissar. Not only the command and the Red Army men, but also the inhabitants of the village had the greatest respect for Nikolai Nikolayevich. They liked him for the unaffected, sensible, kindly way he spoke; for the fact that he made no empty promises, but once having promised something, always kept his word; and for the fact that there were no disorders in the village, which they rightly attributed to his moral influence over the Red Army men. The soldiers also loved him—most of all because he was always with them on the march, and fought together with them in the lines, lying down under fire and running forward in the attack—always a comrade on an equal footing with them.

It must be said that at that time, at the very beginning of 1919, political work in the Red Army had in general not yet been got under way properly. Form and method were still not clear, and many of the political workers, particularly the junior commissars, were simply the more class-conscious of the soldiers who by their own example showed the men how a soldier of the Red Army should endure hunger, cold without boots or warm clothes, and the ardours and privations of exhausting marches; how to fight bravely; and if necessary, calmly lay down his life with honour. Continual fighting made it impossible for weeks, or even whole months at a time to carry on any concentrated or systematic work. Everything was limited to chance political "flying meetings," while *genuine* political work was postponed till a more convenient time.

At Alexandrov-Gai, the situation was no better and no worse than in other sectors; the reserves were miserably small, and the men were off duty for but short periods, the majority being on the firing-line all the time. The workers in the Political Department, except for those who had "sitting" jobs, were continually leaving the department for the front-lines, taking printed material, fresh orders, instructions, and manuals. They kept in contact there with the commissars and Party units, instructing both. Whenever possible they carried on political work among the Red Army men, and if necessary, they put aside their instructions, took up a rifle and went into battle. Just at that time, at the beginning of March, it happened that three of the workers of the Brigade Political Department had been killed fighting against heavy odds as they retreated along a gully with a handful of Red Army men, attacked by a horde of mounted Cossacks.

The political workers in the peasant regiments maintained their authority only due to the fact that they were excellent, brave and staunch soldiers of the Red Army. In this regard, Nikolai Nikolayevich was particularly respected, and among the soldiers, he was always held up as the finest example of what a Red Army man should be.

At the beginning of March, the forward positions were near Port Arthur, a small hamlet, by then completely destroyed, situated on the road to the Cossack village of Slomikhinskaya, itself a few dozen versts from Algai. By going through Slomikhinskaya, one could come out on the highway: Uralsk—Lbishchensk—Sakharnaya—Guryev. The army, at that time based in Uralsk, intended to launch a general offensive in the near future, and by combined action, first to drive the Cossacks as far as possible away from Uralsk, and then to wipe out the White Cossack army. From Alexandrov-Gai, the offensive was to be spearheaded against the village of Slomikhinskaya, and then it was to be developed through the Chizh swamps and out on to the Uralsk-Guryev highway. This manoeuvre would cut off the retreat of the Cossack forces withdrawing from the Uralsk sector under pressure from the Red troops. The day for launching the offensive was near. The Algai Brigade was making its preparations in feverish haste.

As soon as he arrived in the village, Fyodor went to the Political Department. There he was taken to Nikolai Nikolayevich. The latter was sitting buttoned up tight in a black fur over-coat, with the shaggiest of fur caps on his head, and felt boots on his feet. His office was high-ceilinged, bare and absolutely unheated. He was sitting alone at his desk rummaging through a pile of papers with shaking fingers red from the cold.

The room was miserably furnished—a desk and a chair, nothing more. On the desk there was the stub of cheap pencil, an icon lamp suspiciously black and evidently containing ink, a besmeared penholder that looked more like a brownish wax taper, a makeshift blotter, two political booklets, some kind of a ledger, and a big sheaf of papers, large and small, jumbled loosely together.

They exchanged greetings and introduced themselves. Fyodor showed Nikolai Nikolayevich the telegram in which Frunze had written, "Comrade Klichkov to take charge of political work in Alexandrov-Gai army group." (The brigade was being expanded into a group, other units were being attached.)

Yozhikov looked at the scrap of paper absent-mindedly, somehow, and silently returned it to Fyodor. Then he suddenly exclaimed:

"Let's go! I'll get you settled. I guess you'd like to have some tea and to rest up a bit after your trip."

Fyodor wanted to begin a serious talk with Yozhikov at once—he wanted to get a clear idea of the military situation, the state of political work, prospects, measures taken, possibilities—in a word, he would have been off at full gallop, but Yozhikov so quickly and solicitously steered him to his flat, so zealously hunted up hot water and bread for him, that all serious conversation had to be postponed for the time being. Nikolai Nikolayevich was living in one room of an enormous vacant apartment; in the middle there was a hall with smaller rooms opening on to it; Fyodor settled in one of them. There was a grand-piano in the hall, and Yozhikov had no sooner seated Fyodor at the table, than he went to the piano and began to thump out revolutionary songs. It was cold and hollow-sounding in the room.

Little by little, they fell to talking. Fyodor eyed the youngish, pale, stern face of Nikolai Nikolayevich in admiration and was glad to know that such a fine fellow was in charge of the political work here. As is usually the case, within an hour they had succeeded in telling each other all about themselves and about their past work in the Party, how they happened to be at the front, and what they planned to do in the near future. Their conversation seemed to be progressing perfectly normally, but Fyodor began to get the idea that either Yozhikov was in a hurry to go somewhere, or was nervous, or was disgruntled about something. From his countenance, one could see that he was an outright, plain-spoken, uncomplicated person, but now he didn't once look Fyodor straight in the eye—he kept blinking and looking at the floor, rubbing his hands; he could not seem to sit still; every now and then he would jump up, laugh artificially and insincerely; he was too obliging in everything, in too much of a hurry to agree with everything the other said.

"What a devil's the matter?" Fyodor asked himself, and didn't know what to answer, how to understand Yozhikov.

They went back to the Political Department, to Yozhikov's cold office, and here the conversation naturally became almost official. Yozhikov himself said little, and didn't tell anything of his own accord. He only listened to Fyodor's questions and answered them briefly—unwillingly, drily, it would even seem, contemptuously. Whenever any of the staff came in, Yozhikov hailed them with joy, and began a conversation endlessly long and apparently absolutely unnecessary. If one could have assumed that Yozhikov was a wind-bag in general, then there would have been nothing surprising in all this, but Fyodor correctly judged that quite the contrary, Yozhikov was very chary of words, especially so when at work— he gave instructions or explained only what was necessary for the matter in hand. This affected talkativeness of Nikolai Nikolayevich's therefore again struck Klichkov as being unnatural, and he was again surprised that Yozhikov should be so pleased whenever any of his fellow-workers entered and took Yozhikov's attention away from his conversation with him.

From Yozhikov's brief answers one could gather that there were Party units everywhere; the "comrades' courts" were working very well; there were leaflets and other literature; lectures and indoor and outdoor meetings were held regularly and with success; etc., etc.— in a word, everything had been excellently organized, and there probably would be no call for Fyodor to "organize and expand" the work, since he had come to a place where everything was ready.

Frankly speaking, it must be admitted that Fyodor himself felt somewhat awkward about beginning this new kind of work. Up to now, he had never been at the front, knew nothing about the situation here, and therefore could not "teach" Yozhikov, and, then, he had come with the sincerest desire to work—*not to command, but to work*. The question of subordination did not bother him in the least. He had said as much to Nikolai Nikolayevich in their very first talk together, but from the latter's vague mumble he couldn't make out whether this honest avowal was received in a good light or bad. Now talking with him in his office and getting forced, grudging replies, Klichkov resolved to be very cautious and tactful, since he suspected that Yozhikov was offended because of his appointment, which made Yozhikov his subordinate and took him off the pedestal on which he had settled himself so firmly, both in the brigade and in Algai itself. Up till now, he had been the *one and only* political leader with authority—he held all the threads in his hands, everyone came to him with every question—to him and to him alone. And here suddenly this Klichkov had arrived—the political head of a whole army group of which the brigade was but a part. The pedestal might begin to wobble. Klichkov might begin little by little to obscure Yozhikov and squeeze him out of his exalted position—these were the doubts, which to Fyodor's mind, must be agitating Nikolai Nikolayevich; these were the causes which made the latter begin to act unfriendly to Fyodor an hour and a half after they had got acquainted.

Klichkov was put on his guard and didn't ask any more questions, realizing with an organizer's instinct what he should do next.

First of all, he decided to get thoroughly acquainted with the actual state of the work in the brigade by looking through the minutes and reports; if this were impossible to do with Yozhikov's help, then he would go to his assistants and fellow-workers and obtain official reports and other information through them.

Next, he decided to insist on calling small meetings or conferences of the Party units, cultural commissions and economic control commissions, meetings of the military committees, etc. This would help him at once to see and understand a lot.

After that he intended to make an inspection of all the units and there on the spot to see exactly just what state the work was in. Finally, he wanted to take an active part in the coming fighting as a rank-and-file soldier, and in this way, win for himself the name of a good and brave comrade. This might be decisive in the success or failure of all his future political work.

In the next few days, right up till the beginning of the offensive, Fyodor stubbornly stuck to the tasks he had set himself. He had already had numerous talks with the people in the organizational, cultural and educational and information departments, but everywhere he was accorded the same prejudiced and unfriendly reception. Yozhikov's influence made itself felt everywhere. Nevertheless, he succeeded in spite of every difficulty in getting a fairly detailed report on the state of the work as a whole. The report was full of commonplaces—Fyodor encountered this defect dozens, even hundreds of times later on when he undertook political work on a still bigger scale. Such accounts usually begin with the Creation, then there is a description of the "chaotic condition of things" at the beginning, after which it is explained that the work is being "got into order," but that in certain departments it is still "not at the desired level"; the report concludes with a reference to the multitude of "fruitful measures taken," which, without any doubt, will "correct all existing deficiencies."

In general, reading between these important-sounding phrases, one could gather that booklets were being accurately and zealously distributed to the regiments, and libraries being organized; that the schools for eliminating illiteracy had completely ceased functioning because of military operations, and when they were functioning, were badly attended; that all kinds of commissions seemed to have been organized everywhere, and did exist formally, but there was no information on their work; that meetings were being held, but not often; that amateur-talent performances, on the other hand, were often put on, and were well attended. The whole report was along these lines. Of course, this dry enumeration gave some idea of the work being done, but Fyodor now placed his main hopes on his personal inspection of the units, and on getting a first-hand knowledge of the work on the spot.

He tried to call together some of the commissars—here, too, he encountered a prejudiced attitude; he called a meeting of Party unit representatives—it never took place at all; he called a general meeting, but the Political Department did not get the word around, and there was only a chance audience of fifty or sixty people.

The work didn't get on. Things couldn't go on like that any longer. Fyodor was impatiently waiting for Chapayev's arrival—this, he believed, would cut the Gordian knot and clear up the confused situation.

The day after tomorrow the offensive would begin; why hadn't Chapayev come yet? Fyodor sent an inquiry to Army Headquarters, but got no reply. Tomorrow the last units would move up to Kazachya Talovka and Port Arthur to be in position for the beginning of the attack.

The last conference had been called at Staff Headquarters—the detailed plan for the attack had been discussed for the last time. It was to be made simultaneously from three points, and relied for success not so much on surprise, as on good organization and on Red superiority in weapons and equipment, particularly machineguns. Fyodor, who at that time was still weak in military matters, listened attentively to everything that was said at this council of war, but himself took no part in the discussion and arguments, only looking into the face of one, another, and yet another of the "specialists" and thinking:

"That one, there—can he be a traitor? Can it be that all these fine words are lying—just for effect—to throw dust in our eyes? Tomorrow, when everything is ready, will they stop being friends and turn into enemies?"

And holding his breath, he particularly scrutinized the face of the colonel in command of the brigade.

"Can it be—?"

But the face of the Brigade Commander was such as does not arouse suspicion—it immediately won people's favour—won their trust.

"But just the same, Commissar—be on your guard!"

The "council" finished its meeting. Everyone left Staff Headquarters.

All that day, and all evening, baggage train after baggage train, caravan after caravan, left for Kazachya Talovka. Alexandrov-Gai began to look deserted. Tomorrow, the last units would leave and the town would be deserted and left defenceless.

V

CHAPAYEV

Early in the morning, at about five or six o'clock, someone knocked loudly on Fyodor's door. He opened it—a stranger was standing there.

"Hullo! I'm Chapayev."

Fyodor was wide awake at once. He quickly looked Chapayev in the face, and held out his hand, too hurriedly somehow, trying hard to remain calm.

"My name's Klichkov. Just arrived?"

"Just come from the station—my fellows are there—I sent horses for them."

Fyodor quickly ran over him with greedy eyes—he was impatient to see everything about him and understand all of him. In just this way, at the front on a dark night, a searchlight on the hunt nervously jabs into every crack, trying to drive the darkness out of corners and expose the shrinking nakedness of the earth.

"An ordinary-looking man, thin, of middle height, apparently not very strong, and with slender almost feminine hands; his thin, dark brown hair is stuck down on his forehead in strands. His nose is short, thin and sensitive. His brows are thin and straight, his lips thin, his teeth shining white; he is clean-shaven except for a big sergeant-major moustache. His eyes are light blue, almost green; they are quick, intelligent, unwinking. His complexion is fresh and clear, without pimples or wrinkles, and is not shiny. He was wearing a khaki tunic, blue trousers and high doe-skin boots, and was holding a cap with a red band in his hand; he was wearing shoulder-belts, and at his side was a revolver. His silver sword and green jacket were thrown on the trunk—" That is how Fyodor described Chapayev in his diary that evening.

Chapayev, though after the road, refused to have tea. He talked standing, and sent an orderly to the Brigade Commander to tell him to go to Staff Headquarters, where he, Chapayev, would follow. Soon the lads who had come with him burst into the room in a noisy crowd; they chucked their things into all the corners; threw caps, gloves, and belts on to the tables, chairs and window-sills; they threw down their revolvers, while some unhooked hand-grenades and carelessly stuck them in among the weathered caps and gloves. Sunburned, stern-looking, masculine faces; deep, gruff voices; clumsy, crude movements and speech; they were cut out awkwardly and carelessly, but with a strong, confident hand. Some of them had a way of speaking so strange that one might think that they were always quarrelling—they would jerk out a question abruptly, and answer as sharply, almost fiercely; they flung things around.

The whole house rumbled with their talk and their arguments—the new arrivals were spreading into all the rooms with the exception of Yozhikov's, which was locked.

Within two minutes, Fyodor saw one of the guests sprawl on his unmade bed, and hoist his legs up against the wall; then he began to smoke, flicking the ash off to one side, doing his best to make it fall on Klichkov's suitcase which was standing beside the bed. Another leaned his full weight on the frail dressing-table, which groaned, cracked, and tottered. Somebody knocked a pane out of the window with his revolver butt, while somebody else put his stinking sheepskin coat on top of the bread on the table, so that when they came to eat it, it smelled vilely.

Along with this mob, seemingly even long before it, strong, robust, noisy talk burst into the room. It was never silent for a minute and never got any louder—a steady drone of voices. This was the ordinary, normal conversation of people fresh from the steppe. Just try to make out who was in command here, and who subordinate! There wasn't a hint to go by—they all talked in the manner peculiar to themselves; their behaviour was equally rough, their language original, colourful, permeated with sound steppe simplicity. One family! But there was no visible attachment of one member for another, nor any consideration, any mutual concern, in even the veriest trifles—nothing whatever. At the same time one saw and felt that this was a single, strongly-knit bunch of people, only bound together by ties that were out of the ordinary and finding expression in an original form. They were knit together by their hazardous soldier's life; they were drawn together by bravery, personal courage, contempt for privation and danger, by loyal, unchanging solidarity and a readiness to help one another out of a tight place—by all their hard and colourful life spent together, shoulder to shoulder on the march and in battle.

Chapayev stood out among the others. He had absorbed a little culture—he didn't look so primitive, and didn't behave like the rest. It was as if he were holding himself tight by the bridle. The others also bore themselves rather differently towards him—it reminded one somewhat of the way a fly crawls up a window-pane: the fly keeps crawling confidently along; it runs into other flies and hops over them, or crawls over them, or they bump together and fly away in different directions; and then, suddenly, it runs into a wasp, and lo!—a flash, and it has flown away! It was the same with the Chapayev lads—so long as they were associating among themselves, they were absolutely free and easy; they would blurt out anything that came into their heads; one might give another a wallop with his cap, or a wooden spoon, or a boot, or splash him with hot water from his tumbler. But as soon as Chapayev appeared in their way, none of these liberties were taken with him. Not from fear, not from some feeling of inequality, but from a particular sort of respect —it was as though they said "although he's ours, he's in a class by himself, and it's not for just anyone to set himself up as his equal."

This made itself felt constantly. No matter how free and easy the others held themselves in Chapayev's presence, no matter how much noise they made or how lustily they swore, as soon as things touched him the picture changed immediately. That was their way of showing their love and respect for him.

"Petka! Off with you to the commandant's!" Chapayev ordered.

Petka, a thin swarthy little fellow whose job it was to "perform special errands," immediately left the others, and without a word, ran up to him.

"I'm leaving in two hours—see that the horses are ready. Send mounted men ahead—Potapov and me'll go in a sleigh—get a move on! Potapov, you come with me!"

Chapayev imperiously jerked his head in the direction of a stoop-shouldered, sallow-skinned fellow. The chap was about thirty-five; he had kindly, laughing grey eyes, but his voice was as harsh as a raven's croak. For all his powerful, thick-set body, his movements were strangely soft and girlish.

Potapov was apparently in the middle of telling something very funny but no sooner did he hear Chapayev than he at once became sober. The smile in his grey eyes went out like a candle; he looked Chapayev seriously in the eye with an answering glance that clearly said. "I'm listening!"

Then Chapayev went on with his orders:

"Nobody else except Potapov! The commissar here'll go too, and send three men on horses. The rest of you follow us to Talovka—don't run the horses for nothing. Be there by evening!"

"Listen—" Chapayev looked round the room, not seeing the one he wanted. "Oh, yes—I've sent him there already—Well, you, Kochnev, go take a look at Headquarters—if everybody's there, come back and let me know."

Kochnev left the room. To Fyodor, he looked like a gymnast—he was so quick, so light on his feet, so agile and wiry. He was wearing a short wadded jacket short in the sleeves; a diminutive cap was stuck on the back of his head; he had boots on with puttees to his knees. He was yet under thirty, but his forehead was all in wrinkles. His eyes were light-grey and shrewd; his nose was broad and damp and he had a way of sniffing with it and twisting it slily to one side. He had enormous white wolfish teeth, and when he smiled, he drew back his lips as though ready to tear something to pieces.

There was also a chap named Chekov. His whole appearance jumped out at one—he had thick red eyebrows, a bushy fiery-red moustache, a crocodile jaw and Mongol cheek-bones. His lower lip hung down like a leech distended with blood. His square, cast-iron jaw was thrust out aggressively, and above it, like a mushroom in an iron kettle, was his nose—sweaty and puffy. Below the red matting that he had for eyebrows, his eyes glowed like live coals. He had a broad, barrel chest, and his heavy hands were like shovels. He was a trifle over forty.

Ilya Tyotkin fussed with the tea-kettles, cut bread and cracked jokes incessantly and laughed at them himself—he made digs at everyone and had an answer ready for everything. A house-painter by trade, he had distinguished himself as a Red Guard; he was good-natured, always laughing and a favourite with everybody, a great one for songs, and games and tomfoolery. He was a little older than Petka—somewhere between twenty-six and twenty-eight.

Vikhor, a dashing cavalryman and the intrepid commander of the mounted scouts, stood beside Tyotkin patiently waiting for some bread. He had lost the little finger on his left hand—a target for much joking:

"Vikhor, punch him with your little finger, you four-fingered old ass!"

"Show us your little finger, and I'll give you a fag."

"You nine-fingered blockhead. You nine-legged he-dog!"

It was hard to get under Vikhor's skin—he was made that way, and was always that way even in battle. That man could do a lot without talking!

The most shoving, the worst swearing and the loudest noise came from Shmarin, the oldest of them all—a man of almost fifty. He was wearing a home-tanned, sheepskin jacket with the fur inside, and felt boots, because he was ill and was always cold. His voice, hoarse as Potapov's, and he was black-eyed, black-haired and swarthy.

Averka, the coachman, just a youngster, was here with the rest of them—leaning on his whip and missing nothing of the preparations being made for tea and something to eat. Averka had a livid red face and an onion for nose. He was blear-eyed from the frost and his lips were chapped and cracked. A scarf was wound around his neck—he never parted with it even when he slept.

Of the orderlies, Alexei was the most permanent and the favourite. He was an old acquaintance of Chapayev's and was a very capable and resourceful chap. When anything was needed they sent Alexei—he would hunt out everything and get everything ready. If food was needed, or a linch-pin for a cart, or a strap for a saddle, or home-made medicine, they never sent anyone but Alexei, the shrewdest lad you could find.

What a motley company they were! Each face was a type in itself—you could sit down and write out a whole epic of the steppe with it for inspiration. No two of them were alike, as no two stones are alike. But all of them together were a single, devil-may-care clan. One family! And what a family!

Kochnev came in:

"The Brigade Commander is at Headquarters—you can go now."

There was a slight rustle in the room—more than one pair of curious eyes were fixed on Chapayev.

"Let's go!"

Chapayev nodded to Potapov, and poked Shmarin and Vikhor with a finger. They went out, spurs ringing and tramping heavily in their iron-rimmed heels. Fyodor went with them. It seemed to him that Chapayev was paying too little attention to him and was putting him on the same level as his "suite." Born of these suspicions, an unhealthy little fear was lurking deep in him somewhere, and he recalled what people said about Chapayev: that in 1918, during some fighting when he and his men had been surrounded, a commissar had lost his nerve, and Chapayev had given him a lashing with his whip. Fyodor recalled this, and a sinister feeling began to disturb him. He knew that it could all have been invented; it could have been exaggerated or coloured up. But still there might be something in it—those were different times and Chapayev himself was different, and then anyone might have been a commissar! Fyodor walked behind, and just the thought that he was walking behind was unpleasant.

Chapayev greeted the Brigade Commander curtly and abruptly, looking aside the while, but the latter gallantly bowed double, clicked his spurs, and drawing himself up, almost fired a report at him. He had heard a lot about Chapayev, but mostly from the bad side, making him out little more than a ruffian, or at best a little cracked; he had heard nothing to show that Chapayev had really done anything and did not believe the rumours circulating in the steppe about Chapayev's heroism.

Curious heads were peering out from all the doors, the way the household at some merchant's home peep out through all the cracks when a distinguished guest arrives. It was apparent that it was not only the Brigade Commander that had heard horrors of all kinds about Chapayev. Today, Headquarters was unusually clean. Everyone was sitting or standing in his place. Preparations had been made to put on the best front possible—perhaps they were afraid, not knowing how Chapayev might take things. When the new-comers came into the office of the Brigade Commander, the latter spread out on the table an excellently drawn plan of the next day's attack. Chapayev picked it up, silently examined the fine draughtsmanship and again put it back on the table. Then he pulled up a stool and sat down. Some of those who had come with him also sat down.

"Some compasses!"

They gave him a sorry-looking, rusty pair of compasses. He opened them up, twisted them this way and that—wasn't satisfied.

"Vikhor, go to Averka and fetch mine out of my bag!"

In a couple of minutes Vikhor came back with the compasses, and Chapayev began to measure out the plan with them. At first, he only worked on the plan, but then he pulled a map out of his pocket and began straddling up and down over it with his compasses. He kept asking about distances from one place to another, and whether the going was hard, about water, the baggage trains, the morning fogs, and steppe snow-storms.

Those sitting round kept silent. Only the Brigade Commander would put in a word from time to time, or answer a question. As Chapayev looked at the map, the thin lines were transformed in his mind's eye into snowy valleys, burned-out villages, skirmish lines advancing in the dusk, columns of troops and crawling baggage trains; in his ears the cold morning wind roared and whistled; before his eyes flashed hillocks, well-sweeps, frozen blue streamlets, broken-down grey bridges and stunted bushes.

Chapayev had begun the attack!

When he had finished measuring, Chapayev showed the Brigade Commander where there were mistakes: here the march was too long; there the place for a halt was badly chosen; here they would have to set out too early; there, they would arrive too late. All his arguments were backed up by notes he had made while measuring. The

Brigade Commander was not too ready to agree with him, and seemed secretly amused at times. Still, he agreed, made notes and altered the plan. When it came to certain questions, Chapayev would turn to Vikhor or Potapov or Shmarin, as though enlisting their sympathy and support:

"Well, and what d'you say about it? What d'you think? Am I right or wrong, I ask you?"

The fellows weren't used to holding forth much in his presence, and besides, there wasn't much that they could have added, so exactly and in such detail did Chapayev always provide for everything. They had even altered the old proverb to fit Chapayev: "Don't ever bother Chapayev. With him, it's this way: 'One head is better than two.'"

This new proverb, they thought up specially for him. And well thought-out it was, too, because there had been occasions when he had listened to other people's advice, and had then regretted it, had sworn and cursed himself. Also, the lads had not forgotten one "council," when in their impetuousness they had come out with the devil only knows what kind of advice. Chapayev had listened and listened for a long time, even egging them on:

"Right, that's right—yes—good—I see—that's fine—"

His listeners had really believed that he agreed with them and approved of everything. However, when they had finished, he said:

"Well, and now here's what we have to do—spit on all the rubbish you've said and forget it. It's no good at all. Now listen to my orders!"

And he began, and began in such a way that everything came out entirely different and there wasn't a thing left of what they had been conferring about so long.

All three had been at that conference and remembered it well—now they were careful about coming out with anything, and mostly kept silence, well knowing when and where they could talk and when it was better not to. "Sometimes," they thought, "it may be a good thing to give advice, that's true, but more often, one word can make a lot of trouble!"

Now they kept silent. Fyodor also was silent most of the time—he was still somewhat at sea in military matters and there were some points which he understood with difficulty or not at all. It was only months later that he became familiar with this battle lore and the front in general, but now—why should they ask him, a muff of a civilian!

With his hands folded behind his back, he stood right up against the table and looked now at the map, now at the plan, with a very knowing air; then he would knit his brows, or turn his head aside to cough, obviously fearing to disturb the business-like discussion. His expression was serious and calm. An outsider might think that he was an equal participant in the discussion. Long before meeting Chapayev, Fyodor had decided to establish a special, subtle and cautious system of relations with him: at first, he would avoid purely military discussions so as not to reveal his complete ignorance; instead, he would hold political discussions with Chapayev in which he, Fyodor, would unquestionably be stronger; he would try to draw him out, make him give his opinion on all matters, including intimate questions, personal peculiarities and details; he himself would talk more about science, education, general development—here Chapayev would listen more than talk. And then—then he, Fyodor, would show himself to be a brave soldier—it was absolutely necessary that he do this, and as quickly as possible, otherwise everything would go to the devil so far as Chapayev was concerned, and probably all the Red Army men also—here no politics, knowledge or personal qualities would be of any use! When he had done this feeling-out—this preparatory work—and Chapayev had opened up so that he could be understood, then he, Fyodor could attempt to become closer friends with him, but for the time being—for the time being—he must be careful. If only his courtesy and consideration were not construed to be fawning upon a "hero" and accepted as such! (Chapayev, of course, knew that his fame resounded everywhere, and that many a one would be flattered to knock up an acquaintance with him.) Only when Chapayev was "intellectually captured," when he himself began to listen to Fyodor, when he began, it might be, to learn something from him, only then would he, Fyodor, be able to meet him halfway in everything. But no putting on airs—not for anything! He must immediately put simplicity, heartiness and a certain rudeness into their relations so that Chapayev wouldn't have the least thought of Fyodor as a lily-livered intellectual, who, at the front, was always looked on with suspicion and unconcealed contempt.

All these preparations of Klichkov's were by no means trifles—they assisted him in the simplest, quickest and surest manner to begin to feel at home in the surroundings in which he had now begun to work, and for the sake of this work to become an organic part of them. He did not know yet, just what the limits of this "coming together" would be, but he understood very well that Chapayev and the Chapayev lads—all this half-guerrilla mass, and the nature of their activities—was an exceedingly complicated phenomenon which one couldn't afford to approach blindfold. Along with good qualities, there were also qualities which must be treated very cautiously and guarded against.

Just what was Chapayev? How did Klichkov picture Chapayev to himself, and why was it that in regard to him, he conceived the idea of establishing a special, subtle system of relations? Was this really necessary?

While working in the rear, Fyodor had of course heard and read a lot about the popular heroes who flashed now at one front of the Civil War, now at another. When he looked closer he saw that the majority of them were from among the peasants and very few from the ranks of the city workers. Worker heroes were always of a different sort. Having grown up in a large industrial centre, used as he was to seeing the broad, orderly, well-organized struggle of the weavers, Fyodor always looked somewhat askance at the half-anarchistic guerrilla undertakings of popular heroes like Chapayev. This did not prevent him from following their careers with the greatest attention, regarding them with the greatest respect and being most enthusiastic about their heroic exploits. But a feeling of apprehension always remained with him. Such was the case now.

"Chapayev is a hero," Fyodor reasoned to himself. "He personifies all that is irrepressible and spontaneous, all the wrath and protest that has accumulated within the peasantry. But the devil knows how such spontaneous elements may manifest themselves. We have had cases (can they be called few?) when just such a fine commander as Chapayev has suddenly gone and knocked his commissar on the head! And not some rogue, blabber-mouth or coward, but a fine, brave revolutionary! And it even happened that they went over to the Whites with their 'spontaneous' bands.

"The workers—that's something else again: *they'll never go over under any circumstances whatsoever*, that is, those of them that consciously entered the struggle. It is of course obvious that there are also people among the workers who yesterday were peasants. There are those who are not class-conscious enough, and there are those who are too 'conscious' and have become tenderfeet; but with the workers, nevertheless, one sees at once with whom one is dealing.

"But—ah, how much there is that's dangerous in this Chapayev's, guerrilla fire-eating!"

It was because of his suspicious attitude towards this spontaneous guerrilla movement that Fyodor came to have the desire to establish his relations with his new surroundings in the most subtle way—to establish them in such a way that he himself would not stew in this juice, but on the contrary, would exert an ideological influence on everything. It was best to begin with the head—to begin with Chapayev, the leader. It was on him that Fyodor concentrated all his attention.

Petka—as almost everyone was accustomed to calling Isayev—stuck his tiny bird-like head in at the door, and beckoning Potapov with his little finger, shoved a note at him, which read:

"Tell Vasily Ivanovich the nags and ivrithin is reddy."

Petka knew that at certain times and certain places, he couldn't just burst in, and on such occasions he always made use of such notes. The note came just in time. Everything had been said, written down, signed—now the order of the day would fly the rounds of the regiments. The formalities of taking charge of the operations occupied but little time.

"I came here to command," Chapayev declared, "and not to potter with papers—for that there's clerks."

"Vasily Ivanovich," Potapov whispered, "I see you're through—everything's ready—we can start."

"Everything ready? Let's go!" Chapayev abruptly rose from his stool. Everybody made way for him, and he went out first as he had come in.

A crowd of Red Army men had gathered outdoors around the porch—they had heard about Chapayev's arrival. Many had fought with him back in 1918; many were personally acquainted with him, and of course every last one had heard about him. They stood stretching out their necks, their eyes full of wonder and delight; their ingratiating smiles stretched to their ears.

"Hurrah for Chapayev!" shouted someone in front, just as Chapayev stepped on to the ground.

"Hurrah! Hurrah!"

From all sides, Red Army men came running up; the villagers approached; the crowd grew.

"Comrades!" said Chapayev.

There was instant silence.

"I've no time to talk to you now—I'm on my way to the front. Tomorrow we'll see each other there because we've got a good appetizer ready for the Cossacks and tomorrow we'll give them a treat. We'll have a talk then, but right now—so long!"

Again there was a thunder of cheers. Chapayev got into the sleigh. Potapov settled himself in after him. Three mounted men were waiting. A spirited black stallion was led up for Fyodor.

"Get going!" shouted Chapayev.

The horses gave a jerk—the crowd made way, shouting the louder. They rode abreast all the way to the edge of Algai.

The snowy desert of the steppe was monotonous and dreary. During the warm days, the hillocks had got bald—the ground had begun to show through, but now they had again been snowed under; the whole steppe was covered over and was crunchy from the frost. The horses trotted along easily and in good spirits. Chapayev and Potapov sat almost back to back. One might think they had quarrelled, but they were thinking over the coming action, preparing themselves for the next day. The three mounted horsemen kept three or four paces behind the sleigh, no closer, no farther away, but always at the same distance as though chained there. Fyodor rode at one side. At times he would let the others get a whole verst ahead of him and then put his horse into a gallop. It was good to gallop over the steppe, the horse was so light in his stride and so willing to go.

"Tomorrow," he thought, riding along at a stiff trot, "will mark the beginning of my life as a soldier, the beginning of real life for me. It will really begin to get going, but will it be for long? Who can know what it will all lead to? Who can name the day of victory? When will it come, our victory? Day after day, day after day will gallop by on the march, in battle, in danger and alarm.... Will we wisps of down be preserved? Who of us will return to his native place, and who will be left here in the dark gullies, in the snowy wastes of the steppe?"

And memories of everyday affairs crept into his mind, and dear, familiar faces rose up before him. He pictured himself killed: he lay on the snow, his arms thrown wide, his temple bloody. He even began to be sorry for himself. Once this feeling of self-pity would have been sure to turn into a protracted fit of melancholy, but now he shook it off, drove away the thought and rode on composedly—he laughed away the thought of his death.

Two and a half hours passed in this way. Chapai* evidently got tired of sitting still, stopped the sleigh, put one of the riders in his seat, and himself rode horseback. He rode up to Fyodor.

"So now we're together, Comrade Commissar?"

"Yes," answered Fyodor and at once noticed how firmly and solidly Chapayev sat in the saddle, as though welded there. Then he glanced down at himself and it seemed as if he was tied on.

"A good bump," he thought, "and I'll fly out of the saddle. Just take a look at Chapayev, there—nothing'll loosen him."

"Been fighting long?"

* Chapayev's close friends often called him simply "Chapai."

It seemed to Fyodor that the other was grinning and he caught a note of irony in his voice. "He knows that I've only just come to the front, and is making game of me."

"I'm just beginning."

"Been in the rear up to now?"

Again the question was sarcastic.

One must know that for such fighters as Chapayev, people in the rear were the most contemptible and despicable of creatures. Fyodor had suspected this before, and during the last few weeks he had become fully convinced of it in travelling and talking with many a soldier and commander.

"In the rear, you ask? I was working in Ivanovo-Voznesensk," Fyodor carelessly dropped the words in a matter-of-fact tone.

"Way beyond Moscow?"

"Yes, three hundred versts at least."

"Well, and what's it like there? How're things getting along?"

Fyodor was glad to change the subject and eagerly grasped at the last question; he explained to Chapai what a hard and hungry life the Ivanovo-Voznesensk weavers had. Why weavers? Were there only weavers there? It was always that way with Klichkov—when he began to talk about Ivanovo-Voznesensk, he saw before him only the host of workers, and was proud of the fact that he was close to this host; in his recollections, he even posed a little.

"That means they live badly," Chapayev agreed seriously, "and all because of the famine. If there wasn't any famine—why, everything would go entirely different—and they stuff themselves, the sons-of-bitches, you can be sure they don't think of those——"

"Who stuff themselves?" Fyodor asked, not understanding him.

"The Cossacks—they don't give a damn about anything."

"Yes, but all the Cossacks aren't that way."

"All of them!" shouted Chapayev. "You don't know, but I tell you, all of them! And don't you tell me otherwise—n-no!" and Chapayev bounced nervously in his saddle.

"They can't all be that way," Fyodor protested. "Maybe just a few, but there are Cossacks who're for us. Why, wait a minute—" and he recollected something with joyful agitation, "what about our mounted scouts in the brigade, aren't they all Cossacks?"

"In the brigade?" Chapayev became just a little thoughtful.

"Why, yes, with us, here, in the brigade."

"They must be from the city—I doubt it could be any from around here," Chapayev stubbornly argued.

"I don't know whether they're from the city, but they're here, and it can't be, Comrade Chapayev, that all the Cossacks, every single one, is against us. It simply can't be that way."

"Why not? You stay a little with us, and—"

"No matter how long I stay—I'd still never believe it," Fyodor's voice was hard and stern.

"As for single people, why talk about them?" Chapayev began to back down a little. "Of course there's one here and one there, but not many—hardly any at all."

"No, not individuals, you're wrong there—they're writing from Turkestan—Cossack regiments there have set up Soviet power over a whole region—and in the Ukraine, and on the Don."

"Well, go on hoping, they'll show you—"

"Why hope—I'm not hoping," Klichkov explained to Chapai. "There's a lot of truth in your opinion. It's true that the Cossacks are a bunch of vultures. Who can argue about that? The tsarist government did not make so much of them for nothing. But you look at the young Cossacks —they're nothing like the old ones. The young ones come to us more. Of course, it's harder for some Cossack greybeard to reconcile himself to Soviet government—at least it's hard now, until he has understood it. Why, the devil knows what they think about us, and they believe everything: the churches, they say, we are turning into cowsheds, our wives are all in common, we force everybody to live together, make them eat and drink together, and it has to be at one table. How can a Cossack reconcile himself to that when he's been used to the Church from generation to generation—been used to having plenty of everything on his fat farm, been used to having other people work for him, and been used to a free steppe life?"

"Ixploiters," said Chapayev, hardly getting the word out.

"Exactly," said Fyodor, repressing a smile. "Exploitation is at the bottom of it. The rich Cossacks not only exploit the Kirghiz and Russians who don't happen to be Cossacks—they're not above exploiting their own Cossacks. That's where they begin to split up. Only the old people, even when they get the worst of it, have reconciled themselves to it—they say that it's God's will. The young people look at things simpler and bolder— that's why it's more the young people who come over to us. You can't change the old ones—the only way you can get at them is with a gun."

"A gun, a gun's not all—" and Chapayev shook his head, "fighting's hard, if it weren't for—"

Fyodor didn't understand why Chapai said this, but realized that he hadn't said it for nothing—that something special was to be read into these words. He waited for the other to develop or explain his thought.

"Our centres—that's what—" Chapayev again vaguely dropped an obscure but tempting phrase.

"What centres?"

"Why, they've stuck in all kinds of bastards," Chapayev muttered seemingly to himself but loud enough for Fyodor to hear everything distinctly. "It used to be they kept me under arms for days at a time, the sons-of-bitches, and when it was freezing cold at that, and now they welcome them with open arms: 'Here's a soft chair for you, General—sit down, please. Command any way you like—you needn't give them any ammunition if you don't want to—let them fight with sticks.'"

Chapayev had got on to his sorest question—that of staffs, generals, orders and court-martial for their non-fulfilment—a question which in those days touched to the quick not only Chapayev and not only people like Chapayev.

"You can't get along without generals," growled Klichkov in a soothing tone. "What would war be like without generals?"

"We'd get along without them." Chapayev gripped the reins tightly.

"We couldn't get along without them, Comrade Chapayev. You can't do much with just daring—we need knowledge and what knowledge have we got? Who'll give us knowledge except the generals? They've studied all that and they've got to teach us. The time'll come when we'll have our own teachers, but we haven't got them yet, or have we? Of course not! And since we haven't, we'll have to learn from others!"

"Learn! Yes! But what will they teach us? What?" Chapayev hotly objected. "D'you think they'll tell us what has to be done? Just keep on waiting. They'll tell you! I was at their Academy, myself—for two months I hung around there like a fish out of water, and then I spat on the whole business and came back here. Nothing for people like me to do there. One of them—Pechkin, his name was—a professor—bald as your knee he was—asked me at the examination:

"'D'you know,' he asks, 'the Rhine River?'

"I'd been all through the German War—why shouldn't I know? Only I thought, why should I answer him?

"'No,' I says, 'I don't know, but do you know the Solyanka River?'

"He didn't expect that, and opened his eyes wide.

"'No I don't,' he says. 'What about it?'

"'Then there's no use asking questions. I was wounded on the Solyanka River, and crossed it and recrossed it five times. What do I care about your Rhine, what the hell does it make to me? But on the Solyanka I've got to know every little bump of ground because that's where we're fighting the Cossacks!'"

Fyodor burst out laughing and looked at Chapayev in amazement. "What baby ideas this Chapayev, this popular hero, has! Each to his own calling—some people can acquire knowledge, but for others it's impossible. Here this fellow spent two months at the Academy and didn't get a useful thing out of it, didn't understand a thing. And he's got brains—only he's terribly raw—he'll take a lot of polishing."

"You weren't at the Academy long enough," said Fyodor. "You can't learn everything in two months. It's hard—"

"Might as well've not been there at all," said Chapayev, with a hopeless gesture. "No need to teach me anything—I know all there is to know myself."

"What d'you mean, no need to teach you," Fyodor objected. "A person can always learn something new."

"Yes, but not there!" Chapayev caught him up excitedly. "I know there's things to learn and I'm going to learn. I want to tell you—What's your name?"

"Klichkov."

"I want to tell you, Comrade Klichkov, that I'm almost illiterate. I only learned the alphabet four years ago, and I'm thirty-five years old! You might say I've lived in ignorance my whole life. Well, why talk about that now—some other time. That must be Talovka, there."

Chapayev spurred on his horse. Fyodor followed suit. They overtook Potapov. Ten minutes later they were entering Kazachya Talovka.

VI

THE BATTLE OF SLOMIKHINSKAYA

Kazachya Talovka was a tiny village that had been burned to the ground. Only three dingy clay huts were left standing; smoke-blackened chimneys were sticking up lank and gawky everywhere. The hovel where they now stopped was packed full of Red Army men, some sitting, some lying; they had jammed in here to wait for the order to march. The new-comers did not order them to leave, or disturb them, or even take any notice of them. Those sitting on the bench squeezed together to make room. They woke up some of their fellows who were snoring with especial zeal and hindering the conversation.

The steppe fog had made the twilight deeper, and it was dark in the hut. The soldiers had got the end of a church taper from somewhere or other and stuck it on to a saucer—they clustered around the table, spread out a map and began to discuss the details of next morning's attack. Chapayev sat in the middle of the bench, both hands on the table. In one, he held his compasses, in the other a sharpened pencil. The commanders of regiments, battalions and companies, as well as ordinary Red Army men surrounded him in a solid ring—some had their elbows on the table, some were bent over it, and all watched attentively as Chapayev measured off the distances, his little nickel compasses striding along with broken steps like a crane. Fyodor and Potapov sat beside him on the bench. This, to tell the truth, was no con-

ference.—Chapayev was simply taking the opportunity to acquaint his commanders with their tasks, to tell them what they would be up against.

All listened in silence, some writing down certain of his orders and advice. The solemn silence was broken only by Chapayev's imperious voice and the whistling and snoring of the sleeping soldiers. One of them, lying in the corner, was whistling away like a reed pipe, and his neighbour slowly and purposefully dragged the dirty sole of his huge boot across his nose. The sleeper jumped up, and still half-asleep looked stupidly and wild-eyed around him, unable to understand anything.

"Quiet, you scarecrow!" his neighbours angrily threatened.

"Quiet? Who?" His sleepy eyes were blank and ludicrous.

They brought him to his senses by giving him a thump on the back; he rubbed his eyes, discovered that Chapayev was here, and himself rose quietly on tiptoe and listened to what he was saying till the very end, perhaps not even understanding the meaning of his commander's speech.

Soon the rest of Chapayev's outfit arrived from Alexandrov-Gai. They piled into the hut which was now crowded to suffocation.

Chapayev went on with his instructions: "If we don't do it all at once, nothing will come of it—got to be all at once! Jump on him so he won't have a chance to move an inch. Send off everyone from here in two hours. D'you understand? Got to be at Port Arthur before sunrise. Have to do everything when it's still dark, no real light, d'you get me?"

They nodded their heads, answering softly: "We understand. Of course, it's got to be in the dark. The dark's what we need."

"You've all got your orders," Chapayev went on. "I've put down the time everywhere—when to make a halt, when to march. You want to believe, chaps, that everything's going to turn out right, that's the most important thing; if you don't believe we're going to win, better not attack at all. I've put down only the time and the places, but that's not enough to win—you've got to finish the job yourselves. First of all, you've got to be careful—we can't let anyone know we're beginning an attack—not for anything. If they find out, it'll all go to pot. If you run across any Cossack or Kirghiz, or any peasant for that matter, hold him, don't let him go—we'll check him up afterwards."

"We've caught some," somebody muttered from the corner.

"If you have, then hold them," Chapayev rejoined briskly. "You have to keep your eyes about you when it comes to the Cossacks—you know what they're like—they'll jump out at you from under the table. Here they're at home—they know all the paths, all the gullies. Remember that, too. And don't mince words with them or they'll have you where they want you."

"You're right there. That's just the way. The Cossack always hits you from behind."

The business part of the discussion was over. The omnipotent Petka produced bread, boiled some water in a little kettle, and found sugar—six greyish, well-sucked lumps. The company fell to noisily. The din in the hut developed into a lusty uproar. The soldiers who had been sleeping the cast-iron sleep of men after a march, woke up bewildered, some from the shouting, some from energetic kicks, some from a boot scraping across their faces, or a rifle, or a great-coat—whatever it happened to be. They all got busy with their pannikins. In a few minutes they had dragged the table into the middle of the room and perched themselves around it on saddles, boards or chunks of fire-wood—some sat on their heels right on the floor. The yellow church taper shone feebly, and nothing could be seen but vague black shadows and waxy blobs instead of faces.

Fyodor felt strange in these new and amazing surroundings. It seemed to him that no one noticed him at all. Why, after all, should anyone notice him? Say he was a commissar—well, and what of it? In military matters he couldn't as yet point out anything and this was no time for politics—why should they notice him? "A time'll come," he thought to himself, "and we'll get to know each other better—right now I can keep in the background."

He even felt lonely among this closely-knit family of soldier comrades. He even began to envy them. Why, even this Petka, the sooty little jackdaw, was closer, more akin, more easily understood than he, Klichkov. How all of them worshipped their Chapai! If he merely said something to anyone of them, the chap was struck silly, and thought it great luck just to talk to him. If he ever praised anyone a little, the fellow never forgot it. To sit at the same table with Chapayev, to shake hands with him— that was a matter of the greatest pride for any of them. Later they would recall it, and tell about it with great fervour and dignity, spicing up what had really happened with fantastic fibs.

Fyodor left the hovel and was about to go out in the field when he heard them singing inside. He went back in, squeezed up to the table again and began to listen.

Chapayev himself was setting the tune. His voice was metallic, with a strong tremor, and at first even unpleasant. But then as one became accustomed to it, one was attracted by the fervent sincerity and feeling with which he sang his favourite songs. There were only a few of these favourites—four or five in all. All his comrades knew them to the last word—one could see that they sang them often. Chapayev could take unbelievably high notes, and at such times one held one's breath for fear his voice would crack. But never, not even a single time, did Chapayev spoil the song—only if he shouted too much he would get hoarse, and for three or four days would go about black as thunder. Chapayev was always gloomy when he couldn't sing, would never get through the day without falling into the dumps. No matter how grim the situation, no matter how worn out he was with the march, no matter how shaky he might feel after a battle, or how sleepy he might be after his work, he would be sure to find at least ten minutes to sing. Another such lover of songs was not to be found; to him, songs were as bread, as water. And his lads, from friendly habit, and never tiring of keeping him company, did not lag behind.

> *Sailor boy, my handsome lad,*
> *You are twenty, I can see;*
> *Love me, then, and make me glad.*
> *Now, what will your answer be?*

The song went on as muddled, trivial and empty to the end. Chapayev liked it mostly for the refrain—it went so well with their nomad, restless partisan life:

> *Over waves, over foam,*
> *One day here, then away from home!*
> *Over the foam, the foam, the foam,*
> *One day here, then away from home!*

This refrain, caught up by them all, rolled out like thunder across the black sky, and filled the steppe with its wild melody.

Then they liked to sing about Stepan Razin, about Ataman Churkin, and now

> *Behind the iron grating in a dungeon's foul air,*
> *The mountain-bred eagle was plunged in despair.*

They sang and palavered till midnight, and then curled up each wherever he could, and fell asleep.

The advance was planned in such a way that they should be approaching Slomikhinskaya when it just began to get light. They were to attack in regimental strength from three sides at once. The regiment now at Talovka was to be in the centre and attack the village itself; the other two regiments were to strike from the flanks, bending around in a half circle.

It had been decided that the regiment here at Talovka would soon leave in waggons—within an hour and a half —but all was still quiet. There were no lurking signs anywhere of the imminent battle.

Fyodor couldn't sleep. He also had tried to make himself comfortable on the floor with his head on a cold Cossack saddle—no, he couldn't go to sleep! Either he wasn't used to sleeping with his head on a saddle, or it was the cold uneasiness that gripped his heart in this, the night before his first battle.

What was it to the others! Dozens and dozens of times they had been in battle—shell-shocked time and again, bones broken, heads punctured, their bodies riddled with bullets, what was it to them! To them this night was nothing at all out of the ordinary. The night before a battle—what of it! No few such nights had they snored through—these nights were no different to them than any other quiet night. But for every one of them, for every single one, there had once been his first "night before a battle." On that night, just like Fyodor, each of them must have been tortured in this chaos of unresolved conflicts and gloomy apprehensions; he, too, must have dumbly ached with depressing thoughts and feelings.

Fyodor couldn't sleep, oppressed as he was by some inexplicable weight that he had never known before. When he looked about him, the dead glow of the candle-end showed him the soldiers scattered about the floor, twisted up and tangled together indiscriminately in one common heap.

"That's the way dead bodies must lie scattered about on the battle-field—in disorder, limbs twisted in agony, here in heaps, there separately, and there again in even rows where they have been mowed down by machine-guns."

In the dim light, the faces seemed pale as in a morgue, and the snores, now escaping in a sharp rattle, now resounding in drawn-out whistles and sighs, were to him like groans.

Fyodor left the hovel, feeling that he could not go to sleep. Wouldn't it be better in the healthy air of the frosty night? And the night was quiet and black—a steppe night. High in the sky the stars shone green. The wind was light and free, a wind such as blows only in the steppe.

Among the ruins of the fire-gutted village, the regiment had bivouacked under the open sky. Here and there at the dying camp-fires he could see the hunched figures of soldiers sitting alone. These were men on duty, or poor wretches like himself, wearied with sleeplessness, who did not know how to shorten the soul-burning hours before the battle. Absently they threw wet chips into the fire, and sweaty little sticks that they had gathered in the steppe—there is no wood to be found in the steppe. They anxiously scraped together the coals so as not to let the fire go out and leave them in the black impenetrable murk. There, where three or four were clustered about a fire, they were busy with kettles, making soup or boiling tea. There was a roll of laughter dying away like distant thunder—the lads were amusing themselves telling jokes, killing the time before the march in their own way.

The night was black as pitch, and grim. It had crept up close all around, ringed with fears, and scampered off in a million tiny rustlings which only made sharper the sinister silence of the steppe.

In the steppe, beside the ruins, ghost-like camels, enormous, shaggy, moved smoothly and majestically. Strange shadows were moving briskly in the gloom. Out of the inky darkness, human figures dived into the quivering bright fire-light, and then as suddenly disappeared again into the bottomless night. In everything, there was an inexplicable stern concentration, a distinct waiting for something immense and final—a waiting for the battle!

No matter how many times afterwards it befell Fyodor to pass the night waiting for the morrow's battle, all these nights were like one another in their stern gravity, in their profound and gloomy immensity. On such a night, passing along the skirmish lines, stepping over the heads of sleeping Red Army soldiers, his brain was filled with thoughts of their struggle, of human suffering, of these sacrificed men whose dead bodies were left to rot nameless on the battle-fields of the Civil War.

"Here they lie, these soldiers, exhausted from the march, and tomorrow, at the first gleam of daylight, they will go into action in skirmish lines and columns, columns and skirmish lines, now lying down, now rushing forward, again and yet again falling flat in fox-holes hurriedly scooped out with a tiny trench tool, or simply scratched out with frozen fingers. And many will never rise—they will never rise again; they will continue to lie, motionless and soundless in the deserted field. Each of them, so small and lonely, left for the ravens to batten upon; those who had arrived at the front so unnoticeably and left the fighting ranks without a trace; each of them gave all he had, reserving nothing, and silently, with no beating of drums, recognized by no one, honoured by no one, fell out unnoticed, a little cog in a fire-breathing steel monster."

Fyodor saw a curly-headed husky lad bent over the fire, fussing with some potatoes, turning them over, trying to bake them on the dying coals. Every once in a while he would stick his bayonet into the ashes, pull it out with a potato on it, touch it with his fingers and cautiously bring it to his lips—right out of the fire. Then he would spit hastily and flick the potato off his bayonet back into the ashes. He was completely engrossed in his innocent occupation. Probably his head, too, was swarming with persistent thoughts and ever-changing, fleeting recollections. What was he thinking about with such concentration, his stare fixed unchanging on the dying fire? About his village, you can be sure, about his work, the life he had left to go to the front and to which he would have returned—ah, with what joy and eagerness he would have returned! What wouldn't he think over that night! And in the morning, it might be they would bring him back here with a leg torn off, or with a bullet-hole in his chest or with his head laid open. He would wheeze terribly, slowly and vainly, and gritting his teeth, try to straighten out his broken limbs; he would be wild and terrifying all plastered with crimson clots of blood. They would cut off that shock of black curls so well beloved by someone, would shave his broad round head and would begin to fish around in the flinching, bloody flesh with steel knives and needles—Brrr!

And his neighbour—that little peasant with the red beard, no longer young—he must be almost forty. The two said not a single word to one another; they were both thinking their own thoughts—in each of them at that moment his own life, bound up with everyone and separate from everyone, was throbbing more sharply and quickly. They had no time for talking—it would not be in place. The red-bearded peasant was sitting immovable, as though he had frozen in that posture: his hands were folded on his belly, he had pulled his cold feet up under him, and his unwinking sleepy gaze was fixed on the camp-fire. Tomorrow, he, too, might be left lying on the snowy plain among the other bodies, dead like his own, black and crimson on the clean, fluffy carpet of snow. Only in one single spot, under the temple, would the scarlet blood bore a black hole in the snow—there would be no other traces anywhere about.

Those thin, freckled hands would no more be folded on his stomach—they would be thrown out sideways as though in delirium, and it would look as though they had crucified the man and nailed him to the snow-covered field with invisible spikes. His leaden gaze would be as fixed as now—the cold dead gaze of a cold dead body.

Fyodor clearly saw these pictures of death, remaining as they did in his memory from the first war when he had picked up and bandaged wounded soldiers.

"Who goes there?" the sentry challenged.

"A friend, Comrade!"

"Password!"

"Bolt!"

The sentry tossed his heavy rifle over to his other hand, hunched his shoulders from the cold and strode off, disappearing in the darkness.

Fyodor went back into the hut—here there was a furious snoring and whistling. Aiming at the first chink in the heap of sleeping bodies, he contrived to wedge himself in, curled up and lay down. Sleep, surprisingly enough, came at once.

It was still completely dark when they saddled their horses and trotted out of Talovka for Port Arthur. (By the way, does anyone know why they called this little burned-out hamlet "Port Arthur"?) A shivering seized them all; they yawned wildly and nervously from not having had their sleep out. Before sunrise, it was cold and harsh in the steppe—sharp, icy awls pierced through their great-coats and through their shirts.

They rode without talking. Only just before they got to Port Arthur, when the first explosions of the shrapnel flashed in the dusky sky, Chapayev turned to Fyodor:

"It's begun!"

"Yes."

Again they were silent, not saying a word till they got to the hamlet. They spurred up the horses and galloped faster. Their hearts stood still, as though squeezed, from that strange agitation that always overcomes a man as he approaches the battle-field, no matter whether he is timid or brave. No one is *calm*—it is only chivalrous humbug to pretend that there are people who are *absolutely cool in battle and under fire*; there are no such cucumbers among the human race. It is possible to get into the habit of *seeming* cool; it is possible to hold oneself with dignity; one can *control himself and not give way quickly* to the influence of external circumstances—that is a different question. There are no people who are *cool* in battle or just before a battle—there are none and can be none.

Both Chapayev, the seasoned fighter, and Fyodor, the tyro, were now completely in the grip of this strange feeling. This was not terror or the fear of death, but a tautening of all their spiritual strings to the highest pitch, a sharpening of their thoughts to the last degree, and an unbelievable, improbable haste. Where one must hurry to, why this peculiar haste—one doesn't understand or realize, but a man's abrupt movements, his jerky, brief speech, his quick, keen glances—all show that at this moment he is the embodiment of spontaneous haste.

Fyodor wanted to ask Chapayev something, wanted to know his thoughts, his mood, but he saw the serious, almost angry expression of his face, and kept silent. They drove up to Port Arthur. The baggage trains were here, and the peasant drivers sat in clusters among the ruins of the hamlet, pouring hot tea out of their kettles. They were breakfasting with gusto, eating their fill with great appetite. Chapayev jumped off his horse, climbed on to a high wall built of cakes of cow dung and looked through his field-glasses in the direction of the bursting shrapnel. The gloom of night had slipped away and it was quite light. They halted here a few minutes, and then once more they mounted their horses and galloped further. They met a peasant cart with something lying in it covered with a tattered old sheepskin.

"What have you got there, Comrade?"

"A soldier wounded."

Fyodor glanced at the cart, and under the sheepskin, made out the lines of a human figure. He turned his horse and rode alongside. Chapayev rode on.

"Seriously wounded?"

"Yes. Head and legs."

"Did you bandage him?"

"Of course we did—wrapped everything up."

At that moment, the wounded man groaned, slowly poked a bandaged, bloody head out from under the grey covering, opened his eyes and looked at Fyodor with a dull, heavy gaze as though saying:

"Yes, brother—half an hour ago I was as whole as you—and now, look! I've done my bit and now I'm leaving—crippled. Let others now ... it's their turn. I've got nothing to be ashamed of—I saw it out till the end. You can see for yourself—they're carrying me...."

These fragments of thoughts rushed through Fyodor's head. It was intolerably painful: here is the *first*—there would be others—but what of that? It would be easier to look at them—that's the way it goes in battle. But this *first*—how painful was this first, fresh loss!

And other thoughts galloped through his head as swiftly as these, not thoughts, but pictures, and recent pictures—yesterday's—at that: there in Kazachya Talovka by the camp-fire. Maybe this one, too, like the one yesterday, and not yesterday, even, but last night, had been absorbed in baking half-rotten potatoes somewhere, sticking them on a bayonet, and pulling them out to try them smoking hot with his lips.

Fyodor galloped off, hoping to catch up with Chapayev, but the latter had apparently turned aside. They met only at the skirmish line.

Carts crawled up to the front and carts crawled back from there. Those coming up were loaded with shells and cartridges, or were empty, to pick up the wounded. Those going back had only one invariable load—bleeding human bodies.

"Our men very far?"

"Not very—about five versts from here."

On the right, across the Uzen River, there were some Kirghiz villages—the Cossacks had been driven out of them with gun-fire. Across the river, two Red Army scouts were wandering up and down, peering into gullies and looking behind piles of stones and dried dung cakes to see if any wounded comrade was lying there. Nearer and louder roared the Red battery, nearer and more distinctly exploded the shells. Now, the skirmish lines could be seen black in the distance. What did he mean, five versts? To be exact, it wasn't even two. Under artillery fire, the road must have seemed long to the driver!

Fyodor rode up to the second skirmish line, and here he saw Chapayev. The commander of the regiment was walking beside him and they were earnestly talking about something.

"I sent a man—he didn't come back," the commander of the regiment said in reply to a previous question.

"Send another man!" snapped Chapayev.

"I did—no result."

"Send a third!" Chapayev insisted.

The commander of the regiment was silent for a moment. Chapayev's temper was rising. His eyelids quivered, and his eyes glared wolfishly behind his lashes, on the alert like beasts in a thicket.

"Anyone from there?" Chapayev asked sharply.

"No one from there, either."

"Long time ago?"

"Over an hour."

Chapayev knitted his brows tight, but said nothing, and dropped the conversation. Fyodor understood that they had been talking about communications. There was good contact with one of the regiments, but none at all with the other. Later, it turned out that its men had been in doubt about their commander—a former tsarist officer. They had suddenly decided that he was leading them to slaughter. So they refused to march, but held back for a long time, making an uproar in the attempt to get to the truth, kicking up a row while the precious minutes passed.

Fyodor walked beside Chapayev; they led their horses by the reins. Here Potapov silently appeared, and at a little distance, Ilya Tyotkin and Chekov. How they had got here, Fyodor didn't know. When he rode out of Talovka with Chapayev, he hadn't noticed in the confusion whether the lads had stayed in the hut, or whether they had galloped off earlier in the night, after the singing.

It was now half a verst to the first skirmish line. They decided to ride there, but a bitter wind suddenly sprang up, as often happens in the steppe; heavy flakes of soft snow began to fly, plastering their faces and preventing them from moving forward. The advance bogged down. However, the snow-storm soon stopped, and in half an hour, the skirmish lines were again in motion. Klichkov and Chapayev rode along the flanks—they were now in the first line. To the right appeared the little hamlet of Ovchinnikov.

"I think the Cossacks have dug in there," said Chapayev, pointing beyond the river. "There'll probably be some fighting in the hamlet."

This time, Chapayev was mistaken—the hard-pressed Cossacks had no idea of trying to hang on at the hamlet. After some sham firing they took to their heels without offering any resistance.

They were approaching Slomikhinskaya—only a verst or two were left. They were moving along a wide, flat plain—a place that could easily and conveniently be shelled from the village. But the Cossacks were silent. What could it mean? This sinister silence was more terrible than any shelling. Were they making some crafty preparations—getting a trap ready? The only brush had been on the far bank of the Uzen, but here—here all was quiet.

Fyodor rode in front of the skirmish line, smoking and making a show of gallantry—"What a brave chap I am," he seemed to be saying, "just look at me riding horseback in front of the skirmish line, and not afraid that a Cossack bullet might pick me off." This was only an eruption of childish vainglory. But perhaps at that moment it was necessary. In the first place, it raised the commissar's authority, and then, too, this youthful ardour unquestionably encouraged the skirmish line. When a horseman rides in front of the skirmish line, it bucks up the men—any soldier who has been in a skirmish line knows that. This dashing bravery, to be sure, is only possible before the battle. When the enemy opens fire and the men begin to advance in short rushes, it's no time for prancing about on a horse.

Chapayev galloped by headlong, bent on establishing contact between the regiments, giving orders about the supply of shells and asking about the baggage trains.

Fyodor rode from one end of the skirmish line to the other, then returned to the right flank, dismounted, and walked along with the men, leading his horse by the bridle. The Red battery was concentrating its fire. The village was still silent, and Fyodor walked calmly along, joking, making somewhat of a pose of his coolness and his sham familiarity with such matters. He all but made himself out to be an old veteran begrimed with powder smoke. This, of course, was only his baptism by fire—what could be expected of a "muff of a civilian"?

It would be better to see what became of the veteran in five minutes.

Letting them approach to within six hundred metres, the Cossacks opened up with their artillery, and then machine-guns lashed out from the windmills on each side of the village. Fyodor was immediately thrown into confusion, but didn't let anyone see that something had suddenly turned over inside him, sunk and gone cold, as though a whole bottle of ice-cold peppermint drops had been poured into his warm insides. He walked a bit farther as before, but then began to detach himself a little from the others, to lag behind slightly; then he walked behind the line, hiding behind his horse.

The skirmish line dropped down, then sprang up, rushed forward, and then again dropped down, the men hastily burrowing shallow pits in the snow, and lowering their heads into them as if they were already dead. Hiding behind his horse, Fyodor also made two rushes, but then he jumped into the saddle and galloped off. Where to? He didn't know himself—he didn't want to gallop away from the battle, but only to get away from there, from that place—to go somewhere else where the bullets might not be whistling so shrilly, where the danger was not so terribly near. He galloped along the skirmish line but now he was not in front of it but behind; for some reason he galloped to the extreme left flank.

His expression at that moment was most serious and business-like. You would never have thought that the fellow was galloping away from fright. They would have been sure to think that he was taking some very, very important message, or was galloping to some tough spot on some urgent mission.

On his way, he met Potapov riding to the right flank. What for? Perhaps for the same reason that Fyodor was galloping to the left. Who knows—in battle it is impossible to tell whether a person has gone off on business, or if he has lost his head from fright and is dashing about senselessly, frightened out of his wits, seeking safety. They met head on, and stopped. Restraining their lively horses, they hurriedly asked each other:

"Are there any cartridges? Are there enough shells? Where's Chapayev? Where can I find him?"

All these questions were nothing but a blind.

While their horses were dancing in one spot, they were noticed by the Whites in the village, who decided that these two horsemen couldn't be privates, but were high-ranking officers. They trained their guns on them, and the shells began to explode all round, nearer and nearer. One fell at a distance of perhaps fifty metres, another—thirty metres, and the next still closer. It was obvious that the village was getting the range! The shells were falling in a ring around them, and the ring was narrowing, the fiery links were tightening up.

"Got to get away from here!" Potapov whispered hurriedly and audibly.

Another shell burst near them.

Fyodor didn't answer Potapov a word, but suddenly dug his spurs into his horse and galloped to the rear, away from the skirmish lines. Potapov galloped after him, but then turned and disappeared in the direction of the right flank. Fyodor galloped to a little hillock behind which about a dozen carters were lying. He lay down with them and watched the shells bursting at the exact spot where two minutes before he had been dawdling with Potapov. He tied his horse to the nearest cart, and lay listening to the screaming, wailing drone of the flying shells. Whenever the drone seemed to get nearer, Fyodor fell on his face in a flash, hugging the frozen, snow-covered slope and lay prone without stirring. Then, slowly, cautiously, he would raise his head and listen in agony to see if another shell wasn't whining somewhere near. Who knows how long he lay here? It was in just this spot that he might have been killed by the stray shell that later maimed three of the peasants who were now lying with him in the snow. But before this happened, he had got up, again jumped into the saddle, and thought for a moment where to go. As though to help him out, a young Red Army man briskly galloped up from the flank and hastily muttered in a breathless whisper, not speaking to anyone in particular.

"Where's the machine-guns? Where's the machine-guns here?"

"What machine-guns?"

"We've got to have machine-guns—the Cossacks are charging on the left flank!"

Fyodor decided at once that this was a warrior of his own stripe, but glancing in the direction indicated by the cavalryman, he saw a black mass sweeping over the snow not far away. His hair stood on end.

"I'll send some from the baggage train!" he shouted, and whipping up his horse, galloped away to the rear.

He galloped up to the baggage train and didn't know what to say. The carters looked at him slily or scowled; they exchanged knowing smiles, apparently suspecting why the brave lad had come there. Maybe it only seemed that way to Fyodor, and the peasants had other things to think about besides him—they may have been laughing and joking, trying to make the time pass more quickly —to hurry these endless slow terrible hours when they had to stand there and wait, no one knew for how long;

to stand there and wait until they got the order to move; while all around the shells are whining and flashing, hunting out their prey. Stray shells fly far, they may land right in the baggage train. It is only in jest that people say that they send the cowards to serve in the baggage.

Try it yourself and then you'll see what a snug nest the baggage is for a coward! The soldier in the skirmish line has it fine—there, everyone has a rifle, and hundreds and hundreds of them march breast to breast, and those hundreds have their machine-guns in front, and the machine-gunners have the bark of the big guns to support them. Yes, it's easier in a skirmish line! There, you have someone to talk to, someone to rub up against—in the skirmish line, there's help all around. But take a look at the baggage train—two hundred carts, two hundred peasants, and for the whole two hundred—eleven rifles! Eleven rifles, and practically no cartridges at all. There's a machine-gun in reserve, but it needs repairing. And besides that, of the two hundred, one hundred and fifty can't shoot worth a damn, and those that do know how to shoot are cripples or feeble; some of them are too weak to hold a rifle to their shoulders and are only good for shuffling the reins on their mare's back. That's what a baggage train is! And the Cossacks have a hankering for baggage trains—why not take them if they can do it with their bare hands! If a squadron swoops down, who's going to protect you, who'll back you up, where's help to come from? The Cossacks will gallop in between the carts, and chop off the heads of all the drivers. Eleven rifles, and they are silent—the Cossacks will have knocked them out of the peasants' hands in a twinkling. That's what a baggage train is—that's the kind of a nest it is for cowards. The carters go through terrors unknown in the skirmish line.

And so it is wrong and insulting to say that there are only cowards in the baggage trains. Cowards are terror-stricken wherever they are, and the terror of the baggage train is incomparably worse than that which shakes the soldier in the skirmish line!

Klichkov's conscience would give him no peace; a sense of shame galled and tortured him; he couldn't start laughing or talking with the carters, nor could he ride away—where could he go now? He loitered around the baggage train for an hour and a half. He asked for a light, and asked about forage, axle grease, bread, tinned food; he asked about their villages—were they near or far? But nothing came of all this; his questions were empty and stupid, and meant nothing to anyone. The drivers seemed to have no stomach for Klichkov's talk and sheer away from him rudely and insultingly. The minutes crawled slowly and sluggishly by, eating out Fyodor's heart like poisonous worms, tormenting and riddling it as though taking vengeance on him for his cowardice, for his shame.

The thunder of the guns blanketed the whole neighbourhood. Their roar hurled itself about the steppe, as if a giant beast, brought to bay, was rushing madly about, bellowing in mortal anguish. The gallant skirmish lines, encouraged by the firing, advanced through the groaning, whistling and roaring. In his black fur cap with the red band, Chapayev galloped from one end of the line to the other, his black felt cloak flapping in the wind like a demon's wings. Everyone saw his lean figure, welded to his Cossack saddle, appear first here, then there, and as quickly disappear. He gave orders on the fly, passed on whatever information was necessary, asked questions. The commanders, who knew their Chapai well, answered him briefly and quickly—not a superfluous word, not a moment's delay.

"All the machine-guns safe?" shouted Chapayev, on the gallop.

"Safe!" somebody shouted from the lines.
"How many carts of shells?"
"Six!"
"Where's the commander?"
"Left flank!"

He galloped away to the left flank.

The skirmish lines threw themselves forward at a break-neck run. Instantly, the Cossack machine-guns went mad. The men fell flat, digging into the snowy crust; they lay as though dead, waiting for the next command.

Chapayev was galloping behind the lines, imperiously shooting out his orders and snapping up the answers.

Now he pulled his horse sharply around, and flew to the commander of the battery:

"Shell the mills!"

"Blast the machine-guns out of the mills!"

"Don't touch the village till I give the word."

Then quickly turning his horse, he galloped back to the lines. The guns began to speak faster, louder and more angrily. The Cossack village feverishly attempted to halt the lines dashing forward in short rushes. There was a wild howl from the mills which suddenly seemed to be rent asunder with a sharp crackling noise; all the machine-guns began to bark at once. Both sides intensified their fire. The Red Army men were getting closer and closer every minute. The shells from the White battery fell and exploded nearer and nearer. The heart stood still at the thought that death was so near, that the Cossacks were so near, that they must be smashed, that the village must be entered on top of the enemy.

Chapayev flew from one end of the line to the other, his eyes blazing. He sent messengers to the machine-guns, to the carts with shells, to the Commander of the Regiment, or would gallop off somewhere himself; the soldiers saw his wiry figure darting everywhere. Now a cavalryman galloped up and fired some words at him.

"Where? Left flank?" Chapayev flung out.
"Left flank!"
"A lot of them?"
"Yes!"
"Machine-guns in place?"
"Yes, we've sent for help."

Chapayev galloped to the left flank where danger was bearing down threateningly—a horde of Cossacks were charging in mass formation. Their galloping horses could already be seen very close. Chapayev flew up to the Commander of the Battalion.

"Don't budge from here! Everybody in the lines—fire in volleys!"

And he galloped along the lines of soldiers who had thrown themselves down tight to the ground.

"No panic, lads, no panic! Keep down—let them come close—wait for the command! Everyone in his place. Wait for the command to fire!"

The soldiers had real need of a stout word these last crucial moments. They heard his voice—they were calm; they saw that Chapayev was with them and were confident that everything would come out all right.

As soon as the mass of Cossacks had galloped up to within range, a volley rang out, and then another; the nervous rattle of machine-gun fire sprang out to meet them.

"Rat-a-tat! Rat-a-tat! Rat-a-tat!" the machine-guns played an endless tattoo.

"Crackkk! Crackkk! Crackkk!" echoed the distinct, sharp, regular volleys.

The mass of horsemen lost their stride—became confused—hesitated for a moment.

"Crackkk! Crackkk!" came the terse volleys. Another moment, and the mass had stopped moving; still another moment, and the horses had turned their noses in the opposite direction. The Cossacks were galloping away, and in their wake: "Rat-a-tat! Crackkk! Crackkk! Rat-a-tat! Rat-a-tat!"

The attack had been beaten off. Pale faces were raised, still alarmed and agitated. A frightened smile began to hover on some of them. The lines were already at the edge of the village. Quicker, quicker, quicker came the rushes. The Cossack machine-gun fire beat against the lines, the bullets screeching shrilly. As soon as the men jumped to their feet, the Cossack volleys rang out, but the sound was again drowned in the excited, staccato firing of the machine-guns. Now the soldiers had run past the first mills, knots of them hiding behind mounds of earth or fences—deeper, deeper, deeper they pushed into the village.

Suddenly there rang out:

"Comrades! Hurrah! 'raaa! 'raa!"

The line shuddered, started, and with rifles atilt, bounded impetuously forward in the final attack.

The Cossack machine-guns were heard no more—the gunners had been bayonetted where they lay. Noisy waves of Red Army men engulfed the village. The last of the horsemen disappeared in the distance. The Red Army entered the village of Slomikhinskaya.

Embarrassed and abject, Fyodor Klichkov rode out of his shameful hiding-place. Again he rode towards the skirmish lines. He didn't know what was happening there, but he could hear the firing getting less and less until now it finally stopped altogether.

"Our men must have entered the village," he thought, "or it may be the other way round—they were surrounded and beat off one attack after the other until they finally had to surrender. Maybe even now the Cossacks have begun a bloody massacre. In ten minutes they'll gallop back here to the baggage trains and capture me, the commissar, along with the carts!" What a disgrace! How ashamed Fyodor was to admit to himself that he had been lacking in spirit in his first battle, that he had turned tail like a cur dog, had not justified to himself his own hopes and expectations. Where was the bravery, courage, and heroism he had thought so much about when he was far from the skirmish lines and the battle, the shells and the bullets?

Crushed by the consciousness of his crime, Fyodor rode back at a slow jog-trot in the direction of the spot from which he had so ignominiously galloped away two hours before. He rode past the hillock behind which he had lain with the carters—there, quite close, he saw an enormous shell hole, and the snow was all red. What was that blood there? Whose? He hadn't heard yet that a shell had dropped there and killed three of the carters he had talked with.

Beyond the hillock was an even plain—here the Red line had been advancing. But where was it now? In the village? Or maybe on the far bank of the Uzen? Maybe it had been driven there by the Cossacks? Maybe it had been driven clean through the village?

He was lost in conjectures and surmises.

At that moment a horseman trotted up. Evidently, he, too, had been "looking for machine-guns." He began to rattle off something incoherent and foolish. Fyodor looked him in the eye and realized that they were both suffering from the same disease.

"Where are ours?" asked the new-comer with seeming indifference as he rode up beside Fyodor.

"I'm looking for them myself," answered Fyodor with disgust, and was overcome with shame. They understood each other down to the very dregs of their shame.

"Maybe they're already in the village?" said the stranger with feigned composure and forcing a yawn.

"Maybe they are," Fyodor agreed.

"Well, let's go then, shall we?"

"Where to?"

"To the village."

"But if there're Cossacks there?"

"Not apt to be—ours have probably taken the village—but still—"

"That's it—if they catch us, it's all up with us!"

They went on in this vein, each one proposing to the other several times that they should go to the village, and as many times the other persuading him not to, warning him of the danger, and pointing out that first they must find out in some cautious way who was holding the village.

And so talking, they rode closer and closer to the village without noticing it, until finally they were only half a verst away. They had long been distinctly visible from the mills, and they couldn't have got away at all—if anyone had begun to chase them, there would have been no sense in trying to run away—they would have been mowed down by the machine-guns at the mills anyway.

Thus they rode on, trembling, dreading the unknown; they shuddered, but rode ahead.

Just a little way from the huts at the edge of the village they saw a little urchin of about ten.

"Hey, boy, did the Red Army come this way or not?"

"They took the village," the boy shrilled happily. "Where did you come from?"

"Run along, run along, boy, and play! Military matters are not to be talked about," said Fyodor paternally, trying to sober down the boy's mischievous and inappropriate curiosity.

No sooner had Fyodor's companion heard that there was no danger than he galloped off somewhere. Klichkov, calm, but still feeling humiliated and embarrassed, now rode into the village, which had been occupied by the Red regiments. He kept trying to reassure himself that probably it was the same with all novices in their first battle, and that later he would prove himself—in the second or third battle.

Fyodor was not mistaken—a year later he was decorated with the Order of the Red Banner for his part in one of the Red Army's most glorious operations. This first battle was for him a severe and an important lesson. What happened to him at Slomikhinskaya never happened again during all the years of the Civil War, though he was in situations many times worse and more complicated than the battle of Slomikhinskaya. He cultivated in himself the qualities he sought—courage, outward calm, self-control, the ability to size up a situation and quickly decide what to do. This, however, did not come at once—first, he had to traverse the path which evidently no one can avoid, that is, from patent confusion and cowardice to the habitude everyone considers worthy.

When asking people he met where the staff had set up Headquarters, Klichkov noticed that everybody answered hurriedly somehow, as though unwilling or in a hurry to get somewhere—the whole village was in motion, animated and excited to the last degree. The Cossacks had been dislodged and driven away, and were still being chased somewhere by the units assigned the task. So it was not military danger or military preparations that caused the excitement. Then what did?

Unnoticed, he rode up to Headquarters—the enormous house of a merchant named Karpov. Everybody was here—Chapayev and his lads, and Yozhikov. Fyodor particularly remembered Yozhikov. The latter apparently realized what had happened and met the truant with a half-suppressed smile.

"Been bringing up the rear—Comrade—Klichkov?"

The devil had eyes that were flecked with gold, and they were smiling and deriding him.

"Yes—I was held up there," Fyodor growled out awkwardly, and turning to Chapayev, asked:

"Got word to the Army?"

"Getting ready to do that now. Good news from Uralsk. They've advanced there. Clearing the road to Lbishchensk."

"That would be a good thing. And we, here— what about Sakharnaya?"

His questions seemed unwarranted chatter, just as he himself seemed almost superfluous here. "All of them here were in the lines," he thought. "They fought, risked their lives, and then I appear—by your leave, two hours late." Pangs of remorse harried his soul; his face was aflame with mortification.

Peasant women began to come up to the house one after the other. Gesticulating insistently, they were arguing about something with the orderlies and sentries, and trying in vain to get through to the staff. It could be seen from the window that they would not be let in—the imperturbable, ironical air of the Red Army men showed that. Fyodor went outdoors, and asked what the matter was. He discovered that they were complaining about their new guests—the Red Army men, who, they said, were pilfering their belongings. Fyodor immediately went with them to their huts, asked them what had been taken, looked round, wrote everything down, and promised to find what was gone and have it brought back.

There were cases of pillaging—this can by no means be denied. And Fyodor had many opportunities of observing this, both with respect to his own Red Army units, and to the enemy troops. Pillaging is something spontaneous against which it is difficult to struggle and impossible to root out so long as war itself exists. Plundering by soldiers will disappear only with war. That is a fact. Nevertheless that by no means signifies that it is impossible to struggle against it, and very successfully at that.

Fyodor ran across a number of cases of thievery which were absolutely senseless and without any mercenary motives. A Red Army man, for example, was lugging an enormous bundle of all kinds of rubbish.

"What've you got there? Let me see."

The soldier calmly untied his bundle, and unpacked it on the snow—he dragged out baby-shirts, diapers, various toys, scraps of cloth, an old dress.

"What d'you want all that for, old chap?"

The soldier didn't answer—he saw himself that it was useless to him.

"Why did you take it, I'm asking?"

"Why, all of us took things of some kind or other—we just lugged them away."

"Yes, but what for?"

"How do I know?"

"Some woman was complaining to me—she was crying and looking for her things. That must be them you've got there."

"Maybe they're hers—let her have them," the lad agreed without regret.

"It's not a case of letting her have them—you must take them back," Fyodor said impressively, but in a friendly and kindly tone.

"I can take them back," the other assented. "Of course I can take them back—why should the woman fuss about it? Just say the word, and I'll take them back myself."

Fyodor found out where the soldier had got the bundle and went there with him. The Red Army man brought the bundle in and silently laid it on the iron bed, which had been stripped bare, hesitated awkwardly, then seized the handle of the door and went out without a word.

Fyodor met another Red Army man. This one had a wicker perambulator stuck on his head. He may have been taking it to put in the stove, or it may have been just horse-play. There was always plenty of horse-play among the soldiers—they found various ways to amuse themselves: Massive paws would grab some shock-headed peasant lad, his enormous boots caked with mud, with thighs weighing three poods and with a forest of flaxen curls. They would grab him and drag him up to the most cherubic of baby-carriages. This "baby" would squeal and struggle; his bellowing would frighten the passers-by. This game was always the same, no matter where—in Russian or Cossack village or in town. No matter how loud the victim howled, the game would be played to the end: other lads would come running up from all sides—they would help to hold the fellow, to tie him and to squeeze him into the baby-carriage. They would tie him there tight and then pick out the steepest slope they could find, and give him a shove down it in his baby-carriage, head over heels.

"Ha, ha, ha! What fine sport!"

But here in Slomikhinskaya the perambulator incident ended just as the one with the bundle did—the lad returned the perambulator to Klichkov without the slightest regret—it was absolutely useless to him—he had only been tempted by its pretty adornments.

Much was hunted out, much returned to its owners; the village quieted down and complaints stopped. Chapayev gave orders to call the commanders together. When they had assembled, he ordered them sternly to make general searches among the soldiers and to arrest everyone found with any stolen property. Everything was to be collected at one designated spot; a distribution committee was to be appointed; those who had lost things were to be called before it and their claims satisfied—but only if they were poor people—not one "bourgeois" was to be given back a kopek's worth. All their property was to go into regiment funds, which must be organized now—at once!

Soldiers who turned things over voluntarily were not to be arrested. Besides all this, the soldiers were to be called together in the square in two hours' time—they were to be told that Chapayev himself was to speak—that was how he ordered it to be announced: "Chapayev himself is going to talk."

In two hours, Petka Isayev reported to Chapayev that the Red Army men had gathered in the square and were waiting for him. At this moment the commander of one of the regiments appeared, and Chapayev and he went to the square together. On the way, the commander described the mood among the soldiers.

This was the first time that Fyodor had heard Chapayev speak. He had long got unused to such demagogical orators. As a speaker, Chapayev would have been weak, even absolutely unsuitable for a working-class audience: they would have laughed not a little at his methods. But here it was quite the opposite. His speech was a tremendous success. He began without any introduction or preliminary explanations with the question he had called the men together to discuss—the question of plundering. But as he went on, he dragged in a mass of the most unnecessary trifles—he dragged in everything that he happened to recall which he could in some way or other tack on to the matter in hand. His speech hadn't the least pretension to proportion, or unity or subordination to one single idea—he said whatever came into his head. Still, in spite of its infinite deficiencies, his speech created an enormous impression. And not something superficial that would pass lightly—not at all. Here was something indisputable, something that had a keen and far-reaching effect. His speech was sincere through and through, permeated with energy, purity and a somehow naïve, almost child-like truthfulness. You listened to him and realized that this incoherent speech, with its chance details, was not empty drivel, and not posing. It was the passionate, sincere profession of faith of a noble soul, the cry of a warrior, outraged and protesting; it was a clear and convincing call, and, if you like, a command. In the name of truth, he knew how not only to appeal but also to command.

"I order you," he said, "never to steel any more—only scoundrels do that—get me?"

The crowd of many thousands responded to this command with deafening and joyous shouts of approval, coming from the very depths of their hearts. The enthusiasm was indescribable. The Red Army men took their oath in deep sincerity; they honestly swore to their leader that they would never permit plundering, and that they themselves would shoot those guilty on the spot.

The sad thing was that they didn't realize that this was *impossible*—that plundering can't be *rooted out* in *wartime*, but they swore with conviction, and they undoubtedly *did cut down* the amount of pillaging to the very minimum possible at the front.

Odd snatches from Chapayev's speech stuck in Fyodor's memory.

"Comrades!" his harsh metallic voice filled the square. "I won't stand for what's going on here! From now on I'll shoot anyone who's caught pillaging. I myself'll be the first to shoot the scoundrel with this hand!" He shook his right fist in the air threateningly. "If you catch me at it, then shoot me, don't have any pity on Chapayev. I'm your commander, but I'm only your commander in the ranks. At other times I'm your mate. You can come to me at midnight and after midnight. If it's necessary, why, wake me up. I'm always with you, I'll talk to you, say what's necessary. If I'm eating, sit down and eat with me; if I'm having tea, sit down and have tea with me. That's the kind of commander I am!"

Fyodor was embarrassed by this brazen, childish

boasting, but Chapayev waited a moment, and, absolutely unruffled, went on.

"I'm used to this life, Comrades. I never went through any of those academies—I never finished them, that is—but just the same I've knocked together fourteen regiments, and in all of them I was the commander. And everywhere there was order. There wasn't no pillaging, and nobody dragged the priest's surplice out of the church. What are you—a priest? Do you want to wear it, you son-of-a-bitch? Then what did you steal it for?"

Chapayev looked threateningly from one side to the other, even leaned over backwards, his glance quick and penetrating, as though he wanted to find the rascal he was talking about among the grey mass of the thousands of soldiers.

"Priests, naturally, all lie," Chapayev declared with great conviction. "They live by cheating—what kind of priests would they be if they didn't cheat? The priests tell you not to eat flesh during Lent, but they'll stuff themselves on roast goose—all you can hear is the bones cracking. Don't take what don't belong to you, they say, and they themselves live by stealing—we're sick and tired of them because of all that. That's true. But still, leave other people's faith alone—it don't hurt you any. Am I right, Comrades?"

This was a winner. Chapayev realized this, and so it was here that he shrewdly put his question.

The peasant Red Army men, excited to fever-heat by Chapayev's speech, burst into wild shouts, as though giving vent to feelings stifled during their long silence. That was what Chapayev had been waiting for. The sympathy of his listeners was now completely on his side—no matter how he put together the rest of his speech, success was assured.

"You carry off something from someone else's house, but everything there is yours—as soon as the war's over, where'll it go if not to you? If we take a hundred cows away from some bourgeois, we'll divide them all up among a hundred peasants—a cow to a peasant. If we take away clothes—we'll divide them the same way. Am I right?"

"That's right! That's right!" the answer thundered.

All around, animated faces blazed up, and eyes darted about glowing with rapture. In flying scraps of phrases, nods, jokes, and lively glances, the soldiers expressed their sympathy, agreement and satisfaction. Chapayev held the soul of the multitude in the hollow of his hand and made them think and feel the way he thought and felt.

"Don't take anything!" he shouted, and made a convulsive gesture with his left hand. He hesitated a minute, not finding the word he wanted. "Don't take anything, I say, but put it all together in one heap and turn it over to your commander, turn over everything you took from the bourgeoisie. The commander'll sell it and put the money in the regiment fund. If you're wounded, they'll give you a hundred rubles from the fund—if you're killed, they'll give your whole family a hundred apiece. How's that? Am I right or not?"

The ensuing scene was indescribable—the soldiers went mad in their enthusiasm, their shouts rose to a frenzied, rapturous howl.

"See to it that everything is turned over," Chapayev finished, when the excitement had calmed down a little. "Turn over everything you've taken down to the last scrap. Then we'll see what's to be given back, and what's to be left to help you. Understand? Chapayev means what he says. So long as you do what you're told, I'm your friend, but if you don't keep discipline, then don't say I haven't warned you."

There was a frenzied clapping of hands as he finished his speech, and prolonged "Hurrahs."

A Red Army man jumped on to the box which Chapayev had just left, and opening up his great-coat in a flash, pulled up his tunic and with a quick movement undid the heavy silver Cossack belt that held up his pants.

"Here it is, Comrades," the lad shouted, waving the belt over his head, "seven months I've been wearing it—got it in battle—killed the man myself and took his belt off him. But I'm turning it over. I don't need it—what's it to me? Let it go into the pot to help everybody. Hurrah for our brave commander, Comrade Chapayev!"

Again the crowd thundered its applause.

Fyodor saw what a profound impression Chapayev's speech had made; he was glad to see this effect, but kept worrying about the "hundred cows" and the clothes that were to be "divided evenly"; then, too, he wasn't quite sure about the regiment committees.

"Comrade Chapayev," he said, "I'd like to get acquainted with the Red Army men, and then I'd like to tell them in a few words something about the general situation in the country. Only you tell them yourself that now the commissar, Comrade Klichkov, is going to speak."

Chapayev at once mounted the box and introduced Fyodor. The latter began to tell about the fighting on the other fronts—the fighting against Kolchak, Denikin and all the other White army leaders. He touched briefly on the international situation and said a couple of words about the country's economic life. At different points he cited Chapayev's examples, as though merely in passing and by way of illustration. While not openly rejecting them, he "explained" them in such a way that little if anything remained of the original proposition.

Fyodor was very cautious in going about the demolition of Chapayev's theses; he was constantly dropping such asides as "our enemies would of course say that the good idea, the correct idea, expressed by Comrade Chapayev about our *common* property, means that we seize, carry away and divide up everything and in any way we like. But Comrade Chapayev and I, and of course you, too, we don't think that way." And here Fyodor would undermine and topple over the "sharing" which Chapayev had probably had in mind. At least, his striking example of "a hundred confiscated cows will be divided among a hundred peasants, a cow apiece," could have been developed and understood that way. Such principles could not be left without any explanation.

Chapayev's having been in a group of Anarchists—for a very short time, it is true—his peasant origin, and his daring nature, unrestrained, irregular, undisciplined—all this inclined him to an anarchistic manner of thinking, and incited him to guerrilla deeds.

Yes, words are a powerful thing: there were no more cases of pillaging in the village, no more outrages or violence.

As soon as the meeting was over, Fyodor hunted up Yozhikov, and wanted to have a talk with him—should they organize the village Revolutionary Committee right away or leave it till the next day? But Yozhikov mumbled something unintelligible and evaded a straightforward answer. Fyodor decided to act alone. He had the villagers informed that they were to get together at once at the office of the village administration. He invited three political workers to go with him, outlined the questions to be discussed, and decided to try his luck at this new business—he had never had to organize such committees in the theatre of hostilities before. A large number of the villagers turned out—the office couldn't hold them all. When Yozhikov discovered that the Revolutionary Committee would be organized without him, he appeared himself. Fyodor didn't at once understand this manoeuvre, only later did he suspect what lay behind it—Yozhikov longed to collect as much material as possible about Fyodor's inactivity, his unsuitability, weakness, etc., so that he would be recalled, while he, Yozhikov, would be left commissar of the army group. He had wanted very much but didn't have time to organize the Revolutionary Committee himself, and then to confront Fyodor with the accomplished fact.

The villagers who came to the meeting were very hesitant as usually happens in such cases. There was nothing surprising in that. Yesterday, the Cossacks had been there; yesterday they had been called together here and their government elected for them. Today, the Reds had come and were appointing a Revolutionary Committee, and tomorrow maybe the Cossacks would return— and then what? Wouldn't they make short work of the villagers who had been appointed to administer the village affairs?

Out of fear nobody would agree to work in the Revolutionary Committee. Those who were not afraid and understood events in all their complexity and gravity, had long ago left the village; they had gone to the towns and joined the Red Army. Army political workers were appointed to the Revolutionary Committee.

Then they began to talk about their work—what to do first, what to do next, what could be postponed. They decided to take up a collection among those present to get the money for their immediate needs—let everyone give what he could—after that they would pass the hat around in the village. Then they would get in touch with Uralsk and get instructions and orders from there, and maybe even material assistance.

Fyodor explained to them with great fervour the work of Revolutionary Committees, at the same time explaining the tasks of Soviet power. The villagers listened, agreed with what was said and endorsed it. Soviet power was proclaimed in the village. A small red flag was hung above the porch of the old office of the Cossack administration.

Towards evening, the scouts returned empty-handed. They had poked around in various directions, snuffed and felt and looked about, but the floods along the river Chizh precluded any thought of travelling by sleigh to the Uralsk highway. It was true that there were hard night frosts; it was true that the steppe was covered with slushy, sticky snow. Still the roads had already got perceptibly soft and mucky—the warm March days had left them completely bald. Any further advance must be halted while they waited for fresh orders. All the commanders gathered at the merchant's house. Chapayev ordered a guard to be stationed, and the baggage trains to be brought up; order was to be established in the Soviet village. At this moment some prisoners were brought in. For a long time they questioned a Kirghiz who had been captured in the steppe, but without result. It became known that the Cossacks were getting busy around Shilnaya Balka, a hamlet a few dozen versts away, and had all but captured it. Part of the forces must be sent there. That was discussed. There were all kinds of matters to be discussed—where is the space to be found to tell about them all?

The twilight came down black with fog. Exhausted with the march and with the alarms of an eventful day, the commanders had gone to sleep. Fyodor was also asleep. Chapayev soon woke him up to sign an order. Fyodor woke up, signed the order and again fell asleep. Again Chapayev woke him up. That amazing man sat up all night, right till the very morning. Fyodor would wake up and see Chapayev sitting alone, the lavender-coloured lamp shining dimly. He was sitting there bent heavily over the map, the same favourite compasses in his hand that he had had at Alexandrov-Gai; he kept measuring and writing something down. All night long until the cocks began to crow, he measured distances on the map to the lusty snoring of his commanders. At the door, the sentry dozed, his rifle clutched in his hands, his grey forehead nodding against the black rib of his bayonet.

They spent four days at Slomikhinskaya. Frunze informed them by direct wire that the brigade was being transferred to the Orenburg front. However, the situation soon necessitated a change in this decision, and the brigade was transferred not to Orenburg but to Buzuluk District. Frunze summoned Chapayev and Klichkov to Samara for detailed consultation with them.

They got ready in four minutes. They knew that they would never come back. They threw their little travelling bags into the sleigh. Their three spirited horses couldn't stand still—the very best and most mettlesome had been selected.

Averka was already sitting in his place, ready for the gallop through the steppe, the reins drawn tight like an old woman's lips—dry and firm. On the porch Potapov, Chekov, Ilya Tyotkin, the whole Chapayev outfit, had come to see them off.

'Hurry up and get us out of here, Comrade Chapayev."

"I'll send for you as soon as I get there."

The horses sprang forward. Shouts of farewell were drowned in the flying snow. The sorrow of parting was reflected as in a mirror in the eyes of those standing on the porch. Someone yelled, someone cracked his whip, someone threw his cap in the air. Soon the porch disappeared in the snowdrifts.

Steppe, O steppe! The sunset red as bunting, the snows a cradle of white down! The wind is like a sigh, and it blows in cold and fragrant waves—blows over the white snows, over the snowy wastes, and disappears in the pure blue of the early March sky.

From Slomikhinskaya, they headed back again towards Alexandrov-Gai, over the same road they had come a few days ago with the regiments. They rode and were silent. The steppe is like a cradle to the rider—it lulls him to sweet slumber.

Here was Kazachya Talovka already. Why, had it been long ago that they made their preparations here for the battle, studied and measured the map with compasses, discussed the situation, racked their brains hunting for a way to crush the Cossacks? And then the night —with songs, with lively talk, and then dead silence broken by the loud snoring of the exhausted soldiers.

Fyodor recalled the camp-fire and the red-bearded man beside it, and the big curly-headed chap who had been turning potatoes over on the coals and fishing them out with his bayonet. Where were they now? Were they still alive?

And so all the way to Alexandrov-Gai—absorbed in memories of what he had lived through, and accounting to himself for his actions.

They did not stay long in Algai—they had something to eat, rested a little, and again set out. They sped across the steppe, post-horse, all the way to Samara.

VII

ON THE ROAD

Chapayev was one of those people with whom it is easy to become friends. But this friendship might fly to bits just as easily. He would shout and storm, wound deeply with insult, berate, infuriate, spare nothing, break everything; in rage and blind frenzy, he saw no farther than his own nose. In a minute it would all pass and he would regret it. He'd begin painfully to recall everything and to comprehend what he had done—to examine and sift out the important and serious from random chaff and thistles. He would think everything out and be ready to back down. But not always and not with everyone—he would only make concessions if he *wanted* to, and then only to those whom he respected—those whom he reckoned with. At such times, one must boldly and persistently try to get him to be outspoken. He was easily drawn out and at times would open up his whole soul.

He was a noisy man and liked to shout, and was so strict that a person who didn't know him would think twice before approaching him; he'd be afraid that he might give him a lashing with his tongue and even give him a punch if he got angry. And this was quite possible —that is, with a stranger and one who was timid to boot. The more afraid a man was, the more Chapayev's soul would rage. He couldn't stand a timid person. A stranger might take him for a brute of a man, but when you looked closer, you saw a most artless and affectionate companion, whose heart was sensitive to every stirring of another's soul, and throbbed joyfully and warmly in response. Look closer and you'd see that after this violent abuse, after this scowling harshness, nothing was left, not the slightest rancour—he had used up all his ammunition in a single volley. And when you finished talking something out with him, whether you agreed with him or not, you knew that the question was exhausted to the very bottom. With Chapayev, no questions, no matters, were ever left open—with him, everything was always finished. He pronounced his decision, and that was that.

Chapai held his head high and proud. And not for nothing: the steppe rang with the fame of his exploits. This glorification clouded his vision; it painted him to himself as an unconquerable hero, and the wine of vanity turned his head.

It was the lads immediately surrounding him that made the most noise about Chapayev's exploits, both to his face and behind his back. It was they who first spread tales about what had really occurred and what they had made up; it was they who painted everything in such brilliant colours; it was they who first of all began to sing paeans to him, to burn incense at his altar, to tell him about his invincibility. When people lied to Chapai skilfully, or even flattered him, he lapped it up, licked his chops like a tom-cat after a saucer of milk, himself egged them on, and even embroidered the story a little. On the other hand, he would at once drive away an empty twaddler and petty toad-eater who couldn't lie glibly, and give orders not to let him come near him in the future.

There was another remarkable trait in Chapayev's character—he had a childish belief in rumours—he believed them all, serious and trivial, even the worst nonsense. He believed, for example, that in Samara they were issuing ten pounds of shag on the ration cards, while the men at the front weren't being issued an ounce. He believed that at the Front Headquarters and the Army Headquarters it was one continuous drunken orgy day and night; that the only people there were whiteguard specialists, and that they were betraying the Red Army to the enemy every second. He believed that shells, boots, bread, rifles, reinforcements—whatever you liked—all was slow in getting to the front because of the malicious interference of certain individuals, and not because of the general shortage, dislocation of transport, destroyed bridges, etc., etc.

He believed that typhus was spread by birds, that the more birds there were, the more typhus there was. He believed that sugar all but grew in loaves; that if you didn't beat your horse, you would spoil it. What didn't he believe in his open-hearted simplicity!

He believed the wildest rumours even when it concerned a close comrade—such as Potapov, for instance. Potapov was a brigade commander, a hero who had been with Chapayev in all his scrapes: had been in many an attack, had been wounded and shell-shocked more than once—in a word, it was not for nothing that he was a brigade commander.

And then something might go wrong in a battle—Potapov wouldn't bring up the baggage waggons in time, or would be late in coming to the assistance of another brigade, or he would retreat five versts, only to advance ten later. And someone would whisper to the credulous Division Commander, "Potapov's a coward—ran away—failed to help—lost his head completely. Was drunk all week, the scoundrel. He's talking about you, Chapayev. He's jealous."

And the trustful Chapai would soak it all up greedily, fanning his rage to fiery heat.

"I'll show the rascal! Why, I'll take his head off! I'll have him shot for drunkenness! What does he think—that he can have my men killed while he's on a spree! And Chapayev has to answer for it all. Call him in at once!"

And, insane with rage, he begins to wait for Potapov, who drops everything as soon as he hears the ominous summons. Potapov gallops up, and in the corridor, inquires:

"Angry?"

"Ughh, how angry he is!"

"Just at me?"

"Only you."

"Somebody said something, maybe?"

"You can depend on that."

"Well, let's hope it'll blow over."

Hurriedly tightening his belts, straightening his pants, patting his holster, and drawing himself up in a martial way, Potapov goes in.

Chapayev does not look at him, and doesn't answer his greeting. His smouldering eyes under his thick eyelashes are cast down. Chapai jerks his moustache and is silent a full minute. And then—like the cork flying out of a bottle:

"You've been drinking again!"

"Why, I didn't even—"

"Silence! Letting yourselves go, you sons-of-bitches!"

"Comrade Chapayev, I—"

"Silence! Shooting's too good for you, you loafer! At such a time, and to let yourselves go the way you have, you devils! What do you mean by it! What do you mean by it, I'm asking you? What are you trying to do to Chapayev?"

Potapov keeps silent. He knows that once the gas has escaped the cork will come out without any fuss. He knows that Chapayev will shout out all his anger and calm down so that you can tell him just what happened, explain everything and refute the slander and lying rumours. At first, he'll jib, refuse to listen from pure stubbornness, but you keep right at it, drive away, go ahead, till you get what you're after. If you can only chip off a little from the very edge of his belief in the slander, he will suddenly become as soft as good white bread, look you kindly in the eye and say guiltily:

"You understand, I—"

"I understand—"

"Yes, you see I, you understand—well, they said you retreated—then they said you were drinking—"

"Yes, yes."

"And so I believed it—how could I help believing it? Wouldn't you have believed it in my place? Of course. Why, anyone would have believed it!"

And now Chapayev begins to laugh. He begins to clap Potapov on the shoulder, his manner is again friendly. He sits him down to have tea with him—can't do enough to make up for it all.

Two days would go by, three days, and if the same thing happened over again with respect to Potapov, Chapayev would again believe from beginning to end all the slander and lying rumours, would fly into a rage, shout, threaten, and then—and then make up with him guiltily.

He was as credulous as a little child. This caused him much trouble, but he couldn't cure himself of it. But there was one thing he never believed: he never believed that the enemy was strong, that it was impossible to smash him and make him retreat in disorder.

"There's no enemy can stand up to me!" he would declare firmly and proudly. "Chapayev don't know how to retreat! Chapayev has never retreated! Tell that to everyone—I don't know how to retreat. Tomorrow, attack along the whole front! Say I ordered it! And if anyone dares to go against it—bring him here to me at Headquarters. I'll teach him damn quick to keep his ass pointed in the right direction!"

In his line and on his own scale, Chapayev was an expert, a master hand. He had an excellent knowledge of his whole division—the soldiers and their commanders. He knew less about its political composition and wasn't interested in it in the least. He had a perfect knowledge of the theatre of operations; he knew it from memories of his youth, or from the inhabitants by questioning them, or from studying it on the map with the right people. His memory was fresh and retentive—it would clamp on to facts like a vice and would hold them tight until no longer needed. He knew the inhabitants, especially the peasant soul. The townspeople interested him less. He knew what sort of peasants there were here, what could be expected of them, what they could be depended on to do and where the pitfalls lay. All that was necessary he knew—about bread, and boots, and clothes;

about sugar, cartridges, shells and shag—he knew about them all. You wouldn't catch him napping on any question.

But when it came to questions of a different kind—political questions and especially questions that went beyond the scope of his division, he didn't understand them—he didn't know and didn't want to know anything about them. Moreover, there was much that he simply didn't believe.

He considered the world labour movement, for example, a pure fiction; he didn't believe in it and couldn't imagine that it could exist in such an organized form. When facts or reports in the newspapers were cited to him, he only grinned knowingly: "The papers—we write the papers ourselves—they've thought it up so that it'll be more fun fighting."

"Not a bit of it—here are people's names, towns, numbers and figures. Here's facts you can't dispute."

"What of it? I can think up figures myself."

At first, he stubbornly believed this, and refused to listen to anything to the contrary. He would only smirk. Later, after frequent and long discussions with Klichkov, he changed his view on this just as he changed it on many other matters.

Then, he considered all the trouble with the Anarchists to be unnecessary and stupid: "We ought to let the Anarchists do what they like—they won't do us any harm at all," Chapayev would say.

He didn't know the least thing about the programme of the Communists—and he had been listed in the Party for a year now—he hadn't read it or studied it and didn't have the slightest understanding of any of the questions it dealt with.

Finally, mention should be made of Chapayev's attitude towards the "staffs," as he called all the bodies from which he received orders and directions, as well as men, cartridges, clothes—everything that he was supposed to get. To the very end, it proved impossible to change him very much where this was concerned. Chapayev was profoundly convinced that the "staffs" were composed of tsarist generals that had entrenched themselves there, that they "were selling the Red Army right and left" and that the "people" under the leadership of such chiefs as he, Chapayev, were not to be fooled, and if they went against the orders of the "staff," they usually did not lose by it but gained. Distrust of the Centre was something innate in him and he had a mortal hatred for all tsarist officers; it was very, very seldom that he allowed some shabby little officer of the lower ranks to be enrolled in his division. There were, by the way, a few officers (very few, to be sure) who recommended themselves in battle. He remembered and valued them, but was always on his guard against them.

He also had no respect for the intelligentsia. Here what displeased him most of all was their *big talk* about things, and the absence of the real, visible deeds that he loved so much and at which he was such a master. He considered those of the intelligentsia who *did things* as the greatest of exceptions. From this attitude of his towards officers and towards the intelligentsia arose quite naturally Chapayev's desire to put in his *own* people everywhere—in the first place because they were people of deeds, not words, and reliable. In the second place, because it was easier to work with them, and finally, as he often said: "The peasants and workers must be taught right away, and they can only learn by doing things themselves. I tell someone to be the Chief-of-Staff and the fool refuses—doesn't know I'm doing it for his own good. I command him to, I put him in there, and he thrashes around for a week, and then, before you know it, he begins to work, and does good work, better than any of your officers would!"

This was always his main line—to advance his own men everywhere. That's why his whole apparatus was so flexible and obedient—it was his own devoted people who were in command everywhere. Moreover, it was people who greatly respected him as commander.

It didn't take long for Klichkov to discern these traits in Chapayev's character, and having discerned them, he was even more convinced that he must first of all win his respect and only then begin to change his ideas, to curb him and direct him along the path of conscious struggle, and not only blind and instinctive struggle, however picturesque and heroic it was, and however resounding and glorious.

How could he win Chapayev's respect? He must take him captive in an intellectual sense. He must awaken in him a desire for knowledge, and for an education, an interest in learning and in larger horizons—not only confined to military matters.

Here Fyodor knew his superiority and was convinced beforehand that when he had succeeded in awakening these desires, Chapayev's song as an anarchist and guerrilla would have been sung—it would be possible little by little, cautiously but persistently, to interest him in other ideas, to arouse his interest in other matters. Fyodor had a strong belief in his own strength and ability. Chapayev was out of the common run—not to be compared with other people. It was true that it would be as hard to break him as a wild steppe horse, but wild horses are broken! Only the question arose: wouldn't it be better to leave such a colourful, original and vivid figure to destiny—to leave it absolutely untouched? Let him shine and parade and sparkle like a many-faceted jewel!

This idea had occurred to Klichkov, but it seemed both ridiculous and childish against the existing background of titanic struggle.

Chapayev was like an eagle with hooded eyes—his

heart was restless, his blood hot, his transports of feeling were splendid and fervent, his will was indomitable, but —he did not clearly see his road in life.

And Fyodor took it on himself to enlighten him, if only a little, to help lead him out on to the true road. Perhaps he wouldn't succeed—never mind, there's nothing like trying, and at least it wouldn't make things any worse. But if something did come of it—oho! How much the Revolution needed such people!

No sooner had they left Alexandrov-Gai than memories of Slomikhinskaya, and the recent battle, and all the other events of the last few days, faded into the background. In their place arose something new—the tremendous, unknown matter for which they were now hurrying to Samara. They didn't yet realize the full extent of the harrowing danger that had arisen on the Kolchak Front; they were not informed of the recent serious reverses near Ufa. But even so it was obvious that it was not for nothing that they were being summoned so precipitately for a discussion—evidently something big was being planned, and the role they were to play in it was not the smallest.

"What d'you think we're going for?" Klichkov asked.

"To Samara, you mean?"

"Yes."

"They'll transfer us. Need us somewhere else," Chapayev answered with assurance.

Neither knew anything for sure, and they didn't want to engage in idle conjectures; the conversation stopped of itself. Each thought his own thoughts, and they were endless and unspoken.

They came to the first village along their way, and stopped at the Soviet. As soon as the peasants heard that Chapayev had arrived, they jammed into the hut, shoving and jostling one another in their desire to see the famous hero. Soon the whole village knew of his arrival. There was a stampede in the street, everybody hurrying to get a glimpse of him before he left. A big crowd gathered around the porch—women and kids and old people—even grey-bearded, white-headed, dried-up grand-daddies crawled out. All of them greeted Chapayev like an old and close friend. Many of them called him by his name and patronymic—Vasily Ivanovich. It seemed that here, too, as was the case near Samara, there were veterans who had fought beside him in 1918. Everywhere, there were radiant and touching smiles. The grey faces of strangers shone with joy. Others stared at him seriously and fixedly as though they wanted to look their fill and imprint for ever on their memory the image of the heroic commander. Some of the women stood in ludicrous bewilderment, not knowing and not understanding what in particular was happening—who it was everyone was looking at with such curiosity and why—their men had run to the Soviet, and they had run after them. The little boys weren't making a racket the way they always do, but were standing quietly, patiently waiting for something. Everyone was waiting for something—they evidently wanted to hear what Chapayev was going to say. Isolated chance phrases jumped from mouth to mouth in the crowd. The words were distorted and garbled, but flew farther and farther.

"Maybe you'd say something to us, Comrade Commander," said the chairman of the Soviet. "The peasants, you can see, would like to hear a good speech."

"What'll I say?" asked Chapayev with a smile.

"Why, tell us how everything's getting along round about. You can think of something."

Chapayev was never one to be asked twice. He knew, and could very well see, that the peasants wanted to hear him—why shouldn't he say a few words?

While the horses were being harnessed, he made a speech to the peasants. It would be hard to say what the main theme was; he repeated commonplaces about the Revolution, about the dangers threatening it, and about the famine. But even this pleased his listeners—just think, Chapayev himself was speaking! They listened with rapt attention to the last word of his intricate and confused speech, and when he finished, nodded their heads in approval, murmuring:

"That's something like!"

"Why, what else could you expect from Chapayev himself!"

"Fine fellow, that!"

"You said a lot of good things, brother—thanks, thanks a lot!"

No matter how many villages and hamlets they rode through, Chapayev was known everywhere, and everywhere he was met with the same deference and joy—at some places the meeting would become quite a solemn affair. All the villagers would pour out to look at him. The peasants would begin a lively conversation, while the women would gasp and whisper, and the boys would run for a long way behind the sleigh, shouting wildly. Here and there, he made "speeches." The effect and success were assured. It was not the speeches themselves that were important but the fact that it was Chapayev who was making them. His name had magic power—it made everyone feel that behind the "speeches," which in themselves might be empty and of no significance, were hidden big, important matters.

This is an amazing trait in mankind, but it is always so—the chance and sometimes *commonplace* words of an outstanding and famous man always carry more weight than an undeniably *wise* comment of the colourless and inconspicuous "ordinary" person.

During one of the stages, Fyodor and Chapayev talked about personal matters—where each of them was from, what they had done before, and in what surroundings they had grown up—about an infinite number of things. Fyodor told Chapayev about the sooty industrial city where he had been born and received his first childish impressions—where he first realized that life was a stern struggle; then about his migratory life right up till the Revolution. When he had finished his short biography, Chapayev began to tell Fyodor about himself. So as not to forget, Fyodor wrote down all of Chapayev's little tale from memory at the first hamlet they came to.

CHAPAYEV'S BIOGRAPHY

"Chapayev has told me about himself," Klichkov wrote. "Whether to believe it all or not, I don't know. On some points at least, I have my doubts. For example, as to his parents—it's too obviously coloured up. I think that here his imagination was at work, but still I have put it all down as I heard it—why not? I don't see any harm in it, and whoever wants to establish the exact facts can prowl about in the places I'm telling about—there are friends and relatives of Chapai's left there. They will be sure to tell a lot about the life and exploits of the steppe commander.

" 'D'you know who I am,' Chapayev asked me one day when we were riding in the sleigh together, and his eyes twinkled naïvely and mysteriously. 'My mother was the daughter of the governor of Kazan and my father a Gypsy actor.' I thought that Chapayev was joking, but after waiting a moment and not hearing any exclamation of amazement from me, he went on: 'I know that's hard to believe, but it was all just like I said. That Gypsy got my mother to run away with him and then left her expecting a baby—left her to get out of it all by herself. Well, what could the poor thing do? She tried this and that but there was nothing for it but to go back to her mother. Her mother was a widow by that time—my grand-dad, the governor, had died. So she came home to her mother, but died very soon afterwards, when I was born. I was left like a pup nobody wants. They wondered how to get rid of such a treasure. Then they thought of something. They called in the yardman—he had a brother in the country. I was given to this brother like I was a toy of some kind. I lived and grew up like all the village kids did. The man had a family himself—a pack of kids! We'd fight and squeal so you'd want to leave home. I don't remember hardly anything about when I was a kid—I don't suppose there was anything to remember—in the village it's pretty much the same for everyone.

" 'When I got to be nine years old, I was put out to work, and I've been working for people all my life. First of all, they set me to herding pigs—I practised on them—they don't give a boy cattle to herd right off. When I'd broken my hand in on the pigs, I got to be a regular cowherd. Then a gang of carpenters took me on to teach me their trade and I worked at that for a while, going around with them to their various jobs. Then I left the carpenters and went to work in a shop. I learned how to sell things, and tried to cheat, but nothing came of it. With me, cheating went too much against the grain. Merchants only live by cheating—if a merchant doesn't cheat he'll soon starve to death. It was then I understood it all, and I saw through it so well nothing could make me want to cheat, so I left the shop. And if I've got it in for merchants now, it's all because I see right through the devils—on that point I'd make a better Socialist than Lenin, because I've seen all the merchants at work, and I know once and for all that everything should be taken away from them, they should be stripped clean, the curs.

" 'So I spat on trading then, and I thought to myself, what am I going to do now—me an orphan. I was going on seventeen then. I thought and thought, and finally decided to tramp it along the Volga. I thought I'd see all the different cities, and the people, and how they lived—find out everything for myself. So I bought myself a barrel-organ. And then there was a girl with me at that time—Nastya, her name was. "Nastya," I said, "let's go up and down the Volga. I'll sing and grind the organ, and you can dance. That way we'll see our fill of the Volga, and we'll go to all the different cities together, me and you." So we set out. At different places where winter would catch us, we'd live for quite a while. We even worked if we got too hungry. But what kind of work was there—only flunkeying—whatever could be picked up in winter. But as soon as the sun began to shine on the green April grass, and Mother Volga began to push the ice into the Caspian Sea, we'd forget we were hungry and set out along the bank. And the organ would play, and the larks above would sing, and Nastya was there, and I'd be singing. I'll never, never forget how beautiful it all was. I'll never forget those days in the spring.'

"Suddenly Chapayev bowed his head and his gay voice became sad:

"'There's lots of sun in April, and from the sun the ground begins to steam.... I didn't guard my sweetheart against the damp and she wilted like a little green leaf. Only my barrel-organ was left. I buried my little dancer on the shore at Volsk. I sold the organ to a Gypsy, and so I was left all alone.

"'But life always picks out people like me, and it picked me out, too—my time was coming round to serve the tsar. My time of service came, and so I went into the army; and when I went into the army, the war came along. Up till this very day, I've been under arms all the time. That's what my life has been like.'

"'Weren't you married?' I asked Chapai. 'I seem to remember you saying something about children.'

"'Oh, yes—that was before the war. It's true I was married but not for long. As soon as the German war started they took me right away. I came home once on leave—I found that people were talking about my wife. I didn't know what to believe. "Tell me," I said, "just how it all happened." "I haven't done anything, Vasily," she said, "it's spiteful gossip." There was a lot of spiteful gossip, but in between everything I discovered that she really had been carrying on something shameful. "Well," I said, "you green snake, I loved you once, but now you get out of here, you bitch. I don't want ever to see you again so long as I live. I'm going to keep the kids." It hurt me a lot—for two years I hadn't seen her, and as to other women—why, I didn't so much as move a finger. I never had anything.... I was waiting all the time to go back to her and was keeping myself for her. Who wouldn't have been upset—her husband comes home, and how has she been behaving herself!

"'I went back to the front, and I was so cut up that I began to poke my head into the very hottest fire. What difference does it make if I'm killed, I thought, if nothing comes of living. They gave me all four St. George crosses, made me a sergeant and then a sergeant-major, and still nothing would kill me. I was wounded more than once, but I kept on living. There was only one trouble—I knew how to fight but I didn't know my letters at all. It bothered me a lot. I was ashamed and jealous. The lads would be reading and writing all round, and I didn't know anything. I remember once the ensign called me an "ignorant devil," and I gave him a round of good old Russian cursing—it got under my skin so. So they tore off all my stripes, and I was again a plain soldier down at the bottom. However, I learned my letters there—learned how to read and write. Meanwhile the war began to drag out, and now the Revolution came around. They hustled me off to serve in the garrison at Saratov.

"'What the devil, I thought. All round me I heard sensible talk about why the people was moving, and I was the only one who didn't know. So I thought I'd join a party. I asked one clever fellow, and he kept trying to get me in with the Cadets, only I soon left them and joined the Socialist-Revolutionaries. I saw those S.-R. lads really wanted to do something. I was with them for a while and went to some of their meetings and then I discovered the Anarchists. These people are really doing things, I thought. People would get everything right off, and there wouldn't be any making anybody do anything— everybody would do whatever they liked. At that time, Kerensky was organizing a volunteer detachment of Serbs, and they made me commander. And it was me who spoiled the whole detachment—turned it against Kerensky, I did. So they demoted me, a fine fellow that I was, and sent me to Pugachov to command a company. You know what the times were like then. In Pugachov we had our own council of people's commissars, and the chairman was a... in a word, he was a fine chap. You could see he liked me a lot, and for my part, he was a lad after my own heart. When I listened to him talk, it even made me want to live sensibly myself. This chap began to teach me and give me an eddication. Since then I look at everything different. I threw all that Anarchy overboard and entered the Bolsheviks. I began to read other books—I'm a great reader. In that war, soon as I learned my letters, I'd lie in the trenches, and read and read. The chaps would begin to laugh: "You'll soon be a psalm-reader, you read so much," but I didn't see anything to laugh at. I read about Ataman Churkin, Razin, Yemelyan Pugachov, and Yermak Timofeyich. Then I got a book about Hannibal, and I read about the Italian, Garibaldi, too, and about Napoleon himself. You know, I like best of all that a man should know how to fight and that he shouldn't spare himself if it's necessary. I know all about those people. And then I read other things. They said that Turgenev had some good stories, but I couldn't get hold of them. I remember everything of Gogol's, and I remember Chichkin.* Oh, if I could get more eddication, then my head would begin to work different. As it is, I'm just plain ignorant. I always was ignorant and I'm still that way.

" 'I hadn't any time to learn—at Pugachov, you had to watch all the time, or the Cossacks would make a raid. And then, whenever grain had to be got somewhere or some uprising put down, they always sent me.

" 'Chapayev here?' they'd ask.

" 'Here,' I'd say.

" 'Get going.'

" 'That's all they ever said—they didn't have to teach me—I knew myself what to do.'

"Chapayev told about his life right up to the October Revolution. Whether everything was as he told it, I don't know. He liked to brag. That was a weakness of his. It may be that he added something for the effect. Only if he added anything, it was the merest trifle.**

"His biography would seem to be nothing out of the ordinary; there is nothing remarkable in it, but at the same time, if one looks closer, one will see that all the circumstances, all the needs and events of his personal life pushed him on to discontent and protest."

Fyodor had some other things written down, but we'll stop there and not quote his ideas about Chapayev. As for Chapayev's life after the October Revolution, the information is very conflicting—this period of his life was too picturesque. He flew over the steppe like a whirl-

---

* Properly, Chichikov, a character of the *Dead Souls* by N. Gogol —*Ed.*

** What Chapayev said about his mother being the daughter of the governor was evidently pure invention; later everyone doubted it.

wind. Today, he might be seen in one village, and tomorrow a hundred versts away.

The Cossacks quaked at the bare mention of Chapayev's name, and tried to avoid fighting against him—they were so completely bewitched by his daring raids and his constant successes and victories.

It took Chapayev and Fyodor four days to get to Samara. They passed through many villages and hamlets on their way, but wherever the name of Chapayev was pronounced it always had the same effect. Chapayev held himself with inimitable self-assurance. One day, it happened that they drove into some village or other late at night. There was no one in the streets—not a soul to ask where the Soviet was. They were thinking of barging into some hut, but didn't want to climb out in the cold; they drove straight to the church, thinking that they'd find the Soviet "somewhere there on the square." At last they met someone.

"Comrade, where's the Soviet?"

"Over there, across the gully," and he pointed in the opposite direction. They turned round and went to where they had been sent. They found an enormous building that looked like a shed; it was old and solitary and wild, and it stood in a wild place across a gully, at the edge of the village. It could be seen at a glance that it was quite neglected. They knocked and knocked—it was all they could do to get someone to open the door. A feeble, deaf old man came out.

"What d'you want, young men?" he asked.

"Where's the man on duty?" Chapayev angrily demanded.

"There isn't anyone, they're all at home; people only come here in the day-time, nobody here now."

"Call the chairman right away."

In such cases, Fyodor never protested against any insistence or even sharpness in talking to people: in those times civility would not get a person very far. Sometimes when people noticed that they had to do with a shilly-shally kind of person, they deliberately shoved him aside; they tried to get the best of him, and not do a thing for him. The times were harsh, and one had to act harshly, and not bandy words if he wanted to get something done.

They sent for the chairman—the latter found out from the messenger that it was "Chapayev himself" who wanted him. He came up timidly, pulled off his cap, and bowed.

"What's this, brother, is the Soviet a pigsty to you?" Chapayev greeted him sternly. "Why the devil have you stuck it here at the edge of nowhere. Couldn't you find a place in the middle of the village?"

"The people won't give me any other place," the chairman timidly interposed.

"What people? It isn't the people, but the kulaks that don't want to give anything; the people have nothing to do with it. You back down too easy."

"But I wanted—"

"What d'you mean 'wanted'?" Chapayev interrupted. "This is where you've got to do something, and not just want. And you call yourself the administration! Move the Soviet to the square tomorrow, take over a good house, and say that it's Chapayev's orders. D'you understand?"

"I understand," the other mumbled.

"If I come back from Samara and find you in this hole, then look out."

The inarticulate chairman, apparently an ineffective "dummy," began to fuss and bustle about the horses. They didn't even want to spend the night "in such a place," and pushed on, late though it was.

They arrived in Samara and reported to Frunze. He asked Chapayev and Fyodor in a friendly way to come to his quarters that evening so they could have a good talk about the coming operations. They went to his place. Frunze explained the situation at the front, and told them what decisive actions were necessary and what kind of commanders the moment required. When Chapayev left the room for a few minutes for some reason or other, Frunze said to Fyodor:

"This is a serious matter, Comrade Klichkov. I'm thinking of appointing Chapayev commander of a division. What do you say? I don't know him very well, but you know yourself the reputation he's got. What is he really like? You've at least worked with him a little."

Fyodor told him just what he thought. He told him his high opinion of Chapayev but stressed his political immaturity.

"That's my opinion, too," said Frunze. "He's, of course, quite out of the ordinary. He can be of enormous service, only there's still a lot of the guerrilla in him. But you try—it doesn't matter that he's hot-tempered—hot-tempered ones can also be tamed."

Fyodor briefly explained to Frunze that he was working along just these lines, that he was sure he had won Chapayev's liking and trust, and that he hoped to become closer friends with him in the future.

Chapayev came in. After a little talk, Frunze informed him of his appointment and told him that he must go to Uralsk and wait orders there, since the general plan for the offensive was still far from clear. They said good-bye to Frunze and left. Within two hours they set out from Samara. Before leaving, Chapayev had asked permission to stop in at Vyazovka, his native village, on their way to Uralsk. Frunze agreed, and so they made for Vyazovka.

"You have folks in Vyazovka?" Fyodor asked.

"All of them in Vyazovka—the old folks are there, my father and mother—foster ones, that is. Two boys and a girl—they're living with a widow. She's got two kids of her own, and they all live together."

"A good friend of yours?"

"Very good friend—very good," and Chapayev smiled slily. "A friend of mine died and she was left. He willed her to me."

At Vyazovka, they were met with great ceremony. The chairman of the Soviet at once called a meeting in honour of the renowned guest. Chapayev made some of his "speeches." That evening, at the public hall named after him, a performance was given by "local talent." The acting was terrible, but the zeal that went into it was colossal. The actors wanted to win Chapayev's praise. They spent the night in the village and in the morning—forward march to Uralsk.

It seemed to Fyodor that Chapayev was not very affectionate with his children, and asked him about it.

"That's true," said Chapayev, "since I had that trouble in my family life, nothing suits me—even the kids. I almost look on my kids as someone else's."

"Then how will you bring them up?"

"How can I bring them up? I never have any time, and here, who knows how they get along—I don't even ask about it. I send them money out of my pay, and that's all."

"Money isn't everything."

"I know it's not everything—and then, too, I haven't got my pay for November and December, and now look—March is half over already. They're not paying."

"Things are bad."

"Nowadays everybody's losing something, Comrade Klichkov," Chapayev said seriously. "Without that, you know, there can't be any revolution. Some people lose their property, others their families, others spoil their eddication, and us, why, maybe we'll lose our lives, even."

"Yes," Fyodor said musingly, "we may even lose our lives. It's a strange thing—there seems to be no end to the war. More and more enemies on all sides. Danger all around. Will you and me be travelling around together for long? There'll soon be new campaigns, you know."

"I don't give it a thought," Chapayev waved his hand. "Who knows when the end'll be? Sometimes you get into such a mess that it looks like there's no way out at all, and still you're not killed. Better not to think about what's coming. One day I rode into a village right into the hands of the Czechs by mistake—that was back in 1918. I thought it was our soldiers and our village, and it was all the same to the driver—he'd go anywhere you liked. We just entered the village—Jesus, it was the Czechs. 'Well,' I said, 'Babayev'—that was the driver—'get us out of this the best you can,' and I grabbed the machine-gun. 'Turn her round,' I said, 'and I'll begin to shoot. If you'll make it in time, we're safe, if not, we're goners.' He began to get the machine round, and I opened up. He kept driving, and I kept firing. As soon as he got the machine round, he gave her her head, and here about fifteen cavalrymen rode out after us. I got busy on them—Such a cloud of dust, you couldn't see a thing, but I could hear them blazing away on the gallop—they were firing at us, and I kept shooting in their direction. I finished up both belts. Well, if a tyre had burst then, what would have been left of me? At that time, the Czechs were offering a price for my head—'bring in Chapayev's head,' they said, 'and we'll pay you gold.' My lads would read the bills and laugh at the Czechs. Once they wrote them a letter: 'Come to our Stepan Razin Regiment, and we'll give you his head for nothing.' They wrote that and sealed it up and gave it to a village youngster to take it to them. Yes, I've had all kinds of adventures."

"And, you see, you're still alive," said Fyodor. "Why are you still alive—is it just by chance or because you had your wits about you? Who knows? I guess you've been within a hairbreadth of death dozens of times."

"You're right there," Chapayev immediately agreed, "dozens and dozens of times. I'm always asking myself the same question: Why is it I'm so hard to kill, just as though something's keeping me alive on purpose. Some chaps, just as soon as the first bullet flies—smack, and they're done for."

"Well, then," asked Fyodor, "you yourself, what do you think—is it just chance or something else?"

"Oh, no—it's not all chance. You've always got to have a head about you. That's the most important thing. Why, it happens sometimes that if you hesitate a minute, it's the end of you, and not only you, but a hundred other people, too. Once the Czechs caught us asleep in a village. I was spending the night at the other end of the village. I jumped out just in my pants, and began shouting, 'Hurrahhh! Hurrahhh!' We didn't have anything—practically no arms at all, but the lads took heart and made a rush at the Czechs and took away their guns. We not only freed our men that had been captured, but took some of the Czechs prisoner. You've got to have a head on you, Comrade Klichkov. Without that, you'll be killed right off in a war."

"And nobody wants to get killed?" Fyodor joked.

"There, too, it's not the same with everybody," Chapayev answered gravely. "D'you think everybody sets much store by his life? And not only that, but the same man may not always look at it the same way. Take me, for example. I was an ordinary soldier—what was it to me whether they killed me or not, wasn't it all the same? Who needed such a louse as me? People like me were being born all the time, as many as you like. I didn't value my life a kopek. The enemy trenches were three hundred paces away, and I'd jump out and yell: 'Come on! Try and get me!' Then I'd jig on the parapet. I didn't even think of whether I might be killed. And then I saw that people began to take notice of me—it meant I was getting to be somebody. And you mark this, Comrade Klichkov, the higher I rose, the more I began to set store by my life. I won't try to hide it from you, but I'll say right out, that I've begun to think to myself: you're not just some bug, you rascal, but a real man; and I've begun to want to really live the way a man ought to live. That doesn't mean that I've got to be a coward, but that I've got more sense. I wouldn't dance a jig on the parapet now—no tricks now, I don't want to get killed for nothing."

"But in action?" asked Fyodor.

"In action? I swear to you," Chapayev exclaimed hotly, "I'll swear by whatever you like that *in action* I'll never be a coward. In action all other thoughts leave my head. What did you think?"

"Oh, I was just wondering."

"That so? Maybe at Headquarters they've said something about me?"

Fyodor didn't understand what Chapayev was talking about.

"Those damned colonels?" Chapayev continued, hardly able to contain his irritation. "There, of course—"

"I'm telling you seriously," Klichkov soothed him, "I haven't been talking to any 'damned colonels.' What are they to me?"

"They'll tell you plenty, of course."

"Don't like you?" asked Fyodor.

"They hate me," Chapayev said slowly and impressively. "I sent them such telegrams and nice little notes that they wanted to have me up before the Tribunal. The war interfered or they might have had me up for trial. They have it fine sitting there at their desks. They want me to stick out my neck, but I won't ever stick it out for any of those fellows. Great commanders they think they are. If you need cartridges, there aren't any, but orders—oh, they're great on them. Well, I gave it to them hot and heavy. They said I was a hooligan, a guerrilla—what could be expected of me."

"Why, Comrade Chapayev," Fyodor said in amazement. "D'you mean to say you think it's those colonels that are running our Red Army?"

"Who else?"

"What d'you mean, 'who'? What about the revolutionary military councils? What about our commissars and Red commanders?"

"Those councils half the time don't seem to understand anything. Somebody tells them a pack of lies, and they swallow it all."

"It's not that way at all," Fyodor retorted. "You've got the wrong idea about the revolutionary military councils. It's our people there, and people who understand things. You're all wrong when you think—"

"All right, you'll see when the campaign begins," Chapayev answered softly, but his voice had lost some of its confidence and insistence. Fyodor explained to him how the revolutionary military councils were organized and what the idea behind them was, what their functions were, and what their structure. He saw that Chapayev didn't know anything about it, that all this information was a revelation to him. He listened very attentively, not missing a word, and remembered everything almost word for word—he had a wonderful memory. Fyodor was always amazed at Chapayev's memory. He would remember even the smallest details, and then stick them into the conversation some time or other.

Fyodor liked these long endless talks. He talked, and he knew that the seed was falling on fertile soil. He had noticed of late that Chapayev would sometimes put forward Fyodor's thoughts as his own—that is, in conversation with some third person, and seemingly by chance. Fyodor saw that the other recognized in him a person who knew things, and that he had apparently decided to make use of this contact. From questions about the organization of the army, and from technical and scientific questions they went on to the question of Chapayev's lack of education—a very sore point with him. They agreed that Fyodor would teach him as much as time and circumstances would permit. Naïve people—they wanted to study algebra in the smoke of battle! Of course, they had no opportunity to study even one day, but they spoke of it many times afterwards. They would be riding up to the front-lines together, and after talking about various things would hit on this subject.

"You remember, we wanted to study together," Fyodor would say.

"There's a lot of things we wanted to do but we can't do everything we want," Chapayev would answer sadly and regretfully.

Fyodor saw that Chapayev greedily caught every new word—and for him, how very much was new! He had been in the Party for a whole year; it would seem that everything should have been clear to him in respect to religion, and then one day Klichkov suddenly noticed Chapayev cross himself.

"What are you doing, Vasily Ivanovich?" he asked Chapayev, using the familiar form of address to which they had gone over after two weeks' acquaintance. "A religious Communist! Are you in your right mind?"

Chapayev was embarrassed but answered with spirit:

"It seems to me that a Communist can do what he likes, too. You don't believe, that's all right, don't believe. But if I believe, what harm does that do you?"

"It doesn't do me any harm, I'm not talking about myself," Fyodor went on doggedly. "What I'm surprised at, is you. How can you, a Communist, believe in God?"

"Maybe I don't."

"If you don't, why are you crossing yourself?"

"I just want to, that's all—and so I cross myself."

"How can you do it? You can't joke with such things," Fyodor admonished him seriously.

Then Chapayev told him an incident from his early childhood, and insisted that it had all begun with that.

"Once when I was a little boy," Chapayev began, "I stole a two-kopek piece from a plate in front of the ikon—there was a wonder-working ikon in our church. Well, I stole two kopeks, bought a water-melon and filled myself up on it. I ate so much that I fell ill right off. Was in bed all of six weeks. First, I had fever and then chills, and diarrhoea kept me running. I just about died. My mother found out that I had stolen that two-kopek piece, and she began throwing money on to the plate. She said she must have put in three rubles, all in ten-kopek pieces. And she prayed and prayed for me so that the Virgin Mary would forgive me. Her prayers were answered—in the seventh week I got up. Ever since then I have always thought that there must be some kind of force that you've got to watch out against—after that I stopped pinching things. I wouldn't take an apple out of someone else's orchard—I don't seem to have the courage. I don't mind being under fire, but when it comes to stealing, fear gets the better of me. I can't do it."

At the time, Fyodor didn't say very much, but later he came back to the subject of religion on numerous occasions; he told Chapayev about the origin of religion and about God. Chapayev never crossed himself after that. Not only did he stop crossing himself—he once confessed to Fyodor that he had been "an out-and-out fool until he understood what it was all about, but once he understood there was no going back."

As a result of these discussions, Chapayev came to look entirely differently on religion, God, the Church and priests. He had, by the way, hated the priests before, only he was just a little afraid to think about them. It had always seemed to him that they were "nearer to God than we, although they were pretty thorough scoundrels."

Fyodor became more and more convinced that Chapayev, that stern man of iron and guerrilla hero, could be taken in hand like a child; that he could be moulded like wax, only it was necessary to approach him cautiously and skilfully. One had to know what he would "take" and what he wouldn't want to accept at once. Learning was the sphere in which he could be led most easily; here he followed willingly, even enthusiastically, to meet the stream of quickening thought. But that was all. In other things, he was firm, inflexible, at times even mulish. The circumstances of his life had held him in ignorance, but now he saw—he realized that there existed other ways, other explanations to everything—and he began to ponder on these new things. Slowly, timidly and softly he crept up to the sacred, barred gates, and as slowly they opened up before him, revealing the path to a new life.

VIII

AGAINST KOLCHAK

Fyodor and Chapayev were in Uralsk ten days, waiting for orders. The boredom was unendurable. They had absolutely nothing to do. They lounged in and about the Headquarters of the Uralsk Division which was stationed there, and maintained contact with the brigade of their own division that was in Slomikhinskaya—it had not yet been transferred to Buzuluk District. They were bored to death. Only once, and that for but a few moments, did

Fyodor see Andreyev, who was travelling about the front almost continuously and only looked in at Uralsk for very brief spells. He had got thin and sallow, and his fine blue eyes were deep sunk and seemed almost black. It was obvious that he didn't get enough sleep and had many worries; it may be he didn't get enough to eat. Klichkov met him in the corridor of Division Headquarters dressed for travelling—ready to set out again, in spite of the fact that he had only arrived half an hour before. The two surveyed each other with a long and searching look, as though asking: "Well, and what has this new life brought you—what have you gained and what have you lost?"

And it seemed that both noticed this something *new* which lays an indelible seal on the face, the look and the movements of anyone who has been in fighting.

They hurriedly exchanged a few words and said goodbye till next time.

Chapayev chafed excessively—he always did when he had nothing to do; whenever it happened that he had to stop and wait for something for a day or two, Chapayev was unrecognizable. When in such a mood, he would begin to find fault with everyone mercilessly; he would begin to curse over trifles and threaten with disciplinary action. His tremendous energy constantly sought an outlet, and when it couldn't be applied usefully, it would burst out abortively—but burst out it must.

At that time, the Uralsk Division was holding a front somewhere near Lbishchensk. Operations proceeded neither well nor badly—there were no major defeats, but there were also no significant victories. Then, all of a sudden, they ran out of luck. A very large number of men were killed in a battle that didn't go as had been expected. The front beyond Lbishchensk began to waver.

The Novouzensk and Moslem regiments were badly mauled, and the Kurilovo lads were hurriedly sent to their assistance. A real catastrophe. And all so unexpected—like thunder out of a clear sky. No one had foreseen it; there had been no warning. The chief of the Uralsk Division, a very cool and tried commander, lost his head and couldn't immediately grasp what had happened and decide what to do. He asked Chapayev's advice, and together they did their best, but they were unable to restore the front. Uralsk was soon encircled, and it held out in this ring for many months.

As soon as the news of the catastrophe was received and forwarded to the Centre, Frunze gave orders for a special commission to investigate the causes of the defeat. The commission included Chapayev, and Fyodor was appointed chairman. Chapayev was apparently offended that the chairmanship had not been entrusted to him, but to the commissar. This, however, made itself felt only later. Chapayev had no idea that here, besides purely military circumstances, a by no means lesser role, if not greater, might have been played by political circumstances. That, apparently, was the view taken at the Centre, and for that reason, Klichkov was put in charge of the entire matter.

They immediately began to collect material of all kinds—documents, copies of orders and instructions, reports, telegrams. From Fyodor, Chapayev got the brigade order that covered the extremely unsuccessful attack on the village of Mergenevsky. This order served as a background for what had happened, and Klichkov accordingly attached exclusive importance to it. Chapayev examined it attentively, drew up his "critical remarks," sat down, and began to dictate to the typist. Fyodor came in.

"Have you had a look at the order, Vasily Ivanovich?"

"Why, yes, I looked at—what of it?"

"I have been thinking about it a lot, too. Let's talk it over," Fyodor suggested.

"You can read this. It's already typed out."

Chapayev's voice and manner betrayed an ill-concealed bluntness, and a certain peevishness that was absolutely incomprehensible to Fyodor at the time.

"Read it out," said Fyodor. "We'll talk it over and maybe make some changes."

"No changes at all," retorted Chapayev. "You can change your own stuff, but I'll send mine off the way I wrote it."

"Why so?" asked Fyodor in amazement, touched to the quick by this unfriendly answer.

"Why, just because. If you're the chairman, then you give your opinion. But me, I'm just an expert. I'm just an expert." He repeated the word in an offended tone.

"Why, what nonsense is that?" Fyodor exclaimed, taking offence. "There's no reason for us to work separately—let's discuss it together, and together we'll send it off."

"No, we won't," Chapayev persisted stubbornly.

Klichkov didn't want to waste any more time on this question. "Well, go ahead and read," he said, sitting down.

Chapayev read out his criticism of the brigade order of the Uralsk Division. His analysis was able, thorough and business-like. Fyodor refrained from discussing it; he had decided to send his opinion separately.

"Well, what do you say to it?" Chapayev asked.

"Why, I think it's good," Fyodor muttered through his teeth.

"Maybe you'll say it's bad?" and Chapayev suddenly raised his voice. "There's plenty that's bad, all right, but it isn't me—I know what I'm about, but those damned penpushers there, the bastards!"

Fyodor didn't understand on whom Chapayev was showering all these epithets.

"The scoundrels," he went on angrily. "Want to keep a good man down, won't give him a chance. Well, I'll find a way to get justice. They'll hear from me yet!"

Chapayev was scoffing at the "damned staffs" which he looked on as a horde of parasites, cowards, careerists, and in general, scum of all kinds.

"Wait a minute, Chapayev, what are you making a show of yourself for?" Fyodor interposed half-jokingly. "All of a sudden, for nothing at all—what the devil! Have you gone off your chump?"

"I've been off my chump for a long time—now it's beginning to show," and there was a note of reproach in his voice. "It's enough to make a person go off his chump.... You can't get anything on Chapayev—he knows his business."

"What are you talking about?"

"About the same thing—the same old thing—that I never finished any acadaymies. But I'll get along without any acadaymies. My peasant way of doing it gets results. I never wore any general's shoulder-straps, but even without them, God knows, I'm a better strateger than lots."

"Now don't brag, Vasily Ivanovich—it's not becoming. Let other people say nice things about you, but you, yourself—" Fyodor put his finger to his lips. His recent unpleasant feeling impelled him to try to get under Chapayev's skin, to get back at him. In what way? Fyodor knew that Chapayev's tenderest spot was the recognition or non-recognition of his bravery, ability and military talent, especially if a reference to "staffs" was slipped in. The moment was such that it was not necessary to goad him any—Chapayev was already beside himself.

"You'd better shut up about strategy," Fyodor blurted out.

"What d'you mean, shut up? Shut up yourself!" Chapayev shouted, trembling with indignation.

Controlling himself, and trying to seem absolutely calm, Klichkov said softly, "Now listen to me, Chapai. You're a good fighter, a brave soldier, a fine partisan, but that's all! Let's be frank. You ought to have the courage to admit it yourself—when it comes to military science, you're weak. Why, what kind of a strategist are you? Just think a minute yourself. How could you be?"

Chapayev's face twitched nervously, and angry flames danced in his wolfish grey-blue eyes.

"I'm a bad strateger?" he almost shouted at Fyodor. "I'm a bad strateger, am I? You can go to the devil after that!"

"Now you just keep cool," said Fyodor maliciously, content with having, if only a little, touched the other to the quick. "Why get excited? If you want to be good in the military line, if you want to know the scientific foundations of strategy, you've got to study and learn all that —and of course you never had the time. Well, isn't it clear to you—?"

"Nothing's clear to me—nothing's clear," Chapayev cut him short. "I could take any army and make good."

"Maybe you could take a front?" Fyodor joked.

"Or a front—what did you think?"

"Why, maybe you wouldn't mind being the Commander-in-Chief?"

"So you think I couldn't do it? I'd look around, catch on, and make good. I can do anything I set my mind to, d'you understand?"

"Oh, naturally!"

The unpleasant feeling Fyodor had had when he commenced the conversation was gone, as was even the derisive tone in which he had asked his questions. Chapayev's confidence in his own unlimited ability astounded him.

"Your belief in yourself is a good thing," he said to Chapayev. "Without it you couldn't do anything. Only aren't you puffing yourself up too much, Vasily Ivanovich? Isn't this too much empty bragging on your part? You let your tongue run away with you. That's the trouble."

Chapayev's eyes blazed up still more, and glittered savagely. He seethed with indignation, but waited for Fyodor to finish.

"Me!" he shouted, "Me, bragging? Who was it that fought in the steppe against the Cossacks, without cartridges, bare-handed? Who was it?" He moved up close to Fyodor. "What is it to them? The bastards! All their talk about a strateger...."

"I don't consider you a strategist, either—that means that I'm a bastard, too?" Fyodor caught him up. Chapayev immediately fell silent; he was confused and his face flushed. He was at once helpless, as though caught in some ludicrous and stupid childish prank.

Fyodor had purposely twisted the question this way with the aim of curing Chapayev in some way of his arrogant, blind abuse of no one in particular. This was not only because it was "unseemly," but because it was extremely dangerous for Chapayev. He might be overheard by his enemies. They would remember it, and then drive him to the wall with witnesses and documents. His position would be most dangerous, and he wouldn't be able to get out of it. And Chapayev could constantly be heard giving it hot and heavy to the staffs, and revolutionary military councils, and the Cheka, and the Special Departments, and the commissars—anyone who might display the least authority over him. He would rave, abuse, curse and threaten, and all for nothing. If you explained things to him, he would understand everything, even at times revise his opinion and agree with you, though slowly, unwillingly. He didn't like to retreat, even in what he had said. To tell the truth, he never changed his orders; this was the reason for their particularly convincing force.

Now that he had cornered Chapayev, Fyodor decided to go on with the process of training him to the end—to go away and leave Chapayev to think it over.

"Let his doubts worry him—he'll remember it longer—"

And when Chapayev, recovering somewhat from the unexpected blow, began to assure Fyodor that he "hadn't had him in mind, but was only talking about 'them,'" and so on, Fyodor said good-bye and walked out.

When Klichkov came home at midnight, he found Chapayev sitting in his room. He was sheepishly crumpling a paper of some kind in his hand.

"Here, read this," and he handed Fyodor a little typewritten note. When Chapayev was excited, offended, or was expecting insult, he often went over to the formal form of address. Fyodor noticed this now, both in his speech and in the note to him.

"Comrade Klichkov," the note read, "I beg you to take notice of my note to you. I am very much upset because of the way you left and how you took what I said in reference to you about which I would like to inform you that you have never done me any wrong, and if I'm so open and a little hot-tempered, and don't stand on ceremony in your presence, and say everything that comes to mind about certain people, which insulted you. But to keep from having any differences between us I am forced to write an application to be removed from my post, rather than be in disagreement with my closest co-worker, of which I now inform you as your friend.

"Chapayev."

That was the note. It has been reproduced here without the slightest change. It might have had the most serious consequences. The application was already written, and in a moment, Chapayev showed it to Fyodor also. If Fyodor's attitude had been in the least disapproving, or if he had kept silent, the matter would have gone "higher," and who knows what the consequences might have been! It is strange that here Chapayev didn't seem to set the least store by his division, although it included the Pugachov, Razin and Domashkin lads—all those valiant regiments which were so dear to him. Here, a fundamental trait of his character revealed itself—he was capable of sacrificing even what was dearest to him in a flash, without a thought, without looking back, and all because of something of no importance whatsoever.

Inflame him at such a moment, and he'd probably go to lengths still more absurd.

Fyodor read the note and turned to Chapayev with a smiling, radiant face and said: "Why, what do you mean, Chapayev, old man? I wasn't offended at all. If I was upset a little, it was for an entirely different reason."

Fyodor said nothing more, and only the next day made a clean breast of his view of the matter.

"Here's a telegram," and Chapayev handed it to him.
"Where from?"
"Orders from Headquarters to set off tomorrow for Buzuluk. We're not going to Orenburg. Have to wind up everything here and leave."

After thinking things over, they decided not to put it off till the next day, but to finish their affairs immediately and leave that night—the investigation of the unsuccessful operation of the Uralsk Division couldn't be finished in one day anyway—it would have required their making a trip to the front, the obtaining of certain additional documents, etc. They made their decision, and went immediately to Division Headquarters. They had the people they needed called in, and talked things over. In an hour and a half, they left Uralsk for Buzuluk.

What took place in those days along the roads and railways leading to Samara, defied description. Trains were continually flying or creeping into Kinel from all directions: from Ufa and Orenburg, from near and far, some with troops, others with shells or provisions, and some—armoured trains. In the opposite direction went empty trains, and hospital trains, and again troop trains, troop trains, troop trains. Transports were crawling out of Uralsk, and troops were marching away.

A hurried re-grouping was under way. Enormous masses of men were being shifted. Fresh troops were being sent up, while badly cut up and demoralized units, temporarily unfit for action, were being sent to the rear. Kolchak had already taken Ufa and was approaching the Volga. The situation was becoming menacing. Samara was threatened, and along with it, the other big centres along the Volga. The situation was such that it might possibly be necessary to retreat across the Volga. That would have been a serious blow to Russia. The Red Command did not want this withdrawal, and took up the defence energetically. They decided that the existing situation must be changed at all costs, and changed in their favour. They must seize the initiative from the enemy and drive him away from the centre of the Soviet state. A powerful striking force was being gathered in Buzuluk District; from here, the first blows were to be struck. Chapayev's division, the Twenty-Fifth, was entrusted with an important task—to strike Kolchak in the centre and, together with other divisions, to drive him away from the Volga, Ufa being the immediate objective.

Besides the units moving in from Slomikhinskaya, and the brigade led by the talented young commander, Sizov, which had been operating in the Uralsk sector and was now being hastily transferred to the Sorochinskaya sector near Buzuluk—besides these units, another brigade was included in the Twenty-Fifth Division, under the command of some officer or other who deserted to the Whites within two weeks. In this brigade, which was grouped near Samara in the Krotovka sector, was the Ivanovo-Voznesensk Regiment.

Kolchak was moving along a very extended front against Perm, Kazan and Samara. In these three directions a White Army of one hundred and fifty thousand men was on the march. The opposing forces were almost equal, the Red Army being a little inferior in number. Through Perm and Vyatka, Kolchak aimed at linking up with the British; through Samara, with Denikin. He was making haste to strangle Soviet Russia within this fatal ring.

The first telling blows were dealt Kolchak on the road to Samara. It was here that the initiative was wrested from him; here part of his divisions and corps were smashed. This marked the beginning of the demoralization of his troops. Neither the officers' battalions, nor the drilling of his troops, nor equipment—nothing, after the first blows received, could stop his spontaneous recoil to Ufa and then, beyond Ufa, to Siberia and final destruction. The regiments of the Kappel Corps, the flower and hope of the White Army, engaged in the fighting at Belebei. They were defeated by the Red troops, as were the other White regiments. The Red wave swept on irresistibly, triumphantly welcomed everywhere by the harassed and impoverished population.

The railway stations, large and small, were like bottles filled with ants, all of them crawling, hurrying, bumping into one another, falling off, getting up and again hurrying, hurrying, hurrying. Trains would arrive; whole crowds of Red Army men would jump off like madmen, and rush in all directions. Throngs would jam up in front of the little brick sheds where boiling water could be got. Queues would be formed, and tea-kettles would rattle. Some would hurry and scold and shout their indignation, and mill about as they waited for boiling water. Others would scatter out about the station and the surrounding settlement, buying matches, cigarettes, dried fish—whatever they happened to come across. They would drink milk offered by the market-women and buy bread —big loaves, medium loaves, little loaves—all kinds of loaves. A madly protesting crowd which never seemed to grow any smaller, jostled and pushed one another in front of the commandant's little window. They cursed the system and the lack of system in fits of exasperation. They showered the thrice-ill-starred commandant with abuse. They demanded the impossible, swore to the nonexistent, expected the unobtainable. Now they demanded a train crew, now an engine-driver, now a new engine, now better goods waggons or carriages instead of the goods waggons given them. When they were told at the commandant's office: "Impossible, there won't be any," threats were added to the storm of protests and insults. They swore to get revenge or to call up their ferocious commander.

Suddenly the gong would sound.

"Which bell?"

"The third!"

A frantic gang of protesting soldiers would suddenly break away from the commandant's window and gallop along the tracks, knocking people off their feet, followed by yelps of amazement and indignation, threats and curses.

The third gong had sounded. Now a whistle, and the troop train would begin to move off. Groups and single

Red Army soldiers would race behind it for a long way, trying to catch up with it. Some would catch on to the ladders and steps and climb on to the roofs of the waggons. Others, exhausted, would give up in despair and sit down on the rails. They would hang around the station until another train came along. They might be there a day, or two days—who knows how long! One train they didn't notice, another wouldn't take them on, still another went off under their noses.

It was pitch dark in the goods waggons. There were neither candles, nor lamps, nor lanterns. The Red Army men lay on bare boards that had been muddied by boots and bast shoes, smeared with greasy kettles, splashed with cabbage soup and tea, spat upon and cluttered up with shag cigarette butts. The nights were long, and long they lay in the cold and inky darkness, half-covered with old, worn-out great-coats, a canvas kit-bag stuck under their heads. At the stations the waggons were shunted back and forth for a long time—they were reshuffled, coupled on to other waggons, and uncoupled from other waggons, while the buffers bumped mercilessly enough to make one's very brains rattle. People with tiny lanterns yelled and cursed in the darkness. Then the train would be left on some far siding to "settle out." And there, there would be other such trains, also packed chock-full of Red Army men—they would be peering out of the high tiny windows, jumping off, running out, crawling in, clambering up. The bustle around the "frozen" trains never stopped, night or day. Some people would be hurrying about their "business," others running around just to keep warm, still others would be prowling about on the look-out for badly-hidden firewood, rails, boxes—anything that would burn in their stoves. Finally, there were some who loitered idly about the station all night in search of excitement of any kind.

After a journey lasting many days, after many trying experiences and exasperating stops, after brawls, and it might be, fights and even shooting incidents, they would arrive at last. The soldiers would throw their things out of the wide open doors of the goods waggons. They would pile them up high and leave a pair of men with bayonets to guard them, while the others went to help unload. Horses would be led down planks, and hobbled, hitched together, driven to one side in droves. They would be surrounded and guarded to keep them from running away. Guns would be slowly rolled down off the trucks, and also motor-cars and waggons loaded with all sorts of baggage—everything they possessed. At last everything would be unloaded. The empty train would be deserted, its empty waggons still colder than before.

A deafening uproar, squabbling, confusion—here and there orders which no one obeyed. At last the final "Fall in!" A running back and forth would begin—anxious and hurried. Men would be hunting for companies, platoons, squads. At last all would be drawn up in marching order. They would strike out. The ranks would sway—broad, well-ordered; carts would rattle and creak; restive horses would snort and whinny; gun carriages would clang; here and there chance shots would be fired. The first versts, they would march with even ranks; the first versts, they would march briskly, in step, and with loud, ringing songs; but farther on, the soldiers who fell behind, the sick and exhausted, were put in the waggons; the ranks became confused, and no more songs would be heard. Now, there was only one thought—to get to the halting-place as quickly as possible. Here it was at last—a halt and a rest. In a few minutes some would already be sound asleep and snoring lustily, while others, indefatigable, would even now begin to sing, to play the accordion, to dance jigs, leaping about and squatting down on their heels to their mates' rhythmic shouts. And so it went from halt to halt, from halt to halt, and then—the trenches!

Trench life would begin.

Potapov was given the brigade that came to Buzuluk; Sizov commanded that at Sorochinskaya, while a little later, Shmarin was entrusted with the brigade whose inglorious commander had deserted to the Whites. The division was concentrated, and still other divisions were concentrated. Armies were concentrated and poised; the whole front stood still, waiting to deal the first blows.

"To be or not to be," that was the significance many people at the time attached to these first blows. "If we don't seize the initiative, if we are thrown back across the Volga, and Kolchak closes up the fatal ring in the north and in the south (and that is possible), then is Soviet Russia to be or not to be?"

Yes! All these dangers were at the time closer and more serious than many people thought. The first gusts of spray from the enormous whiteguard wave had already reached Vyatka, Kazan, Samara, Saratov.

For Kolchak, the most desired and vitally important route was through Samara. It was the shortest route to the heart of Soviet Russia. It was not for nothing that his railway carriages had been marked "Ufa-Moscow."

Mounted patrols had already begun to appear near Buzuluk. In the last few days, Buguruslan had also been lost. The situation was becoming more and more tense. The enemy was approaching closer and closer, and the position was becoming ever more dangerous.

The Red Army had not quite finished its preparations —not all the equipment and supplies had been brought up, not all the troops had arrived; there weren't enough shells; the spring thaw made troop movement difficult. Still it was impossible to wait; every day the skies were getting darker—a terrible black thunder-storm was bearing down upon us.

The Red Army stood prepared for battle, overflowing with energy, filled with determination. The bayonets of its divisions, brigades and regiments were bristling. It was waiting for the signal. At this signal, it would throw itself upon Kolchak along the whole front, breast to breast, and try its strength in fateful single combat.

April the twenty-eighth was the memorable day that marked the beginning of operations of the gravest importance. The Red Army began its offensive against Kolchak.

IX

BEFORE BATTLE

There was no thought of evacuating Buzuluk. All was mobilized, and preparations made for the encounter. The Party Committee, the Buzuluk Executive Committee and the trade unions rallied around the division stationed there and turned all their energies to help the Red Army. The stern battle-cry "All for the Front!" was perseveringly carried out—probably in the same way as it was carried out in hundreds of other besieged centres.

Buzuluk was threatened. Enemy patrols appeared only a few dozen versts from the town. Lone Soviet and Party workers fled here from all directions, but chiefly from the direction of Buguruslan. They were ones the Kolchak patrols had missed, or their own village White scum had had no chance to betray. Many of them immediately enlisted as soldiers in the army and then, advancing with the victorious regiments to their villages, again took up their old work. Some never left their regiments but marched off with them into the far-away unknown as rank-and-file Red Army men.

In this atmosphere of suspense permeated with blood and powder, one felt the approach of a new epoch—a new stage—an important day that would mark the opening of a new and important era. The last orders were being given; every effort was being exerted and all forces gathered and directed towards a single goal. Chattering motor cycles whizzed through the streets of the little town, usually so quiet and sleepy. Motor-cars rushed by; cavalry galloped in all directions; columns of soldiers marched past with heavy regular tread.

Division Headquarters was situated at the corner of the two principal streets. In this centre, activity never diminished, day or night. All the noisy, hurried, strenuous life of those days was focused and reflected here.

Chapayev and Fyodor, now close friends and inseparable workers, seldom went to their rooms; their life was spent at Headquarters. Orders and instructions were continually arriving from the centre. Reports and inquiries were also received from their units. Endless conversations by direct wire were held over the telephone. Of course, the most protracted and noisiest negotiations were those that centred around the various shortages. At that time, there were as many shortages as there were needs, and for that reason, talks with the units (as well as with the centre) were usually accompanied by raised voices, and were full of assurances, entreaties and threats "to resort to the strictest measures." It seemed to Chapayev that it was enough to bring pressure to bear on "the different national-economic councils there," and everything required would momentarily appear in abundance. If he saw or heard about twenty or thirty carts somewhere in a warehouse, or four barrels of axle-grease, or a hundred metres of cloth, or a few caps, felt boots or sheepskin coats, he would fly into a towering rage and importune the authorities to turn it all over to the army. The slogan, "All for the Front," he interpreted in too literal a way. He seemed to think that with these scraps and crumbs, it would be possible to clothe and feed the many millions in the Red Army. He often talked about the economic collapse and the inevitable shortages, but apparently couldn't picture it all to himself concretely, and drew no conclusions whatsoever from his own words. Usually, Klichkov talked him out of his claims and thoughtless attempts, and, it must be said, dissuaded him without much trouble. It was always sufficient to bring forward a couple of weighty arguments, and Chapayev would silently agree. Silently, only silently. It was useless to wait for Chapayev to abandon what he had said, or take back what he had said, or to admit that he had been wrong in something and acknowledge it openly—no, that he would never do. Moreover, to influence him, the arguments themselves must be presented categorically and convincingly—he couldn't stand people that hemmed and hawed, and as a rule never took their remarks into consideration, no matter what the merits of the remarks might be in themselves.

He was a man who loved a firm and decisive word. Still more, he loved a firm, decisive and sensible deed.

In two days, Sizov's brigade was to attack. It was only forty versts from Buzuluk, and it was necessary to pay it a visit.

Exhausted from continual fighting, twice wounded, a man who had lost the ability to think or speak calmly—such was Sizov, Brigade Commander. He was only twenty-two but already looked like an old man.

Back in 1917, Sizov had said good-bye to his little farm and joined the Red Guard. Fate soon brought him into contact with Chapayev, who liked his sensible talk, his decisive actions and his amazing bravery bordering on foolhardiness. Chapayev appointed him commander of the infantry scouts. There had been instances when Sizov and two or three others would creep up to the sleeping

Cossacks, or still more often to the Czechoslovaks, would open fire, rout and disarm the enemy and sometimes bring back as many as a dozen and a half prisoners. He had many such affairs to his credit—the same reckless and fantastic operations which Chapayev engaged in and loved so well. In a brush with the Czechoslovaks at Gusikha on the Irghiz River, Sizov was shot through the leg, he was ailing for a while but soon recovered. As soon as his wound had healed a little, he was back in action again, but not for long. He was shot through the arm in another battle. He thought nothing of the wound itself; he was not frightened by the operation, the pain, the excruciating medical treatments. All that was nothing to him, but he hated to leave his friends at the front. Again they couldn't keep him in bed and he returned to his unit before he should.

The heavy and continuous fighting on the Uralsk front had drained his last strength and shattered nerves that were already thoroughly undermined. His brawny, sunburnt face twitched nervously; his broad nostrils quivered like a wild beast's; his coarse, blond hair was dishevelled; his high red forehead, already wrinkled, was smeared with ink. His inflamed grey eyes had a dry, metallic glitter; his broad, peasant hands were hard and horny. His shirt collar was always open as though it was hot—as though he was suffocating; his voice was strained and quavering—in conversation it might break into a high, shrill falsetto. When Sizov talked, it was with his entire thin, wiry, springy body—his head jerked from side to side in time with his words; he stamped his feet; he drummed with his fists. Sizov knew what he was worth, and could always stand up for himself, even against his own commander.

He was disturbed and irritated by the spontaneous and somehow fantastic glory which fell to the lot of Chapayev, and with which the steppe resounded. His head was turned by envy and his breath was taken away by hot hopes and desires: "Why shouldn't I be another Chapayev?" He was possessed by this feeling, and this now took away the warmth and sincerity of their relations and cast a cloud over their recent unalloyed friendship. Chapayev felt this change in Sizov, but he would never have consented to his being transferred to another division. He well knew that his personal fame was born of such people as Sizov, that it rested on them and was enhanced by them. Neither would Sizov have left Chapayev; he cherished the glory the rays of which fell on him, and the broad and glorious path which Chapayev had opened before him, and along which he was carrying him in an irresistible rush.

Their meeting was friendly. Without wasting a minute, they immediately sat down at the table to look at the map and the orders, to telegraph and to telephone. Messengers were sent for regiment commanders, ordnance and commissary chiefs, surgeons, political commissars. The exact situation was made clear. It would seem that now all contingencies had been provided for; nothing should go wrong if only the whole symphony could be played to the score that had been written out. It takes a fine musician to play music exactly as it is written, and Sizov was a master in this line. (Within three days, the news came in that he had crippled an entire enemy division.) Now, they sat and measured, and discussed, and argued; they wouldn't agree with each other; they would caution one another; and then finally everything would be settled and they would agree to what seemed most sensible to everyone.

"Well, now we ought to see the regiments," said Chapayev. "Maybe we'll explain a few things to them."

"Right!"

Sizov got up and ordered all the commanders to call their men together immediately at the biggest cinema house. "And tell them that Comrade Chapayev is going to make a speech!" he shouted after them. "Let them get ready to listen."

It would be hard to decide why he said this, whether he was serious joking, knowing how Chapayev loved to make "speeches." You couldn't tell from his tone—it was the same for a joke as it was for a command.

In half an hour, the vast, damp, uncomfortable hall of the cinema was packed tight with Red Army men in their grey great-coats. Still more weren't able to get in and stayed outside. On the stage, there was a table, and on the table, as usual, a decanter of water and a glass, and a shiny bell with a wooden handle. As soon as Chapayev appeared, there was a whispering and a hurried clearing of throats, and a setting of caps to rights—they wanted to show that they were fine soldiers. As soon as he pronounced the first word, an affectionate and resounding "comrades!", the faceless crowd closed up tight and became dumb and strained, waiting for the words they wanted so much to hear.

"Comrades!" Chapayev began. "We're about to set out against Kolchak. Together we've beaten lots of Cossacks in the steppe. We're used to victory. Admiral Kolchak won't get away from us either."

The crowd which up till now had been silent, could not contain its delight, and burst into a storm of shouts and deafening applause. Feeling at once rose to fever pitch. In two minutes, everything made a deeper and sharper impression—a half-kopek word passed for a three-kopek one, a three-kopek word was worth a ruble. Chapayev had several trump phrases, and he never missed an opportunity to drag them into his speeches. As a matter of fact, these were quite tame and were not even colourful, but they produced an indescribable effect on the primitive, excited and sympathetic audience.

"Comrades, I'm not one of your old generals," Chapayev protested sternly. "He'd be sitting somewhere three hundred versts behind the lines, and giving orders to capture some little hillock at all costs. When you'd tell him that nothing would come of it without artillery, and that there were barbed-wire entanglements thirty rows deep, the damned greybeard would send an order, 'You've been taught gymnastics, haven't you? You know how to jump, don't you? Then jump, damn you!'"

At this place, the audience would always burst out laughing, and noisily express their solidarity with the speaker. The naïve picture was one they could appreciate, and it struck home.

"But I'm not a general," Chapayev continued, licking his lips and twisting his moustache, "I'm always with you and in front of everybody. If there's any danger, it's to me first of all—the first bullet'll hit me. And dying's not easy. Who wants to die? That's why I pick out a place where everybody'll be safe and where I won't be killed myself for nothing. That's the way we fight, Comrades!"

His whole speech was based on the same lines—the same tone, the same expressions. To his credit it should be noted that he didn't like to jaw for long at a time— not that he couldn't. He merely understood the superiority of short speeches.

When he had finished, it was hard for Sizov to speak, and Fyodor, too, didn't make much of an impression. After the speeches, there was a programme. It was one of those delightful improvisations which could only be met with in those days, and probably only at the front.

The last speaker had hardly uttered his last words— they seemed to be hanging in the air, and everyone was waiting for the next speaker—when an accordion crashed out. Where the accordion-player had come from, or when he had climbed on to the stage, no one had noticed, but he had unquestionably acted at some one's unseen and unheard command. And what did he strike up? Why, the *Kamarinskaya*! And in such a spirited way that your very feet began to itch with the desire to dance. Chapayev, with a dashing swagger, sprang out into the very middle of the stage, and how he danced, how he did dance! At first, he glided smoothly around the circles with short, light steps, bending over; then he went into a tap dance, coming down hard on his heels. The thousands gathered in the hall were carried away with delight, and began to scream and shout and clap in admiration. At this, he hefted his beautiful silver sword with his left hand, and began to dance, squatting until his spurs rang and his cap slid down on one side. Who can describe the rapture of the accordion-player, a giant from Vyatka, with a shiny, hooked nose and tiny elephant eyes in a broad face! Just think, Chapayev himself was dancing to his wheezy, played-out accordion!

One last bound, one last smart caper, and Chapayev jumped to one side. He pulled out a handkerchief, fairly greasy and greyish-looking, and with a satisfied expression, wiped his jovial, sweaty face.

This went on for a whole hour. Dancers began jumping into the ring not only singly but even several at once. Competition was pretty sharp. Those who danced too long were chased away without any ceremony: "you've had your turn, let someone else have a try!"

The dancers were followed by the story-tellers—the nonsense they came out with was enough to make one gasp. At that time, there were as yet no good booklets at the front, no anthologies, no revolutionary song-books— such things were seldom seen at the front, and the Red Army men knew little besides their own comic verses and mass revolutionary songs. After the story-tellers, the singers went at it at the top of their lungs. They also didn't think much about their repertoire, but sang whatever came into their head.

It was poor artistry, but gay, colourful and hearty. With what eagerness and relish did the soldiers relax after the marching, the drudgery at the front, the monotonous strain of the trenches, their half-starved life! Afterwards, in their huts, walking down the muddy, thawing streets, at mess, in the stables or wherever they happened to be standing about nibbling sunflower seeds—everywhere the talk would turn to that fine evening. Chapayev was the centre of all their talk, of all their reminiscences: what a great commander he was, just the kind the men loved. At daybreak he leads the skirmish lines through the cold and foggy field, in battle, in assault, and in the evening, to the music of the accordion, he foots the *Kamarinskaya* with them!

Evidently, at that time, just such a commander was needed, was indispensable—a commander born of those peasant masses, and embodying all the qualities peculiar to them. When the masses came of age, this need would disappear. Even at that time, a Chapayev would not have been needed for such a regiment as that of the Ivanovo-Voznesensk weavers, for instance. With them, his primitive speeches would have had no success at all. With them, *calm consciousness* was more highly esteemed than devil-may-care recklessness. With them, a meeting or a lecture was preferable to dancing the *Kamarinskaya*. They would have talked with Chapayev as with an equal, without gazing in rapture, without breaking into smiles of joy. For that reason, Chapayev least of all liked to visit the regiment of the Ivanovo weavers, where they were so niggardly with their raptures and triumphal receptions.

When Fyodor first appeared at the Division Political Department, he was aware of a cold, unfriendly and apparently prejudiced attitude towards himself. "What's the trouble?" he wondered, not realizing that the hostile attitude of the political workers to the "partisan and bully," Chapayev, had been mechanically extended to him, "Chapayev's commissar."

This was not all. Here in the Political Department they already knew about the friendly relations between Klichkov and Chapayev, and accounted for it very simply. Either "our commissar" had fallen under Chapayev's influence, was kowtowing to the hero, and was just a puppet carrying out someone else's desires, or "our commissar" had already been just such a guerrilla and "daredevil" as Chapayev, and had not needed his influence to become what he was.

Some were of one opinion, others of another, but all agreed that "the commissar should be brought up sharp" from the very first. Accordingly, when Fyodor arrived at the Division Political Department, the chief, without saying a word about the work, about needs and plans, shoved some kind of a paper into his hand with malicious pleasure, and staring derisively into his eyes, watched what impression it would make on him. The paper, it seemed, was a summons. The Tribunal summoned Klichkov "as defendant." At first, he didn't understand what it was all about, but then he remembered and burst out laughing. Rizhikov, the head of the Political Department, looked at Fyodor in bewilderment, apparently having expected an entirely different reaction.

"You're being called up before the Tribunal for something!" he said to Klichkov through set teeth.

"I know. It doesn't amount to anything. I shan't go. You see it happened this way: the last time we were in Samara, I was walking along the street with Chapayev. On both sides there were high snowdrifts; it was a narrow squeeze—nowhere to get off the road, except into the snow. All of a sudden, some little whipper-snapper comes galloping along in a sleigh. He turned out to be a commissar of communications, I think—I don't remember for sure. But he had such a well-cared-for look about him that you could see he had wriggled into the Party by chance. He was galloping along, the rascal, and didn't give a damn. He pressed us off the road and made us jump into the snow to keep from being run over. Well, I lost my temper and said I'd box his ears for such a dirty trick. He stopped his horse, climbed out, asked us who we were and wrote down my name, and Chapayev's, too. That's all—he's complained to the Tribunal."

As Fyodor proceeded with his unconstrained account of this trifling incident, Rizhikov's face gradually lost its malicious smirk. It seemed that the "incident" actually was very stupid, and there was no cause for elation for those who thought "our commissar has gone and done something there—they're calling him before the Tribunal." Moreover, the very appearance of Fyodor, so simple and friendly, and the way he held himself, and the whole conversation, showed that he was by no means a "guerrilla and bully." Rizhikov's pre-conceived opinion of Fyodor began to waver after his first meeting with him, and later it changed completely. He began to like and trust him as sincerely as he had disliked and distrusted him before.

Fyodor wrote to the Tribunal, explaining that the accusations against him were trivial, and that he had no time to go to Samara, that fighting was about to commence, and that he considered that he was needed more here. Then he added. "Of course, I consider myself in duty bound to submit to any decision reached in my absence, but should like to inform you that the incident occurred as follows—"

Here he went on to give a detailed account of what had happened from beginning to end. The people in the Tribunal understood. They believed Fyodor and agreed with him. Fyodor was not disturbed any more. Later, he heard that the little whipper-snapper had been expelled from the Party during one of the purges, as an interloper.

The best of relations were soon established between Klichkov and Rizhikov, and through him, with all the other political workers. Klichkov soon convinced them that a lot of nonsense had been spread about Chapayev, and that actually he was nothing at all like what they had supposed.

Only once, and that at the very beginning, were there sharp words between them—about competency. During the whole course of the Civil War, the question of competency and the distribution of functions between the commissar and the authorities in the Division Political Department was in general one of the most controversial and confused of all issues. It is no wonder that this question estranged Rizhikov and Fyodor, if not for long.

Rizhikov insisted that the Political Department should be absolutely autonomous and maintain direct ties with the army, and that it was in no way accountable to the commissar. He would agree only to the commissar being kept informed of things to a certain extent. Fyodor, on the contrary, regarded these questions from a different angle, and in support, cited various instructions and decrees, of which he had gathered an abundance while in Samara. He had looked them over, mastered them, and now he pitilessly refuted Rizhikov's arguments on a "legal basis." The question was settled very easily, but it was decided not by polemics, nor by formal principles, citations and various "clauses," but by the realities of army life. The very first days showed Fyodor that it was impossible for one man to take charge of agitation and propaganda, occupy himself with questions concerning the organization of political work, direct systematic and detailed work among the population, see to it that the proper reports were made daily and keep an eye on the work of the statistical and information departments, keep in touch with the Party units, and embrace the unembraceable realm of cultural and educational work.

This was all the direct responsibility of the Political Department, and therefore of its chief. The commissar was sometimes gone for five or six days at a time visiting the brigades, and was not at Division Headquarters at all—he could only see what was being done at the lower levels and how it was being done, what should be done and how it should be done, which were matters of the first importance, and which of secondary importance and third, where forces were needed, where they should be concentrated at a given moment and on what work.

In weighing the situation on division scale and broader, Fyodor limited himself to noting down the main questions, an enumeration of urgent matters, and sent advice of the same nature to the Political Department. There his advice was studied and carried out by the department's own forces and apparatus, and by their own methods. Coming to an understanding on this, Fyodor was not only reconciled with the Political Department, but began to work in close contact with them, and there were no further conflicts, not even a single disagreement, between them up till the very last day. He realized that it was not up to the division commissar to *command* the Political Department, but only to *assist* it and keep an eye on the way the principal directives were carried out.

The Political Department, like an enormous sponge, would absorb the multitude of data and facts and all the wealth of experience received from the units and from the surrounding population, and then, having digested this mass of material at various conferences, meetings or simply by individual cogitation, would release it again in the form of cadres of roving organizers and agitators, in the form of a multitude of leaflets of all kinds, appeals, instructions and manuals.

So it came about that not only the army units but also the population of the zone along the front were in a political sense always attended to in some way, though at times in a not very satisfactory way. Communist agitators went through the villages and hamlets, mounted or on foot, or in "red vans." They told the population where the Red Army was going and why, why it had been created, what was happening in Soviet Russia and beyond her borders. Often, they knew little themselves—the sources of information were limited—and often they did not know how to convey well what they knew. Still they always got the *main* thing across. They were educators, mouthpieces, teachers. Sometimes they would put on shows, would dig out a magic lantern from somewhere or other, potter about with it, and show pictures. Even this was a wonder in some God-forsaken, out-of-the-way hamlet, where half the population were Tatars who had lived their whole lives within a radius of some thirty or forty versts.

It was easier to work with the Red Army men: they were always assembled, ready and organized; and then, there was no comparison between the extent of their knowledge and mental development and that of the rural population. Even without the Political Department, the Party units always carried on work with the Red Army men—the units needed only material assistance from the Political Department, and fresh tips; for the most part, they themselves got along all right with the work.

What kind of work was carried on in the regiments? Different kinds—it depended upon where the regiment was stationed and what it was doing. When it was resting in the rear, that was one thing—then it was possible to work systematically and to work day by day at doing away with illiteracy. Lectures could be given, if not on a very large scale, and public readings could be organized in the units. There was a lot that could be done. And lots was done. But on the march, in battle, you couldn't lay your hands on a newspaper for weeks at a time, there was no time for lectures or meetings. If it was battle, it was battle and nothing else. If there was a halt, the only thought was to flop down, to doze off as quickly as possible, to catch up with lost sleep, or to patch up a hole in a boot, to tie on a sole that was flapping; every instinct was concentrated on recovering strength and getting ready for the renewed march in the morning.

When they made the rounds of the regiments, it usually happened, and that tacitly, without any previous agreement, that Fyodor didn't have time to have a talk with all the commanders, while Chapayev didn't have time to acquaint himself with the Party unit and the political work. But what one didn't have time to do, the other was sure to do, and when they rode on and began to discuss things as they went, the whole life of the regiment unfolded before them plain as day. In friendship and harmony they lived; in harmony and friendship they worked.

When the general offensive against Kolchak was launched, a thaw had set in; the ice on the rivers began to crack and break; the bare ground began to show on the hillocks, and soon in the low places as well; streams and brooks washed away the roads; it was not only impossible for artillery to move through the mud mixed with snow, and across the thin ice, but for cavalry as well; in places a man couldn't pass even on foot. Spring was coming in with a rush. Troop movement was difficult to the last degree. This to a certain extent explains the initial slow advance of the Red forces. But only in part—there were also other reasons.

As a result of the very first brushes, the Kolchak troops stopped as though in hesitation. And now, blow after blow rained on them from all sides. The Taras Shevchenko Regiment, which came over to the side of the Reds, confused the plans of the Kolchak forces in that sector, and at once bucked up the Red forces in action there. Without giving the enemy time to recollect himself, the Red forces began to press more stubbornly, and more in unison. The enemy front was shaken. The initiative passed to the Red Army. A turning-point had come, and this was obvious to more than one keen glance. Hopes soared. Strength was increasing. The developing offensive promised to end in victory.

X

ON THE MARCH TO BUGURUSLAN

It was a memorable day when the general offensive opened along the whole front, but of course there had been individual skirmishes long before that: at the front, there are no intervals between acts.

The first brushes with the enemy took place at Easter time, on and about the twentieth of April. The enemy was then continuing his victorious advance from Buguruslan to Buzuluk. Sizov's brigade, broken up into regiments along the left bank of the river Borovka, contained this thrust. The Red regiments had great difficulty in getting to the positions they were to hold. They were held back by the muddy roads and the spring torrents, deep and swift. It was impossible to move the field guns, and even the machine-guns were taken apart and dumped into sacks so that they could be transported. As soon as they got to the Borovka, the fighting began and never stopped right up to Ufa itself.

In one operation near Buguruslan, Sizov himself almost fell into the hands of the Whites. He was saved by a lucky chance. Along with Vikhor and some seventy mounted men, he had penetrated into the enemy rear, when he noticed a battery moving along a hollow. They set off after it at a gallop, but as they approached, the artillery officers, realizing what horsemen these were, began firing at the Red Army men with grape-shot. They could see that the gunners were refusing to fire. The officers were beating some of them with the flat of their swords or the butts of their revolvers, but could do nothing with them. And now, sending the greater part of the detachment around the other way to divert the enemy's attention, Sizov, Vikhor and a handful of cavalrymen slipped up close along another hollow and darted out at full gallop almost at the very guns. The officers were taken completely aback. They raised their Mausers, but it was too late. Vikhor with one swoop laid open the skull of one of them, another was trampled by a horse, the others were thrown to the ground by their own men who began mauling them or twisting their arms behind their backs. Everything happened with amazing rapidity. It almost seemed as if the gunners had only been waiting for the horsemen to gallop up to the guns. Those who were holding the officers begged for mercy with beseeching looks. The others stood still with their hands up. None of the officers were spared, and not one of the men was touched. The battery opened fire at the regiment it had been hurrying to help, and the soldiers there, seeing the hopelessness of the situation, surrendered to the Red units that were attacking them. Vikhor stayed behind to direct this operation while Sizov with a dozen orderlies galloped on to the White baggage trains. As he flew along past the waggons loaded with boots and soldiers' tunics, his breath was taken away by the happy thought that all this would go to the Red Army men. The carters made no resistance. Some were stunned with surprise while others did not understand a thing, taking the galloping men for their own, and supposing that they were being turned round to go somewhere else "according to orders." So the whole transport, consisting of several hundred waggons, became the booty of the impoverished Red regiments.

At the Division Headquarters of the Whites, which was not far from the baggage train, a great commotion began immediately. In such cases there is always an exaggerated idea of the scale of a raid. This explains the resulting panic which ensures the raiders a cheap victory and often abundant spoils. In the present case, the result was exactly the same as usual. No one thought of organizing anyone or anything; no one tried to size up the situation or find out anything. The only thing anyone had any time to think about was how to save his own hide. One of the first to scamper out of Headquarters was Colonel Zolotozubov, Division Commander. Together with the division priest, he jumped into the waiting gig and dashed away. Everywhere, there was running and shouting, confusion, breathless cursing and threats.

A dozen mounted Red Army men galloped among the terror-stricken Headquarters personnel, and with their shouts, firing and demands for surrender, increased the already uncontrollable panic. Sizov galloped after the Division Commander, and was just about to strike him with his drawn sabre, when the priest turned around in the gig and fired. The bullet hit Sizov's horse in the front leg; it began to limp and fall behind. Then the gig stopped. The colonel jumped out and began to blaze away with his Mauser. His second bullet hit the horse in the head, and it reeled and fell. As his horse fell, Sizov succeeded in freeing his foot of the stirrup, and he was no sooner on his feet than he dashed for a coppice nearby A peasant was driving along the edge of it in a light waggon drawn by a pair of strong farm horses. Sizov ran up to him. There was no time for idle talk. Sizov covered him with his revolver, jumped on to the nearest horse, hacked the traces off, and galloped back to where he had left his comrades. But by now, the panic had begun to subside; the people here realized that the raiders who had galloped up did not constitute a serious threat. Sizov concluded that his comrades had been driven away, or maybe had all been killed—none of them were to be seen. Only when he galloped past the hut that served as Headquarters, he saw one of his orderlies without his horse, and with a bloody cheek. Sizov galloped up and shouted to him to jump up behind on the broad crupper of the big horse. Without wasting any time, the latter made a flying jump and caught on to Sizov, almost dragging him to the ground.

They galloped double behind the baggage waggons, behind the huts, tearing off their Red Army insignia. They galloped towards a distant rise which, according to Sizov's calculations, their regiment should be approaching. In front of them, they saw a body of horsemen right in their way—it was impossible to ride around them. What people were they? When they rode up closer, they saw that it was their own men who had left the baggage train, and didn't know how they could make the dash across the clearing under fire, to their regiment which could be seen moving across the plain. Although the horse under Sizov was a strong one, it was no good for such work. This was clear to Yashka Galakh, one of the best and bravest of the orderlies.

"Comrade Commander," he said, "take my horse and I'll go on foot. If they take me, I'll say that I was mobilized. Maybe they won't do anything to me. Sometimes they don't."

There was no time for consideration. Sizov jumped off the big mare, leaving his companion mounted, and jumped on Yashka's spirited gelding. They drew out in a line and tore off. Yashka Galakh was left alone. He plodded back to the baggage train. (He only returned after three weeks. He had hidden in the enemy's baggage train—the peasant soldiers there did not touch him and did not report him. He hadn't been able to escape very soon because he had been brisked away in one of the waggons that succeeded in getting away from the Red regiment.)

They flew across the field at full gallop. The bullets whined and whistled and buzzed like bees. Two of the riders were cut down in the broad meadow. The others galloped up to their own men unhurt. Among them was Sizov. The mounted scouts were called up from the other flank, and they galloped ahead of the regiment to cut off the withdrawing baggage train. Part of the transport succeeded in escaping, but the greater part fell to the regiment. The goods captured went a long way towards outfitting Sizov's brigade which was barefoot and in rags.

. . . .

It might be mentioned here that the regiments, brigades and divisions didn't at all like to send their booty up to the higher levels for "general distribution." As a rule, they kept it for themselves, accumulating it even in excess of what they needed (though this was rare), and only what they couldn't use—and was burdensome—was passed along "higher." This was true not only of boots, clothing and food, but also of rifles, ammunition, machine-guns and even cannon. In this way it sometimes happened that one regiment could hardly scrape up a dozen machine-guns while in another the number was approaching a hundred, and not a soul there would ever own up; even when there was an inspection, they would manage to hide them; and in making out their various accounts and reports, they hadn't the least thought of giving the correct figures. Such secrecy was maintained in this respect that not even a single brigade commander ever told the truth to "Chapayev himself." Chapayev, by the way, never tried to make them tell the truth, but in giving orders he always had in mind twenty or thirty extra machine-guns, although officially they were not mentioned. Sometimes there might even be a field-piece which hadn't got into the list, but which he had happened to see somewhere, or about which he had heard from simpletons in the regiment who had blabbed about it. In the reports, the number of guns on hand would remain the same for long periods. Not that there never were any losses, but it wasn't to advantage to report them; it was even something to be ashamed of. Accordingly, silence was maintained about losses and they were replaced from the secret, inexhaustible "reserves." If nothing was said about losses, neither was all said about trophies. In this, there was a certain far-sightedness: there was no striving for passing glory. In order to increase the "reserves," the number of captured guns was cut by half or two-thirds, or even more, as the need might be.

How did they get rid of what had been accumulated? How did they account for it? Why, there usually appeared all kinds of "defective" articles, "scrap" and "rubbish." Only what was absolutely unfit for use was turned over to the division, and whatever was a little better was invariably kept for themselves.

When Fyodor learned about this method, he began to be less upset by the bitter complaining about shortages of all kinds, knowing that these wails were usually premature. They were to be understood thus: "Help! Help! Division! My secret reserves are in danger!" And actually, it was only long after these wails that genuine need set in.

Accordingly, Sizov's brigade now divided up among themselves almost all their booty. The division got very little, and as for the army, there's no use even mentioning it.

It was only after Sizov's victory that Fyodor Klichkov found out about all this and drew his first conclusions.

"In the first place," he thought, "I'll keep this in mind every time forces are taken stock of, and in the second place, I'll try to cut down the commanders' lying."

To run ahead, it may be stated that in about half a year he did succeed in accomplishing a little—not much though—in this respect.

At the same time, he took note of another circumstance: Brigade Commander Sizov had been successfully operating in the enemy rear with a group of orderlies—he had captured a battery, hastened the destruction of an enemy regiment, thrown the baggage train into confusion, and almost laid hands on the commander of a White division. All this was very well, but— This "but" had already begun to bother Fyodor, and he came to the clear, convincing and irrefutable conclusion that the commander should never let himself get carried away by tactical details. He should always have before him the *complete* picture—the operation in its *entirety* and his troops as a *whole*, and entrust tactical tasks to others.

Sizov's personal bravery might have led to the destruction of the entire brigade if Zolotozubov had happened to hit him, and if, say, his subordinate had made a botch of commanding the regiments. At that time, Fyodor had firmly fixed this conclusion in his mind, but somewhat in the abstract; actually he himself acted at variance with it on numerous occasions, and never criticized anyone who was successful in some rash deed: that the attempt was a foolhardy one mattered little if only it ended well. So great, then, is the fascination of a daring exploit!

As soon as it became known that things were beginning to happen in Sizov's brigade, Chapayev and Fyodor rode over to see him, along with Kochnev, Petka Isayev, and about fifteen mounted men. It would have been impossible to go alone: wandering enemy patrols might appear at any spot, and besides that, the village kulaks weren't particularly gracious to Red Army men, especially the "chiefs."

It was a holiday, and the weather was bright and clear. In the villages, the young people were out walking along the streets, singing and playing, the girls wearing brightly coloured sarafans, the boys their best shirts—it was something astonishing to see. Bent old women were sitting in front of their houses, coughing huskily now and then. To mark the warm holiday, they had put on heavy fur coats, and crawled out of their holes like so many toads. Now they cropped up here and there like black marble figures. At the village Soviets were crowds of people who didn't know what to do with themselves. Chapayev showed them a sure way to overcome their holiday boredom. The spring runnels had cut deep ruts in the road in all directions; not a few of the brigade's waggons had got stuck in these ruts, and wheels and harness had been broken. In every village, the chairman of the Soviet was called up and given orders to carry out a hasty mobilization and repair the road. This was the signal for an uproar. The peasants protested and refused to go to work, but whoever rode back saw that the road had actually been repaired. So it was, from hamlet to hamlet, from village to village, the road was put in order all the way to the farthest positions.

Chapayev and his staff found Sizov at Headquarters. As a matter of general routine which had become second nature, he at once spread out a much-marked and coloured map on the table, and began to point out the positions held, according to the latest reports, by the enemy. Soon a detail of some ten mounted men rode up to

Headquarters. They were wet, spattered with mud, and evidently very tired. It turned out that this party, headed by Burov, the Brigade Commissar, had been reconnoitring. They had been in four villages on the near side of the river and had even swum their horses across to the other side and brought back much valuable information. Pulling out his note-book from somewhere about his neck, where he had put it to keep it from getting wet, Burov began step by step to disclose the situation beyond the river. The enemy was making preparations to forestall the Red offensive. He was concentrating his forces, bringing up artillery, regrouping units, and was hastily sending long rich baggage trains in various directions. Burov's little note-book revealed that big things were afoot. What had been discovered was immediately sent on to Division Headquarters, and from there to the Army.

It was with pride and joy that Fyodor looked at the muddy-faced commissar, so big and tall and strong. It turned out that he was a Petrograd turner who had gone to the front as a volunteer the year before—in 1918. They stepped aside for a talk.

"Well, and how's the political work?" Fyodor asked.

"Oh, that..." the commissar made a helpless gesture. "I'll be frank with you, Comrade Klichkov, I'm not doing a thing, so help me God, not a thing. You can give me hell or not—it don't make no difference. There's no time for it. What am I supposed to do: go across the river or teach the programme? It's more important to go across the river."

"That's true," said Fyodor. "But I'm not talking about that—nobody can say anything when the situation won't permit. But there are times when you can do something, aren't there?"

"Never!" Burov chopped off the word with conviction, as he rolled a cigarette.

"That's where you're exaggerating," Fyodor retorted unconvinced. "There are times, that's a fact. You only have to know how to take advantage of them."

"You try it then, with our lads," laughed Burov.

"That's a different question—"

"Nothing different about it. You go ahead and try," persisted Burov. "That's a job, I'm telling you, very much of a job." He raised his finger significantly as though he had asked a riddle and was waiting for the answer.

"Tough?" Fyodor asked sympathetically.

The other silently nodded, and then burst out:

"It's not only tough—it's impossible! Absolutely impossible! We've come to fight, they say, we'll read books afterwards. When the war's over, there'll be time for books, that's what—"

"Then that's just where your job begins," Fyodor interrupted. "A commissar should convince them that they're wrong. He should convince them that it's impossible to fight without politics. What kind of an army will it be if it doesn't know where it's going and what it's fighting for? You can find time for that. I don't believe it's impossible. You try. Next time you'll admit yourself that it's possible. Only you'll have to get a little life into everybody here—the regiment commissars and the Party units. And then you, too—you don't know how much depends on you."

"Me—you can see—" He pointed to his wet, mud-spattered tunic.

"Not only that," Fyodor waved his argument aside and said in a serious tone. "That's not enough. It's right there that your difference from a commander begins. Why, one would get the idea that you're just a good fighter and nothing more."

"That's the most important thing for them," the commissar tried to convince Fyodor. "If you're not with them, it's the end of you. What the devil do they need you for. You're great at talking, they say, but you yourself don't do anything. You say—"

"Wait a minute, wait a minute," Fyodor stopped him. "I again repeat—it's necessary. But that's not the *only thing* that's necessary. Who's going to instruct the army if we aren't? Don't you understand *it's not enough to be a brave soldier; you've got to know what you're fighting for*?"

He began to show Burov the possibility as well as the necessity of carrying on political work even in the most difficult conditions. The other didn't protest any more, but it was apparent that not much was to be expected of him so far as this work was concerned. But he would make an excellent commander. Not long afterwards, this comrade was given a post as commander, and someone else was appointed commissar in his place.

When Fyodor and Burov had finished their conversation, they went back to the table. Sizov was telling an incident that had occurred the day before:

"Fifteen men. Dressed the way they should be—no insignia at all, just soldiers. Only the commander had a red star, but he put it in his pocket. They came to a village and right away to the Soviet: 'Where's the chairman?' There were about fifty peasants there, and they were whispering among themselves. They were scared, and were trying to keep to one side.

" 'You boys Kolchak soldiers?' they asked.

" 'Kolchak soldiers,' the lads answered; they had decided to pretend that they were, and see what came of it.

" 'What have you come here for? Are you fighting?'

" 'We're fighting, brothers; right now we're looking

for the Reds. Where are they around here? Does anybody know?'

"Then they began to ask the peasants what Red units there were there and just where they were stationed—where they were going to and how they treated the peasants.

"But the peasants looked glum and wouldn't say anything that made sense.

"'Let Ivan Parfyonich tell. He knows everything—he's the chairman.'

"Ivan Parfyonich came out of the door—he must have weighed eleven poods." Here the story-teller held his hands in front of his belly to show what a substantial paunch Ivan Parfyonich had.

Everybody laughed.

"Oh, yes," Sizov affirmed. "You'll find such people in the Soviets here—as many as you like. The peasants don't understand yet what it's all about, and, then, they're scared, so sometimes they elect riff-raff.

"So this Ivan Parfyonich came down off the porch without blinking an eye. He wasn't a bit afraid. He stalked up to the 'Kolchak soldiers' cool as could be. He kept bowing and saluting all the way from the door, smiling all the time. 'How do you do,' he says.

"'You the chairman?' the lads ask.

"'Exactly so,' he answers, and again smiles, the son-of-a-bitch. 'The rascals there picked me out,' he says, 'and so I'm chairman. We were expecting you last week, brothers. Now, thank God, you've come. They've pestered the life out of us.'

"But the lads pretended not to believe him:

"'Why are you trying to play the fool? Talk sense, now, where are your friends?'

"The chairman stared at them with goggling eyes. 'What do you mean my friends?'

" 'You know very well what we mean. Where are the Reds? Come out with it, you Red devil.'

"Then the chairman fell at their feet and began to swear he was innocent, and called three witnesses out of the crowd (eight poods apiece). They began to stand up for him:

" 'Why, what do you mean! Ivan Parfyonich is a respectable man. He never had anything to do with the Reds. It was the peasants that pushed him into the Soviet.'

"The lads got off their horses and went into the Soviet. They wrote down everything he said and gave it to him to sign. 'We want to take the evidence to our officers,' they said.

"The scoundrel signed everything. Then they put him and his three defenders in a waggon and brought them here. As soon as he understood what was happening, he began to squeal, 'So help me God, I belong to the Bolsheviks myself.' The muzhiks were scared to death and didn't know what to say. People have got timid," and Sizov finished his story with a helpless wave of the hand.

"Where are they now?" asked Fyodor.

"We sent all four to the Tribunal. It's a fact, people along the front are all mixed up; they've had Whites and then Reds four times a week, and don't remember who came first, who last—who it was raised hell with them and who left them alone. Nobody knows how many horses were taken away from them, and as for the waggons broken, sheds burned, dishes smashed or carried away—the least said the better. You'll have to hand it to the peasants for finding out how to save their cattle. They drove whole herds into the very thickest part of the forest and kept them there—they took feed to them at night. When the soldiers came, the first thing they asked was: 'Where's the horses? Where's the cows?'

" 'They've taken them all—didn't leave a thing.'

" 'Who took them?'

"Then if they were White soldiers, the peasants complained about the Reds, and if they were Reds, they put it on the Whites. They used to get by with it. But not always—the soldiers began to find out what the peasants were up to and sent scouts into the woods. They would hunt out the herd and drive it back, and the whole village would begin to howl. Only what can tears do when blood isn't worth a damn?"

On their round of the regiments, Chapayev and his staff rode into a big village.

"Is there a Soviet here?"

"A Soviet?" the peasants were embarrassed. "There used to be a Soviet."

"Where was it?"

"Must have been in that house." And they pointed to a big house that had been boarded up.

"Well, and where is it now?"

"Now? Who knows—somewhere in the village. There, at the end."

"Why, what's the matter? Don't you chaps really know?"

"What is it to us? No, we don't know anything. Ride down to the far end. Maybe they'll tell you there."

"But you, yourselves—don't you live here?"

"Of course, we all live here."

"And you don't know whether there's a Soviet or not?"

"There must be a Soviet."

"Is there a headman?"

"And there's a headman."

"Is there any milk?"

"There's milk, too."

"Well, then, give us a jug of milk, and hurry up with it—real cold!"

"All right. Hey, Ivan!"

They called up a lad, and sent him off for milk. They didn't know how to act, or what to talk about. Two fellows appeared, and recognized Chapayev. But long and stubbornly, the peasants refused to believe that the new-comers were not "from the officers." At last, by various signs, by facts, through mutual recollections, they were convinced. They began to talk willingly and freely. In their talk one felt their sympathy, but at the same time their great weariness, as well as fright— profound, chronic, ingrained.

The peasants talked about wanting "to be left alone" —they were sick of everyone. The war was hard on them however you looked at it.

They rested and talked for over an hour, and when they got ready to leave, the peasants saw them off and wished them luck in a comradely manner.

Mikhailov's regiment had taken up positions in a village on the very bank of the River Borovka. The only way to get there was along the shore. From behind a hill on the other side, where the enemy skirmish lines were, there was continuous shooting. As soon as the enemy soldiers saw anyone, they opened fire and kept it up with a vengeance. It was only a little way to the village, and Chapayev and his party could already see the barns, when the enemy increased his fire. The bullets began to whistle past. One of the riders was shot through the leg. They whipped up their horses and dashed on at a gallop. They broke up single file, leaving twenty paces between each rider. Fyodor recalled how he had run away during the battle at Slomikhinskaya, and at once felt a change: now, he did not experience that panicky terror. Then, it had been shrapnel exploding, now it was bullets, but bullets are sometimes more terrible than shells. Each is terrible in its own way—"bullets for the body, shrapnel for the soul." Fyodor galloped along and didn't believe for a minute that a bullet might hit him. "Of course, my neighbour may be hit, but me—not likely." Why such thoughts ran through his head, he didn't know himself.

On the gallop, two horses were wounded and one of the orderlies got his cap shot through. They hid behind some big haystacks, and dismounted. Then, one after the other, they began to run from stack to stack and from barn to barn, and so into the village. Chapayev was the last to make the dash. From his hiding-place, Fyodor was watching Chapayev, and saw him rush out and break into a run, but then, suddenly turn round and again duck behind a haystack. Then Chapayev waited for the shooting to let up, and instead of trying to run straight to the village, went back in the opposite direction and so made his way to Headquarters by a roundabout path. He was the last to appear.

Fyodor was curious.

"What's the matter, Vasily Ivanovich? It looked like you turned tail. You scooted behind that barn as if you were scared."

"I don't like stray bullets," Chapayev answered seriously. "I hate them. I don't want to die for nothing. I don't mind dying in battle, but here it's another thing." And he spat energetically.

It wasn't easy to get to Headquarters. The village was under fire from the hill across the river. As soon as the enemy noticed anyone between two houses, they would fire whole clips. The Red Army men also gave a good account of themselves. They climbed on to the barns, hid behind the ridges of roofs, or behind wattle fences. They made holes in the walls of sheds, and kept a sharp watch on the other bank. As soon as some figure showed black or moved, or a head was thrust out from somewhere behind the hill, they opened fire. This wasn't a battle but a reciprocal hunt—a firing at chance targets. The amazing thing was that girls in bright holiday dresses were walking around in the village. In places, they were singing and having a good time. The boys were missing no chances and were hovering about them and joining in the singing. One was even going it strong on his accordion.

It should be noted that the river here was not wide, and from behind the hill the Whites could see if it was a Red Army man or a peasant walking along, or a girl skipping about. The firing in the lanes was directed against the Red Army men alone. The peasants went about their business as though nothing was happening, calm and unhurried. If it had not been for the shooting back and forth it would have been hard to imagine that death was constantly on the alert; the village might have been somewhere far in the rear and celebrating its Easter in absolute quiet.

They had intended to advise Mikhailov to make a reconnaissance across the river, but it seemed that he had sent out a scouting party that morning and was expecting it to return any minute. The detail did soon return, having buried two of their number on the far bank. They were killed when they were going down to the ford. At the front there is little to be done without a price! The detail made their report, and a council was held, at which it was decided to make a raid that very night. They knew that this ford would be guarded—another must be hunted out while it was still light. Mikhailov undertook to command the operation himself. They had good hopes of success, one of the most promising factors being that the White forces were already half won over by previous agitation. This agitation was carried on in a simple and original manner. Some ten Communists would crawl on their bellies almost to the middle of the village, and would make their way through the gaps where the

Red Army men were fired upon. They would crawl forward without raising their heads, slowly, without wavering off to one side, all in one direction. They would get to the paling, where holes would have been made the night before. They would crawl through these holes and down to the river-bank. Just before they got to the paling, they would do a little camouflaging, although some did it in the village before they began their crawl. The camouflage was likewise nothing complicated. One would have twigs and sticks and fir boughs stuck into his clothes and tied on to him everywhere or would have rags thrown over him so that he lost all human semblance. This freak would move down towards the water. Sometimes they would have hay thrown over them, or straw scattered over them, or be covered over with matting—each to his own taste. Ten or fifteen such monsters would crawl out on to the bank from various directions, and keeping close behind mounds of earth, or bushes, or any other shelter along the shore, would draw up together and suddenly begin to shout:

"Soldiers! White soldiers! Comrades! Kill your officers! Come over to our side! You've been fooled. They're making peasants fight peasants. Officers are gentry. They're your enemies—we're your brothers. Come over, Comrades! Kill your officers! Come over!"

The river here was not wide, and it was easy to hear from bank to bank especially when the dew was falling. The agitators, of course, crawled out in the dusk, either at morning or evening, when their movements were not so noticeable. The officers on the other bank cursed them with all the invectives at their command: they railed and scoffed and couldn't find words obscene enough for the Bolshevik preachers. They also opened fire but what could you shoot at when there was nobody to be seen?

Swear they did, but still, they were afraid to leave the same units on the bank for long. They changed them, but were in a constant fright and were always expecting something horrible to happen within their own ranks. The White soldiers took to heart the simple and convincing words that came to them from across the river, and it was later said that dozens of them were shot by their officers, who overheard them talking about their "Bolshevik brothers." As time went on, the Whites increased spying among their own soldiers more and more. The peasant soldiers began to understand their tragic position; they realized that they were being forced to fight against their own brother toilers, against their own interests. This reduced to a considerable extent resistance to the Red Army regiments. The work of the agitators completely demoralized the White units.

The officers would keep on firing for a while and then leave off. The agitators would crawl back to the village, slowly and without wavering, as they had come. In the evening, the day before the proposed night raid, the agitation had been particularly successful. In some places, the White soldiers, at the risk of their lives, had even shouted back to the agitators and asked them questions. They told the agitators how hard it was to desert—how closely they were watched and how severe was the punishment meted out.

That night, Mikhailov set out with a picked party on the raid planned. The next day, Brigade Headquarters received the following telegram from him: "Crossed the Borovka at night with 200 picked men, part by ford, part over a temporary log bridge, made surprise attack on sleeping enemy. Captured over 150 men, 4 machine-guns, rifles, ammunition, field kitchens, baggage waggons."

"He captured 150," said Chapayev. "That's what he captured, but how many did he kill? Write!" He turned to the staff officer who was writing a report on the successful action. "One hundred and fifty men captured and two hundred hacked to pieces."

"Listen, what d'you mean by that?" and Fyodor fixed his eyes on him in amazement. "What two hundred!"

"No less," answered Chapayev, not a whit disconcerted.

"What two hundred, I'm asking? What are you making up, old man?"

"I'm not making up anything." Chapayev was offended. "If the fool didn't think of it, does that mean I'm supposed to leave it out?"

"Don't write about it yet! We can make inquiries, if you like, and send it in additional, but now—why, that's invention, Vasily Ivanovich!"

"Well, and what of it?" and the other grinned gaily. "We've got to make them happy."

"Make who happy?" Fyodor objected. "What sort of happiness is that? If they find out about those figures, they'll never believe you again."

"They won't find out." Chapayev again wanted to turn it off with a joke, but Fyodor insisted that these two hundred "dead souls" should not be included, and Chapayev had to agree, though he did so with bad grace.

When they got back to Headquarters they found orders awaiting them. They were to leave immediately, taking with them, this, that and the other. The division was to be transferred to another army. During the campaign there were several such transfers. Units were shoved back and forth, here a brigade would be torn off then tacked on again, depending on the demands of the situation. Chapayev was usually indignant at all these reshufflings, and cursed roundly. He looked on them either as fortuitous, or as a manifestation of malicious intention on the part of some of his "enemies."

His notions in such cases were amazingly naïve. At times, they might have been taken for a joke if they had not been stated so soberly, and backed up with such serious arguments.

In their new surroundings, nothing was really new, and they didn't even have to travel very far, since the armies were stationed close to each other and formed a continuous front. A success or reverse for one army had an immediate effect on the others. Reports spread quickly, some of them bringing despondency, others raising bright hopes. Chapayev was especially glad when he heard about the victory of Sizov's brigade.

"He's a fine chap, the rascal! Not for nothing he's been taught," he declared triumphantly at Headquarters, when speaking of Sizov. He at once sent off a telegram in which, between the matter-of-fact phrases, he expressed his satisfaction. Purely congratulatory telegrams were not supposed to be sent.

The offensive was developing successfully. A large number of inhabited points, large and small, were occupied. Chapayev and Fyodor rushed back and forth along the front. They had to be everywhere at once to give instructions, to help and to caution. At times, they took an active part in the fighting. Fyodor described one of these operations, the Battle of Pilyugino, in his note-book. We give his account in full.

THE BATTLE OF PILYUGINO

1. SETTING OUT

We left Arkhangelskoye at the break of dawn, when the sun had not yet warmed the earth. The night dampness still hung over the meadows, and there was in the air the strained hush that precedes daybreak. One after the other, our regiments came out into the broad field, formed ranks and set out, without shouting, without songs or unnecessary noise, for the high hill that concealed the nearer villages. Advance parties were sent out. The mounted scouts galloped forward and were soon out of sight. We were riding in front of the regiments, Chapayev, the Brigade Commander, and I. We kept sending off orderlies, to pass on or get fresh information. To the left, from behind another hill, came the rumble of artillery—that would be from beyond the Kinel. One of our brigades was supposed to advance there, orders having been given to gain the rear of the enemy and cut off his retreat when we drove him out of Pilyugino. It was impossible to say who was firing—it was somewhere a long way off, twenty or twenty-five versts. It is only at dawn that the rumble of artillery carries so far—in the day-time it would not have been so audible.

It was planned to create panic in the enemy ranks by a sudden blow in the rear, and taking advantage of the confusion, to seize some artillery that had been spotted by a reconnoitring party. The cannonade beyond the river indicated that the enemy had noticed and correctly interpreted our manoeuvre and that chances for success had diminished.

We rode over the crest of the hill. Below us was the tiny hamlet of Skobelevo, the point from which we were to launch our attack on Pilyugino. Some scouts galloped up and reported that Skobelevo had been abandoned by the enemy the evening before. Our regiments entered the hamlet. The peasants clustered round their huts and fearfully watched the troops marching past.

"Whites today, Reds tomorrow," they groaned. "Then again Whites, and once more Reds, and no end in sight. They've driven off our horses and cattle. They've ruined us completely." Then they scratched the back of their necks and added with philosophical resignation, "Of course it's the war, we understand that. We can't complain, but it's hard—we're at the end of our tether. When's the damned war going to stop, anyway? We need a rest."

"When we win," we answered them. "It can't be finished before."

"When will that be?" and they looked at us with tired, glassy eyes.

"We don't know ourselves. You help, now, and the end'll come quicker. If we all pull together, how can Kolchak stand up against us?"

"That's right," the peasants agreed.

"That means you have to help."

"Everybody has to help," they agreed again. "Only try helping. We help the Whites, and then you occupy the village. We begin to help you, and they take the village back. We have to watch out or they'll begin to beat us from two sides at once. Our Skobelevo has seen all kinds of people—there have been lots of your soldiers, and they've chased us around more than once. It's best to hide in the cellars, and not help you or them, either."

Before we rode on to overtake the troops that had gone through the hamlet, we hurriedly explained to the peasants where they were mistaken. We explained what the rule of the officers and gentry set up by Kolchak meant for them, and what the Soviet power meant. They understood, and agreed with us, but it was evident that few had talked with them on this subject, and seldom. Their knowledge of events was very hazy, and all their talk centred around one thing only—a desire to be left in peace.

It was not that way everywhere—only in such God-forsaken places as Skobelevo. The big villages usually split up into two factions of irreconcilable enemies. When the Whites came, half the village began to put on airs; they took vengeance on their enemies, scoffed at them and persecuted them, and betrayed them to the

Whites. When the Reds came, the other half was triumphant and they, of course, did not spare their sworn enemies.

The units passed through the village. One after the other, they crossed a small bridge and spread out over the meadow, forming skirmish lines. The enemy began to shell the meadow from Pilyugino, but on the right flank, the first skirmish lines had run forward a long way, and behind them, other lines were forming in thin ribbons; knots of men appeared and disappeared, making it very difficult to get the range. The results of the shelling were most meagre.

Chapayev and I went into a hut and asked for some milk to drink. The thin, sickly housewife, who had been frightened out of her wits by the firing, fetched a pot of milk and put a big lump of bread on the table. She began kindly and attentively to wait on the Red Army men who were clustering around, and fed them too, telling everybody how terrified she had been when the village was being shelled. When we wanted to give her money for the milk, she refused to take it.

"I'll get along without," she said, "but who knows how long you'll have to fight."

She wouldn't take the money, and so we gave it to the kids, who were keeping close to their mother, clinging to her skirt, and like little animals, peering with shining eyes at the strange men with rifles, revolvers, swords and hand grenades.

"You always pay," said the housewife. "I don't need it, but let it be. Whether it's hay or oats, you pay for everything, but those others, they picked us clean as a bone, and didn't pay a straw, even. And they've taken my son, Ivan, as a carter with our horse. God only knows if he'll ever come back."

There was no servility in her voice or manner—she spoke the truth. She didn't know that our men didn't pay everywhere or at all times, but she did know that with the Kolchak soldiers, it was the same in every village and every hamlet—they took everything without paying and stripped the peasants bare.

As we sat in the hut, we could see the shells bursting in the meadow a hundred and fifty or two hundred metres away. Little clouds of black smoke kept appearing here and there, and after every puff of smoke, the air shuddered, the earth shook, and the window-panes in the little hut rattled like a tambourine. The enemy shell-fire was directed against the skirmish lines, but it was ineffectual. They were firing at random and without any result, the shells falling far beyond the mark. We held up the advance for a little, waiting for our artillery to come up so that it could be thrown into action.

I had left the hut, climbed on to a little knoll, and was lying on the ground, when suddenly a woman ran up. Looking apprehensively around, she pulled something out from under her apron and thrust it into my hand, saying, "Here, take it quick."

I looked down, and saw that it was an egg. Not understanding what she meant, I looked at her in amazement.

"How much do you want for it?"

"Why, what do you mean, my dear!" she exclaimed, offended. "You're half starved, I dare say. What's money got to do with it—you go ahead and eat."

It was obvious from her speech and manner that she was in a hurry to get away. When she said something, she glanced around as though afraid that the villagers might notice—if the Whites came and the villagers informed on her she would get into trouble.

"But why are you giving it to me?" I asked.

"Why, my brother is fighting along with you, he's in the Red Army, too. They said that the Whites had beaten you, and taken Samara. Is that true?"

"No, sister, it's not true," I answered. "Not true at all. You can see yourself who's doing the beating."

"I can see that, all right. Well, dearie, take care of yourself." And she ran nimbly down the hill, glancing around and trying to conceal herself, and so disappeared among the huts. I remained sitting there. filled with a queer feeling of gladness. I looked at the egg, and for some strange reason, I was smiling as I recalled that fine, simple woman. You find our people everywhere, I thought, even in such a hole as Skobelevo. They may not understand very much, but they feel by instinct who stands for what. Look at this woman, here: she waited for us to come, and at last the day arrived; she was happy, and didn't know how to show it, and so she gave me this egg.

2. IN THE SKIRMISH LINE

The artillery came up, and its position was pointed out to it. The straining horses plunged along the hollow dragging the heavy guns. We saw the battery take up its position behind the skirmish lines, and saw the first flash: boommm—boommm. The firing went on without intermission. The men in the skirmish lines heard their own artillery, and pressed on with fresh heart. We mounted our horses and galloped forward, accompanied by the orderlies. We came to the top of a hill and could see Pilyugino spread out below. From here it was no more than three versts away as the crow flies. We separated and rode down to the skirmish lines—Chapayev to the right flank, and I to the left.

"Comrade," said one of the orderlies to me, "what's happening there? Look, our men are retreating, they're running—must be coming this way, aren't they?"

I looked. There really was some kind of confusion. The men were running from one place to another, and the skirmish line would first crowd together and then string out again. We galloped over. Nothing out of the ordinary had happened—simply the skirmish line was being reformed so as to advance in a new direction.

We found ourselves in a field of sunflowers, and it was with difficulty that we made our way between the thick, prickly stalks. We got to the first line and dismounted. The orderly led the horses, keeping some thirty paces to the rear, while I lay down in the skirmish line. On either side of me was a young chap with sunburnt face. Both were stocky broad-shouldered, husky fellows. Their names were Sergeyev and Klimov. It is very quiet in a skirmish line when it is advancing: one doesn't hear the sound of a human voice except when a command is barked out, or someone coughs or spits. Or once in a while someone may utter a chance word. These moments are profound. When you are under fire and the bullets are whistling and droning all around, and you are expecting every minute to be hit in the head, the chest or the legs, you have no time for idle words, or for conversation. Complicated, quickly changing, and usually obscure thoughts race through your head. You become concentrated, silent, almost irritable. You strive to remember as much as possible and as quickly as possible, all at once, without forgetting anything or leaving anything out. And it seems that after all it is the most important thing that you have not remembered, and one must hurry—one must hurry.

Now the skirmish line is making short rushes one after the other, at ever shorter intervals. The enemy is close, very close. Another minute and there will be no more rushes—after the final rush will come the assault. It is because of this terrible moment—the assault—that you must hurry to remember everything at once and as quickly as possible. There, ahead, is the brink—there, the black abyss.

I quietly let myself down between the soldiers. They moved aside, looking at me vaguely and not asking any questions. They continued to lie silently, as they lay before. Lying there, I also said nothing, but the numbing silence began to prey upon me, and I pulled out my tobacco-pouch, rolled a cigarette and lit up.

"Want a smoke, Comrade?" I asked my neighbour.

He raised his head, as though not understanding, and wondering at my question, wondering all the more that *here and now* he had suddenly heard a human voice. He seemed to think a minute, and then I saw his eyes light up and become lively.

"That's an idea, let's have some!" He reached for the pouch. "Hey, friend," and he turned to Sergeyev, "what are you chewing the dirt for? Here, better have a smoke with us."

Sergeyev raised his head as slowly as had Klimov, and stared at us with a stern, heavy glance. Then he rolled a cigarette, began to smoke, and also brightened up. There was no conversation at all—only single phrases, now and then: "It's damp here," "it prickles," "the cig's gone out," "look, a shell."

"Ready!" the command rang out.

We jumped to our feet. The whole skirmish line bounced into the air like a rubber band. The men did not stand erect but froze in a stooping posture.

And at that moment: "Run!"

The whole line leaped forward, the men running with their rifles held well in front of them. I also ran, bent double, and my steps seemed awkward and shambling. The enemy machine-guns began to rattle, and the rifle volleys were stepped up.

"Down!" instantly came the fresh command.

We all threw ourselves on the ground, and lay there motionless a few moments, just as we had fallen. Then the men along the line began to move cautiously. Heads were raised, and the soldiers looked around. Those who had got ahead, now began crawling warily backwards to get into line, those who had got behind, crawled forward, their heads close to the ground—no one wanted to be left alone, either in front of the line or behind it.

Klimov, who had got ahead and had flopped down in front of us, now began to crawl backwards like a lobster, and if I had not moved to one side, he would have landed square in my face with the enormous soles of his American army boots. We lay there silent, waiting for the next command. We no longer tried to smoke; there were no more chance words. Klimov was lying beside Sergeyev. Evidently, Klimov remembered that it had been easier for him when they were talking a few minutes before, and I heard him try to strike up a conversation with Sergeyev.

"Sergeyev!"

"What d'you want?"

"Here's a bug," and he poked his finger at something in the grass.

Sergeyev didn't answer a word; he was morose and sulky and kept silent.

"Sergeyev!" Klimov persisted.

"Well, what?" the other broke out irritably.

Klimov himself didn't answer, but only sighed, and then as though he had collected his thoughts, said softly, "You know they married off Lyuba to someone in Pronino."

Evidently he was recalling some girl from his village, maybe a sweetheart of his. This time, also, Sergeyev didn't answer a word. Realizing that it was hopeless, Klimov stopped talking; he probably had no desire to strike up a conversation with me. He stretched out still flatter on the ground and began to poke his finger through the thin spring grass. He would crush a beetle and watch it dying in convulsions on his broad, dirty finger, and then he would scrape together a little mound of earth, and gathering it up between his fingers, would let it spill out a grain at a time until it was all gone.

"Ready! Run!"

We instantly jumped up and dashed forward, our eyes insane, our faces distorted, our nostrils wide and quivering. And all the time we were waiting.... We ran waiting—waiting for the longed-for command "Down!"

We fell flat, our bodies stiff as corpses; we froze to the ground, our arms and legs tucked under us, our heads drawn in, like turtles; then slowly, slowly we relaxed and made small movements, looking round us with shaky, apprehensive glances.

There, with us, was Marusya Ryabinina, a nineteen-year-old girl. She also had a rifle and moved proudly, trying not to get behind. She didn't know, this dear friend of ours, that in a few days, at Zaglyadino, she would again be taking part in an attack, just as she was then, and that, having forded the river, she would be one of the first to charge, only to be shot through the forehead by an enemy bullet. Her warm body was carried downstream by the cold, blood-stained waves of the Kinel. But now she was smiling as she shouted a friendly word to me, but I couldn't make out what she was saying.

I hadn't seen any of my friends from my home town for two months and hadn't even heard that Nikita Lopar and Terenty Bochkin were here in this regiment; they had got tired of serving in other regiments and had got themselves transferred from their units at Uralsk. I didn't see Terenty at this time, either, but I saw Lopar, at the other end of a swamp, wave his Red Army helmet and shake his heavy red curls.

All around were familiar faces, but there was no time to wait. It was only a hundred metres to the barns. Every second we could expect the enemy to suddenly open fire from there. It was a favourite trick at the front to stand stock still, keeping oneself concealed, to take sure aim, allow the enemy to approach quite close, and then suddenly to open up with machine-guns, and fire rifle volley after rifle volley, mercilessly and without respite, piling up human bodies before one in rows and heaps; and when the enemy faltered and ran back, to keep firing, firing, firing after him, and perhaps throw against him cavalry, hidden somewhere close by, and to slash and kill the running mob of soldiers, mad with mortal fear.

We could expect anything. Suddenly, to the right, there were two short volleys, and a machine-gun began to chatter. The orderly galloped off to find out what was up. In a couple of minutes, he returned and reported that it was our men on the right flank trying to draw the enemy's fire. There was no return fire. It might have been assumed that the village had been evacuated, but taught by bitter experience, our skirmish lines moved towards the barns quietly, cautiously feeling their way. Several machine-gunners, and with them some soldiers, snatched up a machine-gun and ran up to one of the nearest barns; they quickly set up the machine-gun and made ready to fire. But all was quiet. From way over on the right flank, came a hollow "hurrahhh!!!" That was our men charging. They captured almost without a blow the whole enemy detachment that had been left there to guard the village. From behind the hill to the left, came the crash of artillery—three times, one after the other. The roar and the scream of the shells became fainter and gradually died away. Only the boom of the guns was heard—the detonations came as a barely audible echo. That meant that it was not our artillery shelling Pilyugino, but the enemy himself shelling some objective to one side of us. He was firing on the units that were moving from the extreme left flank to cut him off. He had shifted his artillery fire to that sector, and hurriedly retreated, leaving only small rear guards. We found that out later, but now much was still confused, and events might be expected to take any turn. When the machine-gunners had taken up their position behind the barn, the Battalion Commander and I rode up to them to find out if they had seen anybody in the barns, but there everything was quiet as before, and neither Whites nor villagers showed themselves. The village seemed deserted, dead. Slowly and cautiously we made our way forward, looking around us on all sides and peering behind haystacks, barns and sheds. There was not a sound, not a rustle. Not a word was spoken, not a shot fired—but how much more terrible was this silence than to be under fire. Silence at the front is something terrifying, harrowing.

Not far behind us, came the men of the Ivanovo-Voznesensk Regiment, their red stars flashing here and there among the barns and haystacks. This movement, hasty, jerky, uncertain, went on in a death-like silence, in constant expectation of a sudden ambush.

In the distance, a woman's figure flashed by. Was it a peasant woman? We must find out as quickly as possible.

I trotted my horse in that direction.

3 ENTERING THE VILLAGE

The peasant woman was standing beside her cellar, staring at me, her dull eyes fixed and perplexed. Her look reflected the horror she had just gone through; it expressed bewilderment and a tense agonizing question—a foreboding of fresh misfortune, inevitable and unavoidable, as though she were expecting a blow which she wanted to turn aside but could not. "Will it be soon?" her tired glance seemed to ask, and it must not have been the first time, and not only at me, that she had stared so wearily, as though asking, "Will it be soon?" Beside her, near the hut, the cellar trap-door was raised, and the grey, haggard face of a woman that seemed half-dead peered out. There were purplish black pouches under her eyes. Her lips were dry, and her hair was straggling out from under a rag twisted round her head. Her sorrowful glance was questioning and filled with entreaty.

"Are the Whites here, or have they left?" I asked them.

"They've gone, run away, dearie," answered the woman who was peering out from the cellar. "Can we climb out, dearie? Will there be any more shooting?"

"No, no—there'll be no more shooting, climb out."

One after another, women began to climb out of the cellar—only women, there were no men. Little children also climbed out. They had been covered up with quilts, matting, sacks—the women had apparently imagined that a flour sack would protect them from shrapnel. They also dragged out by his long, shrivelled arms, an old man with dull, watery eyes and a broad white beard. A long rope was hanging from his belt—they must have let him down into the cellar by it.

When they had all crawled out, they shuffled to their huts in single file, holding on to the wattle fence and looking timidly about them. It made a remarkable picture, the way they moved like shadows along that fence in a dramatic, death-like silence, still fearful, wearied by terror, numbed from huddling in that cold, damp cellar.

At the corner, there was a knot of peasants. They also were at a loss. They did not know whether the fighting was over and they could stay where they were, or whether they must hide themselves in their huts or in the bath-houses, or under the floors of their sheds.

"How do you do, Comrades!" I shouted.

"Good day!" they answered in a chorus. "You've come at last, thank God."

I didn't know whether to believe these words of welcome. I thought they might have met the Whites in the same way out of timidity and fear—so as to be left alone. But then I looked into their faces and saw genuine, unfeigned happiness, such genuine gladness as had no counterfeit, particularly on an artless peasant face. And I myself was filled with joy.

We went on to the centre of the village. Here, there was another crowd but I could see that they were not villagers.

"You fellows prisoners, are you?"

"Yes—prisoners."

"You've been mobilized, have you?"

"Yes—mobilized."

"Where are you from?"

"Akmolinsk Region."

"How many of you?"

"Why, there's thirty of us here, and some have hid in the sheds. There's some over there, running out of the garden."

"So you stayed behind?"

"Yes—we stayed ourselves."

"Well, and where are your rifles?"

"We stacked them over there, by the fence."

I rode over and looked, and sure enough, there was a stack of rifles there. We immediately put men to guard the arms and the prisoners until they could be sent to Division Headquarters.

The prisoners were a sorry-looking lot, and were most shabbily outfitted. Some were wearing worn-out fur coats, some, old cloth coats, and still others, great-coats that were hanging in shreds. Their foot-gear was as disreputable: some were wearing felt boots or bast shoes, all torn and tattered to the last degree. They were not in the least like troops, nothing but a gang of ragamuffins. I was amazed: how was it that they were so badly dressed when the Kolchak forces were so well supplied with foreign equipment?

"Well, chaps, it doesn't look like Kolchak did much of a job outfitting you. Is it that way with everybody?" I asked.

"No, it's only us."

"Why did they treat you that way?"

"We didn't want to fight. A lot of our people got away—part of them ran home, part to the Red Army."

"So you didn't want to serve Kolchak?"

"Why, what's he to us? He put braid on his own people, but look what he gave us to wear," and they pointed to their rags and the holes in their clothes. "And then he kept us in the front-line, where we'd get shot—such riff-raff, he'd say, isn't worth bothering about."

"You should have run away a long time ago."

"We couldn't run away—he put his own men behind us. They didn't fight, only watched to see that we didn't run away."

"Well, and how did you get away this time?"

"We laid down there in the gardens, between the rows. We laid down and waited and then we came out."

"What do you want to do now—do you want to serve with us here in the Red Army?"

"Yes—that's why we stayed, so we could join the Red Army. What else? That's what we want."

That ended our talk.

We galloped through the village towards the hill, in the direction the enemy had made off. Our troops were to be seen climbing up the steep sandy bank, crowding across a little bridge and clambering over a steep ridge.

"Were there many Whites here?" I asked along the way.

"A thousand," the peasants answered.

You can't ever believe these "thousands" right off; sometimes the "thousand" turns out to be five or six thousand, sometimes only two hundred. It is only by comparing a mass of such information and the testimony of dozens of prisoners that you can fix the figure more or less approximately. In any event, judging by the size of the transports, there had been plenty of troops here. The enemy did not hang on to Pilyugino as long and stubbornly as usual, probably because he had noticed the encircling movement on the left flank and was disturbed by it.

"Did the Whites run away very long ago?"

"No, not long ago," the peasants answered. "Just before you came. They can't have got far up the hill.

But our exhausted troops could not pursue them. A try might have been made with cavalry, but we had little cavalry—nothing could be hoped from there. The troops that were ahead and had climbed to the top of the hill still had hopes of seizing the enemy transports, but they only succeeded in capturing a few waggons that had got behind; the rest had long since gone and were now far away.

Pilyugino lies at the foot of a steep hill. From the bridge, it's a hard climb to the top. Here, at the height of the excitement, a dramatic incident took place. Our advance troops, who had climbed straight up the slope, had no sooner stepped out on to the summit than they saw crawling skirmish lines at the other end. They opened fire, and the fire was returned. Our soldiers didn't realize that they were firing at their own comrades. Two men were killed and five wounded. It would have been still worse, if the commander of the regiment that was coming round the hill from the left hand side, had not realized what was up. At the risk of his life, he ran towards the men who were firing, waving his handkerchief and his cap; he ran up and explained what was happening.

When we saw some sixty cavalrymen at the top of the hill, dismounted beside their sweating, foam-flecked horses, we ordered them to split up into two groups, one to ride to the left to see if there were any signs of our encircling forces, the other half to go to the right— the direction taken by the enemy transports. Contact was not made with the encircling forces; it seemed there had been something like treachery there, and it later became necessary to arrest several people and turn them over to the Tribunal. But at the time we suspected nothing and continued to hope that it would be possible to get results with even small blows at the enemy, as soon as our regiments appeared in his rear. The regiments never appeared, and the enemy withdrew, orderly and unpunished, with his transports intact. The scouts that had been sent to the right had proceeded no more than 200 metres when they came under heavy fire from the retreating skirmish lines, and were forced to take to the ravine and make their way through the bushes.

The first machine-gun cart was dragged to the top of the hill. I took charge of it and rode forward to a place where we could see the enemy skirmish lines, swaying in the distance. They were retreating through a level clearing in the direction of the forest, and it was apparent that they were in a hurry. They were probably expecting our cavalry to attack, not knowing that we had practically none. We, ourselves, could of course do nothing, but we still had a sort of faint hope that at any minute firing might begin in the enemy's rear. In that event we could greatly increase the panic from here, even with our one machine-gun, completely demoralize the enemy and seize his baggage train. All our hopes were in vain. We followed on the heels of the retreating enemy for a verst and a half. The reconnaissance detachment on the right, and we on the hill, kept up a constant fire. The enemy returned the fire but continued retreating until he disappeared into the woods. We rode back empty-handed.

The Ivanovo-Voznesensk Regiment had lain down on the hill. As I began to approach with the machine-gunner, we noticed several men put their rifles on their knees and take aim, waiting for us to get nearer. I shouted as loudly as I could that we were friends and began to wave my handkerchief to prevent a fresh disaster. Several men got up and came to meet us and when they recognized me, they shook their heads, and exclaimed in dismay, cursing themselves for their mistake. We rode down the hill and on to the village. There I met Chapayev who was inspecting the units. He had taken part, personally, in the attack before the barn, and from there he had entered the village. Turning my horse, I rode back up the hill with him.

The village came to life. There were Red Army men in all the huts. The peasant women were crowding round the wells and carrying water on the run, hurrying to get their samovars boiling, and treat their new friends to tea. They were no longer shy or afraid, and there were no bounds to the young people's excitement. Village girls get on good terms with Red Army men so quickly, that one can only stare in amazement.

This time was no exception: our skirmish line was on the hill; somewhere in the forest, quite near, the enemy troops were retreating; the air was not yet clear of powder smoke, but from the open windows of a hut, an accordion was already pouring out an enticing air. People were eagerly gathering in response to its call, soldiers and girls, too. There would soon be dancing—an invariable feature on such occasions.

One reason why the Red regiments were so warmly welcomed here was that there was not only no pillaging or violence—there was not a single instance of even the least insult or squabbling. They came as friends and were met as friends; there was mutual respect and spiritual affinity.

The great majority of the men were not lucky enough to find places in the huts, but had to bivouac in the square beside the baggage waggons.

We hunted out a larger, better-built hut, where we set up Brigade Headquarters, and lodged the Division Operations Department, which had been with us all the time during the march of the past few days. Cable was laid, and the telegraph and the telephone began to operate. Here, also, a small samovar soon appeared. Commanders and political workers sat down together at table. They were in a hurry to tell one another what they had done, what they had seen and felt during the battle. They interrupted one another, didn't finish what they began to say, seized upon one thing and then another, made a lot of noise trying to shout one another down, trying to make the others listen when no one wanted to listen.

They all wanted to talk; they were so full of experiences that were still fresh in their minds. Their fatigue had disappeared. About half an hour went by in this noise and talk.

Suddenly there was a sound like a clap of thunder, and then a second and a third. We glanced at one another, jumped up from the table in bewilderment, and rushed to the door. Perhaps someone had dropped a hand grenade? But there had been three reports in a row. Was it artillery? But where could it be firing from?

At that moment there was a rifle shot, and then another and another. A disorderly fusillade began. The Red Army men clustered around the vans had jumped up and were running in all directions. The square was emptied in a jiffy. Over our heads, we saw an enemy aeroplane sailing slowly and calmly away into the blue distance like a silver swan. The bombs had exploded in an enormous orchard nearby, where there was not a single Red Army man.

Soon the whole village had settled down again as though nothing had happened. It was already dusk, and a calm, starry spring night was slowly settling down. The village was quiet. There was nothing to remind one that a battle had just been fought here, and that Death, ruthless and rapacious, was prowling hard by, waiting to pounce on its victims. And tomorrow, when the sun had barely risen, we would again be on the march. Again, like gnats around a flame, we would be circling between life and death.

"Well, and today?" every morning one asks himself the same grim, painful question. "Who will be left alive? Who will be killed? Who will I march out with tomorrow, and who will I never see again after today's battle? And ahead of us are endless campaigns, and every day fierce battles. It's spring now.... This is only the beginning. It's only Kolchak's front-lines that have wavered, and we must smash his whole army of a hundred thousand men.

How dear it will cost! How many victims there will be by autumn! How many of these comrades who are marching with me will be missing!"

After the battle, which has been described here in such detail, the road to Buguruslan was open. Like most towns—not only during these battles but during the whole course of the Civil War—Buguruslan was captured as the result of an encircling movement. It was seldom that there was fighting in the streets of big towns. The principal battle, the last and decisive one, was fought at the approaches to a town, and if this battle went against the defenders, they usually retreated, leaving the town in the hands of the victors without fighting. That was the case at Buguruslan.

XI

ON THE MARCH TO BELEBEI

The Chapayev Division was advancing rapidly, so rapidly, in fact, that the other units, lagging behind for important and unimportant reasons, were through their tardiness ruining the unified general plan for a combined offensive. Having got so far ahead of the other units, and making frontal attacks as it did, the Chapayev Division was driving the enemy before it, rather than destroying his forces or taking them prisoner. The soldiers, tried in many marches, amazed everyone with their powers of endurance, their modest demands, their readiness to fight at any hour of the day or night, no matter what the situation and no matter what their condition. There were cases when they were reeling from fatigue after a march of many versts, and suddenly a battle would begin. Their fatigue instantly disappeared. They would sustain the attack, launch a counter-attack, and pursue the retreating enemy. But there were cases when they were utterly exhausted from constant marching and fighting. Then at the first halt, they would throw themselves flat on the ground and sleep like the dead, often without proper pickets; all of them fell asleep at once—commander, men and pickets.

They marched on victoriously from village to village, through the hills, over narrow paths, fording rivers (the enemy blew up the bridges as he retreated), in the rain and mud, in morning dew and evening fog, one day fed and two days hungry, badly clothed and shod, their feet bleeding, ill, often wounded but refusing to quit the ranks. They were irresistible, invincible; they underwent all hardships without a murmur; they were lofty and steadfast in defence; intrepid and terrible in attack; stubborn in pursuit. They fought like heroes, died like Red knights, and when captured, perished like martyrs, under torment and torture. With such trustworthy forces it would be impossible not to conquer. It required only the ability to command them, and Chapayev possessed this ability to the highest degree—the ability to command such a body of men, in the state it was in, and at the moment in question. This human mass was heroic but it was raw. The moment was a dramatic one, and in the heat of the fighting, much was winked at, or pardoned. It was justified by the unique situation. This human mass was as though in a state of exaltation; its condition was not to be described in words. That condition, one may safely assume, was the first of its kind, because it was the result of a whole chain of events, large and small, which took place earlier or at the time of the Civil War. The Volga will never flow back upon itself and that condition cannot be produced again. There will be new moments, wonderful and profound moments, but they will be different.

And there were Chapayevs only in those days—at other times there have been no Chapayevs and there can be none. Chapayev was born of *that* human mass, at the moment it was in *that* state. It was for that reason that he could so well command "his" division. He himself did not realize how profoundly right he was when he christened the valiant Twenty-Fifth Division *his* division, the Chapayev Division.

In this division were focused and reflected as in a mirror the principal features of the semi-partisan troops of the time—boundless daring, staunchness and endurance, combined of necessity with brutality and harsh ways. The soldiers considered Chapayev the embodiment of heroism, though as you see, there had up to now been nothing exceptionally heroic in his actions. What he did personally, was done by many others also, but *no one knew* what these many did while *everyone knew* what Chapayev did—they knew it in detail, with embellishments, with the particulars of legend and fantastic invention. In 1918, Chapayev was an excellent soldier; in 1919, he was no longer renowned as a soldier but as *a hero and organizer.* But he was an organizer only in a special, relative sense. He could not tolerate "staffs" and relegated to that category all the departments and institutions that did not fight with the bayonet. It made no difference whether it was the commissariat, the commandant's office, the liaison, or whatever you like. To his mind it was only the soldier with rifle in hand that fought and conquered. He also hated the staffs because he understood little about them and could never organize them as they should be. When he appeared at Headquarters, he was more given to upbraiding than to instructing, explaining and assisting.

He was an organizer only in the sense that through his own personality, so well beloved and of such great authority, he united and welded together *his* division, fired it with a spirit of heroism, and a fervent desire to press forward; he spurred it on to victory, and developed and consolidated heroic traditions among his men. These traditions, for example that of never retreating, were held sacred by the men. Preserving these traditions, the men of the Razin, the Pugachov, or the Domashkin regiments endured indescribable hardships, gave battle under impossible conditions, withstood the enemy's attacks, and turned these battles into victories. But they never retreated. For the Stepan Razin Regiment to retreat would have meant to disgrace its heroic name for ever!

How magnificent this was, but how fallacious, harmful and dangerous!

Chapayev was in his element only during battle. A slight lull in the fighting, and he would begin to languish, become bored, nervous and full of gloomy thoughts. But to dash from one end of the front to the other—that was what he liked best of all. There were times when there was no particular need for this, and then he would think up a pretext and tear off for some place fifty or seventy or a hundred versts away. He would arrive at one brigade, and the neighbouring brigade would find out that he was there and telephone: "Come at once: matter very urgent!" And Chapayev would gallop there. To be sure, there was no "urgent matter" at all. His commander friends simply wanted to sit down and have a good talk with their chief. It was they, Chapayev's comrades-in-arms, that proclaimed and gave wide publicity to his exploits and to his fame. Without them, he would never have achieved such fame, and the same is true of anyone in such a situation Great and glorious deeds are not enough for resounding fame— what is necessary are heralds, blindly loyal people convinced of your greatness, who are dazzled and inspired, and who find their own joy in singing your praises. We are always inclined to see more in a "hero" than is intrinsically his, and on the contrary, to underrate the meritorious, it may be even the exceptional, rank-and-filer.

Chapayev's men considered themselves fortunate to be his comrades-in-arms because the rays of glory illuminating him shone also upon them. In the Stepan Razin Regiment there were two heroes who had lost their legs in battle (the word "hero" should not be shunned; it has its right to existence, but must be applied correctly). These men crawled along on their stumps, though one of them could get around a little on crutches. Neither of them wanted to leave his famous regiment and each was happy when Chapayev on his arrival would say a few words to them. They were not an encumbrance to the regiment—in battle both of them were machine-gunners.

Our heroic days will go by, and people will not believe this; they will consider it but a legend, but it was a fact. Two Red Army men who had lost both legs did fight in battle as machine-gunners. There was one man who was blind, stone blind. Through his friends, he once sent a letter to the division newspaper. We still have this letter and reproduce it here, though not in full:

LETTER FROM A BLIND RED ARMY MAN*

"Comrade Editor,

"I ask you to print in your newspaper a fateful event which happened to me—how I ran away from the Ural Cossacks to the Bolshevik comrades I will say in brief explanation that we lived between the Cossacks and the Red Army at the Uralsk railway station My two elder brothers were working on trains during the war between the Cossacks and the Red Army. When Comrade Yermoshchenko made his first attack on Uralsk on April 20 (May 3, New Style) at Semiglavy Mar, an order was given on April 23, that is May 6, by the government of the Cossack army to mobilize the peas-

---

* Nothing has been changed in this letter except the spelling; in places punctuation has been added to facilitate reading

ants and all who were living in the Uralsk region My brothers refused to fight against the Red Army When the Cossacks tried to mobilize them, my brothers declared that they would not go against their comrades the Bolsheviks and so they were shot by the Cossacks on the 23 of June at midnight I was left alone, an orphan, without anybody to take care of me. My mother and father died five years ago and I haven't got any other relatives anywhere. Besides that I am completely blind and can't see anything, and after the shooting of my brothers I went to the Cossack government to ask them for shelter, but the Cossack government told me your brothers wouldn't go to fight against the Red Army so you can go to your Bolshevik comrades and let them give you shelter Then I answered them probably you will never drink your fill of innocent blood, you bloodthirsty beasts, and that's why I was shut up in jail and was waiting to be shot. I was in jail 15 days and then they let me go I spent several days at the city walls without a crust to eat, and then I decided to go to the Bolshevik comrades to ask for shelter, and no matter that I was stone blind I decided to get to the comrades, or lose my way and die somewhere in the steppe, which would still be better than to live in the hands of the Cossacks A friend led me secretly out of Uralsk on to the road and told me to walk so that the sun is always on your back and then you will get to Russia. I said good-bye to my friend and started off. When I had gone a few versts I lost the way that had been pointed out to me and I didn't know where I was going At that time I remembered the death of my brothers, my misfortune and sorrow and trials, my great sufferings I walked six days in the steppe, cold and hungry, and on the sixth day I began to get to the end of my strength. My lips were caked with blood, because I had no bread and not a drop of water, nothing to satisfy my awful hunger. I watered the ground with my bitter tears and had no hope of saving my life. Then I cried aloud 'My dear brothers! You rest in the ground, but you have left me to suffer. Take me with you and put an end to my suffering. I am dying of hunger in the steppe, who will come to help me in my bitter tears, there isn't anybody anywhere' Suddenly I heard a dog barking ahead of me and children's voices, and I went towards the sound, and asked the children what kind of village is this—Cossack or peasant? They told me it was a peasant hamlet, Krasny Tali seven versts from the Cossack border. A peasant took me home and gave me something to drink and to eat and satisfied my hunger, and in the morning led me to the village of Malakhovka, and from here I managed to get to Petrovsk district with difficulty."

Then he went on to tell how well he was received in Soviet Russia, how he was taken care of and surrounded with attention.

"The chairman of the Soviet, Ivan Ivanovich Devitsin, warmly welcomed me and was very happy and delighted Now when I am with my Bolshevik comrades, I have forgotten my suffering and am in safety. They put me in a big room, gave me soft bed clothes, took off my ragged dirty underwear and gave me new shoes and dressed me in a new suit of the economic and food supply department, I am living like a real 'bourgeois,' and I want to express my great gratitude and deep feeling ..."

Here he gives a list of the people to whom he wants to express his gratitude, and then finishes his letter with the following words:

"Long live the All-Russian Soviet Republic, Comrade Lenin, long live the all-conquering hero Comrade Chapayev, long live the District Soviet, its economic and supply departments!"

This is more than a letter—it is a real poem. And this martyr for the Soviet power, this blind Red Army man, who held Chapayev's exploits as something sacred, was the best narrator and minstrel among the Chapayev lads. He told what had happened and what was fantasy, and believed the fantasy most of all because he himself had invented and ornamented it. And who is so strong as not to believe his own inventions?

Chapayev's fame resounded far beyond the Red Army.

We have preserved another letter, one from a Soviet employee at Novouzensk. Read it, and you will see what boundless faith people had in Chapayev's omnipotence. He was considered not only a soldier leader but the all-powerful master in the places where the regiments of the Chapayev Division fought or passed through. This letter was typed on wax paper. It was carefully sealed and sent to Chapayev by messenger. In it the Soviet employee, Timofei Panteleimonovich Spichkin, complained to Chapayev about the injustice of the Novouzensk authorities and asked for assistance. It is only from Chapayev that he hoped to obtain a speedy and just decision in his case. He wrote:

"Urgent

"TO DIVISION COMMANDER COMRADE VASILY IVANOVICH CHAPAYEV,

"From Timofei Panteleimonovich Spichkin, Chairman of the Novouzensk Council of People's Judges,

"S C A N D A L O U S   C O M P L A I N T

"I request you, Comrade Chapayev, to bestow your particular, your *heroic* attention on this complaint. For two years I have been known at the Uralsk front as an honest Soviet employee, but malicious people, Novouzensk thieves and criminals, are trying to slander me and make me out to be insane so that no attention will be paid to my exposures of thieves The matter is as follows: 16 thieves stole. . (here Spichkin gives a list of the people, showing how much each stole) When I, Spichkin, sent a statement about this embezzlement to Samara, the 14 thieves who were not arrested (two were arrested) declared that Spichkin was insane and demanded that the doctors should examine Spichkin. The doctors pronounced me mentally sound Then the 14 Novouzensk thieves and brigands said, 'We don't believe you,' and they are sending me to Samara to the Provincial Committee to be examined by psychiatrists. But bearing in mind that today all truth and justice at the front is in the hands of heroes and Red Army men like you, Comrade Chapayev, I, Spichkin, urgently ask you to give the necessary orders to help arrest in Novouzensk all the 14 thieves mentioned and send them to Samara for trial by the Revolutionary Tribunal, and for that the population will return many thanks, since according to public opinion your name is renowned as a selfless hero and staunch defender of the Republic and freedom. I am completely confident in you, Comrade Chapayev. Defend me also from the 16 Novouzensk thieves and brigands

"April 25, 1919

"Signed: *Timofei Spichkin.*"

In an enclosure, Spichkin informs Chapayev where and how to "unearth" all the material bearing on this case, and concludes with the following words:

"I beg you to immediately arrest without the least hesitation all the remaining thieves, and repeat, your glorious name will be covered with still more glory for this defence of the population from these filthy spiders and microbes"

No less brilliant is Spichkin's "Application," evidently made as a result of his persecution by the fourteen "spiders and microbes":

"You, Comrade Chapayev, are recognized as a hero by all the people, and your fame resounds everywhere Even the children talk about you. I, Spichkin, am also a recognized hero, not in the art of war, but in the civic art I also have my great transports of valour and glory. I ask you to believe this You will be convinced of this by deeds. I, Spichkin, am the embodiment of fiery energy and the embodiment of labour. I would be very happy to meet you personally and for you to become acquainted with me, Spichkin. Being by nature a person of crystal honesty, and loving, as I do, the people, for whom I have given my soul (I can relate to you personally about my great exploits), I would like immediately to become your right hand and devote my fiery energy to your military cause in defeating the bandit Kolchak, who is hated by everyone.

"I request you to immediately enlist me in the ranks of the Red Army as a volunteer, in the glorious regiment named after Stepan Razin

"Signed: *Timofei Spichkin*,

Chairman of the Novouzensk Council of People's Judges."

Spichkin's "Scandalous Complaint," as well as his "Application" are full of contradictions, and ambiguity, and do give an impression of the ravings of a maniac, but everything that is set down in them with such exaggeration was to be found in slightly different form and varying degrees in the Chapayev Division. It was not in Chapayev's nature ever to refuse to interfere in such matters. On the contrary, he got pleasure out of investigating everything himself, unearthing everything, and showing up scoundrels and good-for-nothings. These letters, however, came at the height of the offensive and therefore he could do nothing at all about them, but it worried him. He remembered them for a long time, and had a great desire to go there himself and investigate, but all he could do was to send a formidable letter breathing thunder and lightning at the "guilty." Alas, without the least trial and in their absence, Spichkin's fourteen "spiders and microbes" were condemned by Chapayev as unmitigated scoundrels. He was quick to believe anything and just as quick to change his mind, that is, in everything except military matters; here, it was just the opposite—he didn't believe anyone but relied only on his own wits.

When one pauses to reflect whether Chapayev possessed some unusual superhuman powers which gave him the unfading glory of a "hero," one sees that his powers were most ordinary, most "human"; there were many excellent qualities that he did not possess even in the slightest degree, though those he did possess were remarkably clear and fresh. He made excellent use of his good qualities. Born as he was of this raw semi-guerrilla peasant mass, he could galvanize it to the highest degree, permeate it with the spirit that it desired and demanded itself, and in the centre of everything place himself!

Chapayev's fame stemmed not so much from his heroic exploits, as from the people surrounding him. This is not meant to detract in the least from the colossal role that Chapayev's personality played in the Civil War, only it is necessary to realize and bear constantly in mind that around the name of any hero there is always more that is legendary than truly historical. But people will ask: Why is it that it is around Chapayev and no other, that these legends have grown up? Why was it his name that was so popular?

Why, because he personified, *to a greater extent than*

many others, the qualities of the raw, heroic mass that was "his" men. What he did suited them. He possessed the qualities of this mass and, especially those respected and valued by it: bravery, daring, courage and resolution. Often these qualities were no more pronounced in him than in others, and at times even less, but he knew so well in what light to set forth his exploits, and he was so greatly assisted in this by his close friends, that his deeds were invariably surrounded by an aura of the heroic and miraculous. There were many who were braver than he, and cleverer—more able commanders, and higher developed in a political sense, but the names of these "many" have been forgotten, while Chapayev will long be remembered because he was the child of his environment, and moreover, combined to a remarkable degree the qualities that were scattered among the personalities, the individualities of his comrades-in-arms.

There is no need to describe one action after another, no need to go into detail over operations orders, their merits and defects, or over our victories and reverses. That will be gone into by those who write military treatises. In our sketch, we make no pretensions to a complete narration of events, or to a strict observance of sequence or absolute accuracy in dates, places and names. We limit ourselves to a picture of the life that was born of the times and was characteristic of the times. For example, now, on the road to Belebei, we shall not attempt to give an account of purely military operations, but shall limit ourselves to two or three pictures illustrating everyday life during this period.

Beyond Buguruslan, Sizov's brigade was moving on Tatarsky Kondiz from the village of Dmitrovskoye. There was sharp fighting here. The enemy still refused to believe that in evacuating Buguruslan he had lost the initiative, that an end had come to his victorious advance, and that now it was he who would be driven, and must defend himself, and retreat. He gathered his forces together and met the thrust of the Red regiments with strong blows, but it was already too late. Firm belief in victory had deserted the White armies and gone over to the Red Army men, heartening them and inspiring in them the indefatigability and courage that are the companions of complete confidence in victory.

The moment when the initiative passes over from one side to the other is always striking and portentous—it is only the blind who are not aware of it. One side suddenly begins to pale, to decline, to become flabby, while the other seems to have drunk of some life-giving elixir. It rears up, bristling, its eyes flashing, and becomes menacing and beautiful in its unexpected grandeur. There comes a moment, with the army whose strength is on the wane, that it becomes so weak, and feeble, so anaemic and flaccid, that there is only one thing left for it—to die. The long wasting process that has been acting internally comes to the surface and ends in death. The army of the White admiral, such a short time before, at Buguruslan, mighty and seemingly invincible, was now just a living corpse, doomed to inevitable death. The stern hand of History had already put the shameful brand of an ignoble death upon its low, criminal forehead.

At the same time the Red Army, so resilient and firm, so noticeably re-invigorated by the streams of reinforcements flowing from factories and plants, trade unions, and Party units, was in those days like a shining hero of legend, who has just awakened and who will challenge all, and conquer all, and by whom the forces of darkness will be dispersed.

The Chapayev Division was also imbued with this spirit; it was in this spirit that Sizov's brigade fell upon and routed the enemy at Russky Kondiz and Tatarsky Kondiz.

Frunze arrived at Brigade Headquarters, quickly sized up the situation, enquired about Sizov's latest successful operations, and there, in the hut, wrote the draft of an order of thanks. This still further raised the triumphant spirit of the soldiers, and Sizov, bucked up by the praise, swore to win new victories.

"Well, if that's the case," Chapayev said to him, "you'd better swear to something definite. D'you see those hills?" and he pointed out through the window in a general direction, not giving the names of places, or rivers or villages. "You take them and, I give my word, I'll give you my silver sword!"

"You're on!" exclaimed Sizov, laughing.

And three days after these solemn promises they almost shot one another. Fyodor Klichkov was in bed at the time with a bad cold, and sent his assistant, Krainyukov, to travel about the front with Chapayev in his place. It was on the third trip that this incident took place, but Klichkov, who was ill, was told nothing about it; only vague rumours began to reach his ears. Chapayev also kept silent and gloomily tried to change the subject when asked anything about it. Sizov, on the contrary, was quite willing to tell everything in detail as soon as Fyodor, now well again, arrived at his Headquarters.

"Just a mistake, Comrade Klichkov, a silly mistake," he told Fyodor. "We both lost control of ourselves a little—didn't amount to anything—stupidity—not worth talking about, but I'll tell you—I don't mind remembering such foolishness. You know what he is—red hot! You can expect anything of him! He gets a fire going and may even burn himself up. You've got to keep watch over him, and you weren't here. That fine fellow, your assistant, he only laughs at everything, and doesn't try to argue with him, and then Chapayev's not the one to listen to just anyone. It had to be that we played the fool, and we did, only no harm was done at all. I remember now, I was so tired my legs ached. I was plumb petered out. Well, I thought, I'll have a little snooze, then maybe I'll feel better. As soon as I flopped down, I was dead to the world. Vaska, you remember that boy—bit of a rogue, sort of an orderly to me—well, Vaska managed to find a Tatar shack for us—dirty little room— nothing in it but a bench along the wall. I flopped down on the bench and slept like a log. Before I went to sleep I called Vaska. 'See to it, you little rascal,' I said, 'that you get a hen ready by morning—understand?' 'I understand,' he said, and then I fell asleep and began to dream the devil knows what. Instead of the hen, I seemed to be jabbing at Kolchak with a fork. I'd jab and he'd bend to one side, I'd jab and he'd duck, and then the son-of-a-bitch would turn his head and grin. It made me so mad I gave him a whack on the head with the fork, but it broke in two, and then I saw it was a sword and not a fork. I grabbed the stump and began gouging him on the head, and instead of a head it was a telegraph pole, and letters began jumping out on the Hughes, one after the other, like daws. I knew that this was Chapayev sending me his order of the day before, and I hadn't agreed to that order. 'Smash the enemy,' he said, 'and another brigade will mop him up. You can go to hell, I thought. Am I supposed to get revenge for our losses or not? Who's going to pay me for the hundred men I left on the hill? 'Kurgin,' I shouted, 'write an order!' Kurgin always has a piece of paper in his hand, and a pencil behind his ear. Writes like a whirlwind. Before I could clear my throat he had the heading down. 'Put this in the order,' I said. 'As soon as you've smashed the enemy, you're to drive him back fifteen versts! D'you understand?' 'I understand,' he says. He and Vaska—those devils could understand everything I wanted just by my voice. I knew

I'd get hell from Chapayev, but what could I do when he'd pulled such a blunder? I tried to phone him and explain everything to him and talk it out, but that scoundrel Pleshkov—he was the Division Chief-of-Staff, you know—he didn't even call Chapayev. 'The order has been given,' he said, 'and there can't be any talk about changing it.' Well, I thought, if there can't be, there can't be, but I've got my own head on my shoulders. Kurgin wrote out an order, and I signed it, and the fun began. Only I knew I'd catch it. Chapayev don't like it when his orders are changed. So I slept and had all kinds of dreams. Suddenly I sat up on the bench. The sun had hardly risen. It was still twilight, but here was Chapayev—he couldn't wait—had galloped all night.

" 'What d'you mean, you son-of-a-bitch?' he asks.

" 'I'm not a son-of-a-bitch, Comrade Chapayev,' I answer. 'You be a little careful.'

"He reaches for his revolver. 'I'll shoot you,' he squeals. But as he touched his holster, I already had my revolver out, and I says: 'Mine's cocked—go ahead and shoot!'

" 'Leave the brigade command!' he shouts. 'I'll have you replaced right away. Write an order. I'll put Mikhailov in your place, and you get out, d'you hear! What kind of a commander are you? I tell them to stop and they go on running fifteen versts. What's the meaning of that, I ask you? What d'you mean? Is that what you call commanding a brigade?'

"He gave it to me hot and heavy, the bastard, but he didn't draw his revolver, just the same, and I put mine back. There was no use talking, and so I said: 'Kurgin, write an order.' And he wrote out everything the way it should be.

" 'Four messengers, at once!'

"They galloped up.

" 'Here are letters for Mikhailov. Get a move on!'

They were off before I got the words out of my mouth. We stayed there looking at each other, not saying a word. We began to calm down, we'd said everything we had to say. I was sitting on the bench but there was no place for Chapayev—he was standing by the wall. His eyes, shiny blue and angry, were shooting sparks. That's all right, I thought, you'll get over it, my hawk, you'll cool off. And at that moment, will you believe it, Vaska sticks his head in at the door and squeaks: 'The hen's ready!'

"We'd been quarrelling, but I had to ask him to dinner.

"'Comrade Chapayev,' I said, 'won't you eat with me in the garden?' There was a little garden there.

"'All right,' he said.

"I saw that his voice wasn't friendly, but it wasn't angry. Maybe he would have laughed, but he was ashamed to.

"We went out into the garden, sat down, still not saying anything.

"'Sizov,' he says, 'stop the messengers.'

"'Impossible to stop them, Comrade Chapayev,' I answer. 'How can you stop them, once they've galloped away?'

"'Send out faster ones,' he shouts, and again he got red in the face.

"'There aren't any better. They're the best.'

"'Then you send better than the best! Don't you understand what I'm saying?'

"How could I help understanding—I understood everything. But I says to myself, I'll rub it in a little—why should he call me a son-of-a-bitch?

"'Why did you call me a son-of-a-bitch,' I asked. 'I've got my pride. If I've done something wrong—why, have me tried, turn me over to the Tribunal; let them shoot me, but don't go calling me a son-of-a-bitch.'

"'I lost my temper,' he said, don't pay any attention to all that!'

"Well, we put some more messengers in the saddle—this time six of them. Away they went. In an hour they all came back together. They had stopped the first ones by firing into the air.

"So we tore up all those orders and threw them away.

"'Don't touch your own order,' he says. 'Let them chase the enemy. It's not a good idea to change orders. I'll make whatever changes are needed, myself.'

"And that was the end of it. We ate up the hen, and didn't say one more bad word to each other. It's always that way with us, Comrade Klichkov," Sizov concluded. "We shout at each other and make a lot of noise, and then sit down together to drink tea, and have a little talk."

"Well, and was that all?" asked Fyodor, smiling.

"What else would there be?" Sizov grinned. "Only on my way back, when I'd done everything—taken the hills and captured the prisoners, the ones I turned over to the division a few days ago—he came riding up again.

"'Hullo, Sizov,' he says. And he was in a good humour—smiling.

"'Hullo, Chapayev,' I answer. 'How's your health?'

"He didn't answer, but coming up to me, puts his arms around me and kisses me three times.

"'Here, take it,' he says. 'You've won it.' He took off his silver sword, threw the belt over my shoulder, and stood there without saying a word. I began to be sorry for him standing there without a sword. I pulled off my ordinary one.

"'Here,' I said. 'You remember me, too.' You know when he's promised anything, he keeps his word; you know how he is."

That was the end of their talk. Sizov was called to the telephone: the people in the regiment were asking about something. Fyodor didn't renew the conversation. Evidently everything had been said about what had happened. Nothing serious. Nothing important. However, when they were both excited, they might have done things that would have caused a thousand complications. They needed a nurse all the time, and one that was always on the watch: as soon as she turned her back, you could be sure they'd break each other's necks, and other people's necks, to boot!

The 220th Regiment took Trifonovka by storm, and was billeted to rest up. When some Red Army men went into the end hut, they were surprised to see a lot of blood stains on the floor. They wondered what had happened, and began to question the peasant whose hut it was, but he kept silent and stubbornly refused to say anything. Then they promised him on their word of honour that nothing would be done to him; the soldiers took it on themselves to intercede for him with their commander and commissar "just in case," if only he'd tell them what had happened. Then without any further discussion, the villager led them to an open shed and throwing some manure off the top of a pile, pointed to something bloody and formless, all a dirty crimson: "There!"

The soldiers stared in astonishment, went up closer and saw that this formless, bloody mass was human bodies. They threw off the manure with their bayonets, knives or hands and pulled out two warm corpses.... Red Army men.

Suddenly the hand of one of the seemingly dead bodies moved—those holding the body instinctively jumped back dropping it again on the manure, and saw a leg drawn up and then stretched out and then again drawn up. The swollen, blood-suffused eyelids fluttered and opened slightly, but the deathly leaden look of the eyes showed that the man was unconscious.

The news of the terrible discovery spread like wildfire through the whole regiment. The Red Army men ran up to see, but no one knew what had happened, and they were lost in conjectures and wild guesses. The peasant was questioned. He didn't try to hold back, but told everything the way it had happened.

It seemed two cooks of the International Regiment had come to Trifonovka a few hours before by mistake, taking the village, then occupied by the Whites, for some other village held by their own men. They had ridden up to the hut and asked where the Commissary Department was. The Cossacks sitting in the hut had run out, and pounced with a shout on the bewildered cooks, dragged them to the ground and pushed them into the hut. At first they only questioned them: where they were going and where they were from; what units were stationed thereabouts, and how many effectives there were in each unit. They promised the Red Army men complete forgiveness if only they told the truth. The cooks told them something, but whether true or not, no one can say. The Cossacks listened, wrote everything down and asked more questions. This went on for about ten minutes.

"You don't know anything more?" asked one of the Cossacks sitting there.

"Nothing," answered the prisoners.

"What's that you've got there on your cap—a star? You're for the Soviets? The sons-of-bitches! Look, what they've stuck on to themselves."

The Red Army men stood there without saying anything. They probably felt that things were taking a bad turn. The humour of the Cossacks had changed quickly. While they were questioning the prisoners, they hadn't mocked at them, but now at sight of the stars they began to curse and threaten. They poked one of the men in the side.

"So you're a cook?"

"A cook," he answered quietly.

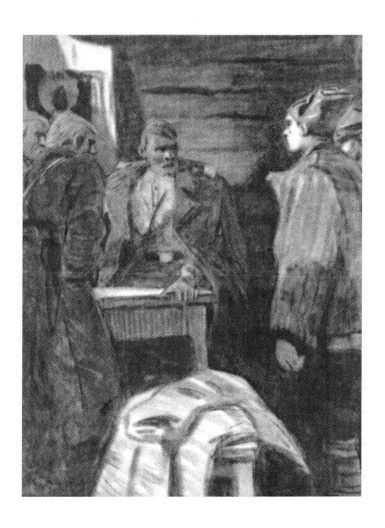

"Fed the Bolsheviks, you scoundrel?"

"I fed everybody," he answered still more quietly.

"Everybody?" and the Cossack jumped up. "We know how you fed everybody, you swine! You've ruined and messed up the whole country."

He cursed obscenely, drew back and struck the soldier across the face with all his strength. The blood gushed from the prisoner's nose. It was as though this was the signal they had been waiting for. This blow in the face loosened their hands, and the sight of the blood aroused in them a wild, insane, bloodthirsty fury. The Cossacks all jumped to their feet and began to beat the Red Army men with whatever they could lay hands on; they knocked them down, stamped on them, spat on them.

Then one of the scoundrels thought up a fiendish punishment. The unfortunate men were picked up from the floor, sat down in chairs, and tied there with rope. Then the Cossacks began to slice off strip after strip of bloody flesh from around the base of their necks. They would cut off a piece and sprinkle the wound with salt; cut off another piece, and salt the place. Mad with intolerable pain, the Red Army men screamed terribly, but their cries only exasperated the frenzied brutes the more. They tortured them this way for a few minutes—sliced and salted. Then one of them stuck his bayonet into the chest of one of the prisoners, and another Cossack did the same. But they were stopped by the others—that way the prisoners might be stabbed to death, and they wouldn't suffer enough! One of the prisoners was killed this way, however. The other was hardly breathing; it was he who was now dying before the eyes of the regiment.

When, a few hours before, the Whites began a hurried retreat from Trifonovka, they had dragged the two Red Army men they had tortured to death out to the shed and hid them in the manure. That was what had happened.

The regiment heard the account of this terrible crime in angry silence. The victims were placed where all could see them, and having done what was necessary, preparations were made to bury them with honour.

At that moment Fyodor rode up with Chapayev. As soon as they heard what had happened, they gathered the soldiers together and explained the absolute senselessness of such atrocities and warned them not to take revenge on their prisoners. But the anger and indignation of the Red Army men knew no bounds. The victims were lowered into their grave, three volleys were fired, and the men dispersed. After the fighting the next morning, not one prisoner was brought to Regimental Headquarters. No speeches, no assurances can prevent soldiers in battle from taking vengeance; there, blood is only paid for in blood. Even on Fyodor, this incident had a remote but undoubted influence. On the following day he signed the death sentence of a White officer.

Probably, it would not be amiss to relate here what happened. This is how it was. They had gone to Sizov at Russky Kondiz. During an attack that morning, he had captured some eight hundred prisoners. There was practically no guard over them.

"Don't worry, they won't run away. You couldn't drive them back to Kolchak again with a stick. They're damned glad to be prisoners."

"Well, Sizov, again you've done it." Fyodor said, nodding in the direction of the prisoners.

"Exactly so," and the other grinned. "I wanted to tickle them a little with the bayonet, but they began to squeal 'we surrender, don't touch us for Christ's sake, we're prisoners,' and so we drove them back here."

"What about the officers?"

"There were some officers, but they didn't want to be prisoners, said it wasn't nice here."

Sizov glanced significantly at Fyodor, and the latter didn't ask any more questions. "Maybe there are some left?" he said.

"Maybe there are, but they're lying low."

"Won't the soldiers give them up?"

"You see," Sizov began to explain. "These prisoners here are from different units and don't know each other—they were some kind of reinforcements."

"Well," said Fyodor, "let's try together. Only first of all, I want to talk to the prisoners—tell them a little about this, that and the other."

When Fyodor began to talk, many of the prisoners listened to him with attention and interest, with unbelief and amazement written on their faces and in their perplexed eyes. It was obvious that much of what Klichkov was telling they were hearing for the first time.

"So now I've explained everything to you," Fyodor concluded. "I have stated the truth without deception, without exaggeration, just as it is, and now you must figure it out for yourselves, the best you can—which is closer to you, which means more to you: what you've seen and what you haven't seen under Kolchak, or what I've been telling you. But remember: we need only brave, unhesitating defenders of the Soviet power, people who know what they're fighting for, and who can always be depended on. Think it over. And if some of you want to fight on our side, come out and say so. We never drive away people like you who have been deceived into fighting for Kolchak."

He finished. There were a lot of questions: political and military and concerning enlistment in the Red Army. It may be mentioned here that over half of them became Red Army men, and Sizov never had occasion to regret that he had taken them into his fine regiments.

The prisoners were drawn up in two ranks, and Klichkov began to inspect them, taking note of how they were dressed, and what sort of boots they were wearing, and asking some of them questions. His attention was attracted to certain of the prisoners who were obviously not workers and not simple village lads. They were taken aside and later at Headquarters they were questioned separately and in detail, so as to establish their identity. One, in particular, aroused suspicion. His expression was arrogant and defiant; he stood there smiling maliciously at the whole procedure of inspection and interrogation, as though he wanted to say, "It's not for you ignorant curs to question us!"

Half his clothes were those of a simple soldier, but there was something suspicious about it—his pants and boots were of excellent quality, while his shirt was cheap and ragged, and was apparently not his own at all. He had trouble in getting his burly, well-fed body into it, and the collar didn't meet on his fat, crimson neck, which was like a leg of pork. He had an ordinary soldier's cap on his head, but again it was obvious that it was not his—it didn't look right on him, and he didn't know how to wear it. He didn't look like a common soldier.

Fyodor first walked past him without saying a word, and then on the way back stopped opposite him and suddenly rapped out:

"You're an officer, aren't you?"

"I'm not—no, I'm a private," the other answered hurriedly and in some confusion. "What makes you think so?"

"Why, I know you," said the cunning Fyodor.

"You know me? Where have you seen me?" asked the other staring.

"I know you," muttered Fyodor. "But see here—this is no time for reminiscences. I ask you once more: Are you an officer or not?"

"And I repeat that I am not an officer," said the other straightening up, and lifting his head high.

"All right, you'll have only yourself to blame."

Fyodor called him out in front, and with him several other men, and then led the whole group down the ranks, but first he made a short, fiery speech, explaining to them the role played by the White officers in the workers' and peasants' struggle against their enemies, and the necessity of destroying their corps, since they were coming out openly against the Soviet power.

He went down the ranks with the suspects, asking the prisoners if they recognized any of these people as officers. When his cap was taken off, the well-fed gentleman was at once recognized by several of the soldiers.

"Of course we know him—he's an officer, no doubt of it." And they named the unit he had commanded.

"We only saw him two days, but how could we help recognizing him. He's had his collar up and his cap pulled down so you couldn't see much of his face, but now anybody could tell him. It's him all right."

The soldiers seemed to get satisfaction out of this "identifying." On this occasion several people were identified but this was the only officer. The others were officials and office employees.

"Well, what do you say now?" asked Fyodor turning to him.

The other looked down and kept stubbornly silent.

"Are the soldiers telling the truth?" Fyodor again asked him.

"Yes, it's the truth. What of it?" Apparently realizing the seriousness of the situation, he had decided to maintain the haughty arrogance he had exhibited during the first questioning when he had tried to deceive them.

"I warned you when I asked you."

"I didn't care to tell you," snapped the officer.

Fyodor had already decided to send the officer off with the group of officials to Headquarters, when he remembered that he had not been searched.

"Give orders to have him searched," said Fyodor to Sizov who was standing silently beside him.

"Why give orders?" Sizov burst out. "I'll do it myself."

He began to turn out the man's pockets, fishing out various trifles.

"Nothing else?"

"Nothing."

"Maybe there's something else?" asked Sizov.

"I said 'no' and that means 'no,'" the officer rudely cut him short.

His insolence and his contemptuous tone irritated them exceedingly. At that moment Sizov pulled out a letter, unfolded it and handed it over to Fyodor. From the letter, Fyodor discovered that the officer was a former seminarist, the son of a priest; for over a year he had been fighting against the Soviet power. The letter was apparently from his fiancée. She had written from the neighbouring town which the Whites had just evacuated. "The Whites will soon come back," she wrote. "Have patience... the Reds give us no peace. God keep you, and you yourself be careful, so you can take revenge on the Bolsheviks."

The blood pounded in Fyodor's temples. "Enough! Take him away!" he shouted.

"To be shot?" asked Sizov point-blank, and with terrible simplicity.

"Yes, yes, take him away."

The officer was led away. In a couple of minutes there came the sound of the volley.

At another time, Fyodor would probably have acted differently, but he couldn't forget the two Red Army men who had been tortured to death; he still seemed to see their bodies with the strips of flesh sliced off, and the deep wounds sprinkled with salt.

And then, too—the officer's stubbornness and his arrogant and defiant tone, and last of all, the letter from his fiancée, depicting, without the shadow of a doubt, the true character of her officer-fiancé.

Klichkov was upset; all day he was anxious and gloomy. He didn't joke or smile, said little, and that unwillingly, and tried to keep to himself all the time. But that was only the first day. The next morning, it was as though nothing had happened. It would have been strange at the front to be upset long by such experiences, when hour after hour, day after day, one sees scenes that are stupendous in their frightfulness, when it is not one person that is the victim, but tens, and hundreds and thousands.

The bloody trail left by war—mutilated corpses, crippled bodies, burned villages, homeless, starving people—this bloody trail along which an army moves and to which it returns again and again, doesn't allow one to suffer long over only one out of the thousands of grim scenes of war! The one scene is crowded out by others. It was that way with Fyodor. The next morning he was calm as he remembered that the day before he had for the first time given the order to have a man shot.

"It is new to you!" Chapayev laughed. "If you'd been with us in 1918—how would you have got along without having people shot? We'd capture some officers, but there'd be no one to guard them—every soldier was necessary for the attack and not for convoy duty. So we'd shoot the whole bunch. It was the same with them—d'you think they spared us?"

"D'you remember, Chapayev, the first time you passed sentence?"

"Well, maybe not the first, but I know that it was hard. It's always hard to begin, but then you get used to it."

"Used to what? Killing?"

"Yes," Chapayev answered simply, "killing. A cavalryman comes to us from some school or other, for example. He can slash this way and that. Yes, as long as it's in the air, he's damned clever at slashing, the rascal; but as soon as it comes to chopping a man down, he forgets all he ever learned. He makes a pass and then another—botches it all up. When he gets used to it, he's all right. It never comes out right the first time."

Fyodor also talked with other war-hardened old soldiers. They all maintained in one voice that no matter what kind of nerves a person has, or what kind of a heart, he always feels timid, upset and remorseful the first time he kills a man, whether it is by cutting him down with a sabre, or by running him through with a bayonet, or by ordering him to be executed, or by shooting him himself. But then, especially in war-time, when he sees blood all the time, he soon gets over being so sensitive, and killing an enemy this way or that gets to be almost mechanical.

"Stepkin, my orderly," said Sizov to Fyodor, "also got a death sentence. I gave the order myself."

"What d'you mean—got a death sentence?" asked Fyodor in amazement.

"It was this way...." And Sizov told him how Stepkin had actually been all but executed on the Uralsk front.

"He was working a machine-gun," Sizov began. "He was a fellow that could be depended on, like all of them. And then, in some Cossack village I saw them taking him somewhere—seems he had raped a woman. 'Wait a minute, lads,' I said, 'we'll find out if it's true—bring the woman here and we'll question her. You, Stepkin, stay here, and I'll question you both together.' Stepkin sat there and didn't say anything. When I'd ask him something he'd only shake his head and mumble some foolishness. But then, just before the woman got there he admitted it all. 'Yes,' he said, 'it happened.' The woman was already on the threshold. He's got a good eye for women—picked out a strapping wench about twenty-five years old. The commissar was there and all the others. There was nothing that could be done—we'd have to shoot Stepkin as an example to the others. Here was the Red Army, on the march to liberate the country, and if anyone raped a village woman, there could only be one end, like it or not. There were cases where we shot our own men—why should Stepkin get off any easier? We reasoned that if we forgave Stepkin, the others would think: 'Go ahead, fellows, you won't be punished.' When I thought of that it was all clear to me what to do, but when I looked at Stepkin, I was sorry for him—he was a fine fellow in battle. The commissar had already sent for the firing squad. They came in:

" 'Who are we to take?'

" 'Wait a minute. I want to do some questioning,' I says. 'So you raped her, Stepkin? Do you confess?'

" 'Why, haven't I admitted it?' he asks.

" 'Why did you do it?' I shout at him.

" 'How do I know,' he says, 'I don't remember.'

" 'Well, d'you know, Stepkin, what you'll get for doing what you did?'

" 'I don't know, Comrade Commander.'

" 'We'll have to shoot you, you numb-skull—d'you understand, shoot you?'

"He answered awfully quiet:

" 'You're the one to say, Comrade Commander—if it has to be that way, why it has to be.'

" 'We have to shoot you, Stepkin,' I try to bring home to him. 'You ought to understand yourself that the whole village will be calling us ruffians. And they'll be right. Because what kind of a Red Army are we if we can't keep our paws off the women?'

"He stood there and didn't answer, only hung his head still more. 'If we let you off, then we'll have to let everyone off—isn't that so?' I asks him.

" 'That's right.'

" 'You understand how it is?' I says.

" 'Yes—I understand.'

" 'You damned fool, Stepkin,' I shouted, losing my temper. 'Why did you have to touch that woman? If you had stayed in the machine-gun cart where you belonged, nothing would have happened. And now, see what you've done!'

"He scratched the back of his head and didn't say anything. Then I asked the woman, 'How was it he got the better of you?' She was a lively wench and liked to talk.

" 'What do you mean 'how'? He grabbed me, that's how. I yelled and I spit in his filthy mug but he... look what a brute he is—how could I keep him off?'

" 'So, you mean.'

" 'That's just what I mean.'

" 'We're going to punish him,' I said.

" 'That'll serve him right, the scoundrel,' the woman chimed in. 'Look at him staring with his ugly mug. A good dressing-down is what he needs so that he'll know better.'

" 'No, it's not a dressing-down he'll get—we're going to shoot him.'

"The woman almost swooned. She threw her arms apart; her mouth was wide open and her eyes popping.

" 'Yes, we're going to shoot him,' I repeated.

" 'What do you mean?' and the woman clasped her hands. 'My God, you can't kill a man that way. Oh, my God, what does it mean!' she squealed, plumb scared, almost falling against the table and beginning to weep.

" 'You, yourself, complained—now it's too late,' I said.

" 'Who complained?' the woman said. 'Did I complain? I only said he ran after me. He almost caught me but not quite.'

" 'So you mean..?'

" 'That's what I mean—that he didn't catch me. As to what he wanted to do, the dirty devil, how do I know? I couldn't read his thoughts.'

"I looked her in the eye, and saw that she was lying, but I didn't stop her. Let her lie, I thought, maybe Stepkin will get away with his life, after all. Only we can't have her making a noise and disgracing us. As to what really happened between the two of them—what the hell did I care. Maybe she led him on herself. If she's crying and begging for him now, she'll spread it all over the village that she was lying because she wanted to get Stepkin into trouble. So I egged her on.

" 'Enough of that,' I said, 'enough, young woman. Everything's clear, so we'll take him away.'

" 'Where are you going to take him?' she squealed. 'I won't let you take him anywhere, I won't.'

"Then she ran up to him, threw her arms around him, and stuck to him, crying and cursing at the same time. She wouldn't let go of him, and was shaking like a leaf.

" 'Of course, you could save him, but you don't want to,' I said. 'Here your husband's been gone two years, and you're a healthy girl. If you married him now, why, then we might forget this business, but if not....'

" 'Why should I marry him? I don't want to marry.'

" 'Well, if you don't want to, then we'll have to get on with our business.' And I got up from the table, as though I was going to leave the room.

" 'But he won't get married in church. He don't believe in God, you can be sure.' All the time she had her arms around Stepkin and wouldn't let go of him. He was standing there like a calf, without a word, as though it didn't concern him in the least.

"'You can do as you like about that,' I answered, 'only tell me, once and for all, do you make it up or not?'

"She opened her arms and let go of her young man. There was a smile all over her face.

"'Why should we quarrel?' she asked.

"Then he began to grin, too, the devil—understood the turn we'd given things.

"To put an end to everything, we shooed them both out of the hut—nothing for the newly-weds to be doing there. Everybody stood around the table smiling at them, and giving them advice of various kinds. Stepkin got out of it easy that evening. But the next morning I sent for him.

"'Listen to me, Stepkin,' I said. 'We went through the farce of marrying you and tomorrow you'll be on the march again. Don't think of carting that woman along with you, if there really is something between you two. To make up for what you've done, I'm setting you a job: earn an award, earn it as soon as there's a battle, or I'll never forgive you, and I'll think you a scoundrel until you've proved otherwise.'

"'I understand,' he said, 'I'll earn it.'"

"Well, and did he?" asked Fyodor.

"Of course he did—he won a silver cigarette case; carries makhorka in it. It was through him and his machine-gun that we took two hundred prisoners at one swoop. He was shot through the leg himself, and it was after that that he was put in the non-combatants. He happened to be assigned to me, so he hangs about doing one thing and another."

"What did he do about the Cossack woman?"

"Why, what could he do about her?" smiled Sizov. "He was at her place that night; she baked him some wheat cakes for the march, and treated him to tea."

"What about the wedding?" Fyodor laughed.

"There wasn't any wedding," said Sizov with a wave of his hand, "no mention of it even. She decided she'd rescued him and kept telling him how she had saved him from being shot. And he just sat there eating and drinking for all he was worth, saying nothing or sticking in some nonsense or other. In the morning we were to march out of the village and he ran up just in time."

Then they began to talk about sexual hunger in general, and of the inevitability of outrages at the front. Examples were cited and reminiscences exchanged. Chapayev, in particular, was extremely interested in this question and kept asking whether it was possible for a soldier to spend two or three years at the front without women. He himself came to the conclusion that "it had to be just that way, otherwise what kind of a soldier would he be?"

From Sizov's brigade, Fyodor and Chapayev went on to Shmarin's. Now if Sizov, envious of Chapayev's fame, would have liked to make himself out his equal, he had plenty of grounds for his pretensions; he really was a hero. Shmarin, on the other hand, only made a fool of himself. He fussed about continually, never giving himself a moment's rest; he was in constant motion and was always anxious about something or other. Even when he was asleep this anxiety was still to be seen in the expression of his face. It was outrageous the way he liked to tell tall stories about his imaginary exploits. He would tell them almost every time he saw anyone. True, there were variations—here and there he would add or omit a wound he had received, or a time he had been shell-shocked, or an attack he had been in—but in general he had six or seven well-learned accounts of his exploits and he got enormous satisfaction out of retelling them. Carried away with his narrative he would literally bubble over with ecstasy at the stormy unfolding of events; he would be amazed at the turn things took and be in raptures over surprises he had just thought up. During his narration he had a strange way of jerking at his thick black hair, and leaning over the table so low that his nose touched it, he would beat time to his speech all the while by tapping loudly and emphatically on the edge of the table with his index and middle fingers. It all gave one the impression that he was not addressing the people present but was reading an instructive sermon to the table, was lecturing it about something.

At first, people listened to Shmarin, and even believed him, but then they discovered that there was much more imagination in his stories than truth, and stopped listening to him. Only it must not be thought that he confined himself to fantasy. Quite the contrary: he would narrate facts, genuine, indisputable incidents that had really taken place. The trouble was not in that, but in the fact that whenever anyone displayed bravery in some operation, or showed real talent, it always turned out that it was Shmarin who had done it all. And then it would come out that the whole incident had occurred on the left flank, while he, Shmarin, had been busy on the right. It would come out that the talent had been displayed by the commander of a battalion, while the regiment had been commanded by Shmarin, or something of that sort. He liked to take the credit for other people's good work. And it was not only Shmarin who had this failing. Fyodor observed it in others—the appropriation of someone else's heroic deed came easy and natural to them. As soon as anyone came to see Shmarin, he would start off, and go on and on—only listen to him, and he'd keep it up till morning, if he began in the evening. He was sure to have been "surrounded," he was sure to have "broken through" from somewhere or other, although everybody knew quite well that the day before, say, there had been no fighting in his sector. His flanks were always being "gravely threatened"; the neighbouring brigades never came to his assistance, even made it harder for him, and always profited by his work and claimed the victories of his brigade. For this they were praised and received marks of approval, or even awards, while he, Shmarin, the real hero, was forgotten by everyone; he was not noticed or rewarded. They evidently thought of him as an insignificant person, not knowing that he, Shmarin, was the one really responsible for great deeds which had been stolen and appropriated by others.

Today, when Fyodor and Chapayev came to him from Sizov, and announced that the latter had taken a horde of prisoners, Shmarin listened attentively, and then pressing his big fist to his dirty, sallow face, he said absent-mindedly, as though musing over something:

"So that's how it was. Well, what could they do? I knew there was no way out for them."

"No way out for whom?"

"Why, those men Sizov took prisoner. Do you know what prisoners those were, Comrade Chapayev? I had smashed them before that—there was a battle on my right flank—you remember, don't you? What could they do in such a fix—all that was left for them was to surrender."

Shmarin had a bad habit of belittling other people's exploits. He would do it even when it wasn't of the slightest advantage to himself.

Seeing now that Shmarin was ready to begin an account of "yesterday's successes," Chapayev at once asked him the most urgent and important question, a question which he couldn't avoid or wave aside:

"What's new in your brigade's sector?"

They went into the little room which served as Brigade Headquarters. It was foul smelling and black and sour with tobacco smoke, as though all the people did there was to smoke and fill the air with fumes. All the lads on Shmarin's staff were efficient and worked very conscientiously. Although Shmarin was a fussy windbag and a dangerous romancer, he always coped well with the tasks set the brigade. He was not at all bad in carrying out orders, but was no good when it came to using his own head. He had absolutely no initiative of his own, and always waited for directions; he was not keen-sighted enough to see what was most important in a given situation.

The people at Headquarters had been well trained, and knew what Chapayev liked. They gave him a detailed account of everything, so that there was little Shmarin could add. When the situation had been made clear, Chapayev immediately decided to make the round of Shmarin's brigade—it was at the time engaged in an attack. Shmarin left his second-in-command at Headquarters, and prepared to accompany Chapayev and Fyodor.

Chapayev remembered with amazing accuracy the number of our own and the enemy's forces, as well as the rivers and roads he had seen on the maps, the green patches that were woods, and the brown spots that were hills. As they rode, he would tell Shmarin what should be behind some hillock, what forces would be concealed behind the nearest wood, and approximately where there ought to be a ford. He knew, and pictured everything to himself distinctly. When they came to a place where two or three roads met, Chapayev without much thought chose one of them and rode along it with as much assurance as though it were a familiar street in a small town. He seldom made a mistake, practically never in fact. He might come to some place where it was necessary to make a detour or would come to a blind alley, but it was a trifle for him to find the way out. He would look about him for a moment; ponder over something, recall various turns and landmarks they had passed, and away he would go. At night it was harder, but in the day-time he scarcely ever made a mistake. When it came to finding his way, Chapayev had an undisputed gift, and as a rule no one ever argued with him—whatever he said, went.

They rode up to the first regiment. The men were in shallow trenches that had just been dug. They were not really trenches but weak little defences more like mole-hills one sees in the woods. The ground had been thrown up in little mounds and they had stuck a pine bough in each mound so that one couldn't tell where they were hiding their heads—behind the bough or behind the mound. Either the enemy really took these boughs for bushes or simply didn't want to bring on himself a rifle duel; at all events he kept silent though he was supposed to be hiding close by, behind the hill.

The men were carrying food to the trenches, crawling on their bellies. They would lie down flat with a kettle or a mess-tin with soup in their outstretched hands and would crawl on their elbows and knees, wriggling along like so many worms, all the way from the field kitchen. Their comrades were eating their dinner and resting —after dinner they would continue the attack. Some of them had dug out a book or a newspaper; terribly old, they must have been, they were so torn and dirty. The chap would lie flat, his head hidden behind the pine bough, his face serious, absolutely calm, and would hold the book or newspaper under his nose and read—it all had such a simple and everyday look that he might have been at home in his village, somewhere, taking shelter from the July heat on a holiday.

Chapayev, Fyodor and Shmarin walked behind the

skirmish line—they were not fired at. This made Chapayev begin to wonder.

"Are the Whites really behind that hill—who knows? Maybe they were there but have gone," he said to Shmarin. "Check up on it!"

Scouts crawled off in various directions. Two got to the hill and climbed up to the ridge, slowly raising themselves higher and higher, until they were standing upright. They returned and said there wasn't a soul on the ridge. The enemy must have slipped away through the coppice that began just beyond the hill.

Chapayev and the others went forward, climbed to the highest point and began to look on all sides through their field-glasses.

"Do you see where that wood goes to?" and Chapayev pointed. "They want to get around behind us from there."

"They won't get around us," said Shmarin. "I've been chasing them for three days—how can they turn back? All they're worrying about is that they won't be able to run fast enough."

"And on the fourth day they'll give you a drubbing," Chapayev answered seriously, not taking his eyes from his field-glasses and continuing to turn them from side to side.

"They won't turn back," Shmarin flippantly continued to assure him.

"And if they do turn back?" asked Chapayev, in a sharp tone. "What if the commander there isn't a fool and realizes that it'll be even easier for him to run, if he plays hell with your rear? While you're getting ready, where'll he be? Blockhead! You try to understand what's happening; use your brains. Do you think he's going to roll along like a pea under your nose?"

Shmarin kept silent; there was nothing he could answer. Chapayev told him what to do so as to foil any possible encircling movement, and ordered him to stay there until the situation had been cleared up. He himself went on with Fyodor to inspect the other two regiments.

And no matter where he went, no matter what he came in contact with, he invariably saw what must be mended and how, where assistance was necessary and in what. When he and Fyodor had already got to the third regiment, on the extreme right flank of the brigade, Shmarin sent an orderly to announce that an encircling movement on the part of the enemy had actually been discovered, but that the enemy, realizing that he had been forestalled, was again retreating in the former direction. Shmarin triumphantly concluded his note with the words, "I put an immediate end to the whole malicious attempt without the loss of a single man."

More than likely, there had been nothing for him to "put an end to"; the thunder clouds had probably broken up by themselves.

Chapayev and Fyodor spent the night with the third regiment. Headquarters had been set up in a village, pickets being stationed all around. In a half circle beyond the outskirts of the village, on the side facing the enemy, a skirmish line had dug in for the night. In the hut which served as Headquarters, there was a smoky little lamp without a chimney which gave so little light that it was hard to make out a person's face. Everybody was tired out and not inclined to talk. People began to curl up in the corners of the hut, stretch out on the benches, or hunt for some place where it would be easier to go to sleep. They crawled through the half-murk like black apparitions.

At that moment, a lad of about fourteen was brought in for interrogation. The regimental commanders questioned him, suspecting that he was a spy. First they asked him who he was, where he was from, where he was trying to get to and for what purpose. The boy told them that he had no father or mother—they had died somewhere during the first war. He himself was a Polish refugee and was now enlisted in the Third Volunteer Red Battalion. No one knew anything about such a unit and their suspicions increased.

"What's your name?"

"Zhenya."

"Didn't you just say it was Alyosha?" someone put in, trying to mix him up.

"Please don't make things up," the boy said firmly, with a kind of natural dignity. "I never told you that my name was Alyosha. You made that up yourself."

"You're good at talking, boy!"

"Why shouldn't I talk?"

"Well, don't talk nonsense, get down to business. You came from the Whites? Well, go ahead and talk—don't pretend. If you tell us all about it, we won't do anything to you."

"I won't tell you anything because there isn't anything to tell." His voice quavered as he defended himself against his persistent interrogators.

"Come, now. Don't lie. There isn't any such battalion. You invented it. You'd better tell us where you were going and why."

And so they kept on questioning him in this manner. They wanted to find out who he was and where he had been sent and for what purpose. They made all kinds of threats, trying to frighten him; they said he would be shot.

"Well, then shoot me!" said Zhenya, through his tears. "Only it's for nothing. I'm on your side. You're all wrong."

Fyodor decided to interfere. He had been lying there, listening to the cross-examination and wondering how it would end. Now it was all the same to him whether the boy was one of theirs or not—he wanted to save him, keep him, and re-educate him if necessary. He told them to put an end to the examination. Then he made a place for the jubilant boy on the floor beside himself. (Later Fyodor did make an excellent and conscientious lad out of Zhenya; he worked in both the brigade and the regimental signal service.)

All was still again at Headquarters. The lamp smoked, and from the corners came the snoring and whistling of the sleepers; from outside the window came the champing of the ready-saddled horses. Before they all made ready to get some sleep, Shmarin, who had by then galloped up from the other regiment, decided to have a "look round" to see if everything was in order, and left the hut. How much time passed, nobody knew, but it was already near daybreak when Shmarin ran up out of breath and shouted in at the open door loudly, stumbling over the words:

"Hurry up, hurry up! They're attacking!"

Everybody at once jumped up, and in a minute they were all on their horses.

"They're already on the hill, two hundred metres away!" panted Shmarin, who couldn't get his foot into the stirrup. His spirited horse kept wheeling, and wouldn't let him mount. Shmarin swung back and hit him across the nose with all his strength.

They galloped through the gate. In the first grey light of dawn, figures were dashing in all directions. Where they were running to, was hard to say, because they weren't running in one direction, but in all directions at once. As soon as the riders were through the gate, they broke up without a word—there was no time for talk. Some galloped away down the road, trying to save themselves. Chapayev quickly decided what must be done and galloped off to the reserve battalion that was stationed nearby. Shmarin, and with him, Klichkov, galloped to meet the advancing skirmish lines, before which they supposed the Red Army men were retreating. Klichkov pounded forward with Shmarin to stop the retreating men and raise their spirits by personal example. There flashed through his memory the arguments he had had with Andreyev in Uralsk about skirmish lines, defence, and taking part in the fighting during a panic; he was instantly filled with a proud, triumphant joy.

"False alarm! There's been a mistake! It's our men on the hill!"

"As you were!" Shmarin suddenly bellowed.

It was impossible to say for whom this command was meant—there was no one around them, except individual Red Army men scurrying in all directions. Chapayev and all those that had galloped down the road were at once sent for. They were stopped by shouting and firing into the air. In ten minutes everybody had reassembled.

This confusion, the shouts and the firing, were heard by the men in the regiment, and caused much bewilderment; they even thought that the enemy had cut them off and that immediate measures must be taken. The men pricked up their ears, began to scuttle about, and prepare for defence. They were making ready to send out new scouts in all directions, when they were informed that it was all a false alarm. When the members of the staff had again gathered in the hut, nobody wanted to sleep any more, although it was still too early to begin the day. They sat down at the table and began to talk. They blamed someone, but just whom, it was impossible to say. Shmarin? No, it had been his duty to rouse everyone, once he had noticed anything dangerous, and there had been no time to check up. Themselves? No, they were also not to blame. What fool would go on sitting in the hut when the enemy was attacking.

They decided that the confusion had been inevitable, and let it go at that. They had not found out who was to blame, but they all seemed to be ashamed of something, and embarrassed. Their talk lacked confidence, and they didn't look one another in the eye. They exchanged short phrases, looking over one another's head, to one side, out the window, or into space.

"Close to a real panic, that time," said Shmarin, bending over the table to get a light at the lamp. "Just try to find out who fooled us."

"Who was it told you?" asked Chapayev.

"From the regimental staff. Met me head on."

"Yes, but who?"

"I don't remember, or rather I didn't recognize him —he galloped past. There was a skirmish line moving —you could see something, so I thought...."

"You mustn't think—you've got to know," said Chapayev gravely. "D'you know what happened to us, one time? Not now—it was in the German war, there in the Carpathians. The mountains there aren't like these little hills; if you climb up, you won't get down in a hurry. We climbed up all right, but the Austrians hid in every hole, or behind stones or bushes; some of them were lying in the sand—they were at home and you didn't have to teach them where to hide. We would be strung out with about as much order as at a bazaar, and the enemy would strike at our rear and make off with all the transports. If there was any artillery, they would make off with that, too. Well, this time we put everything in the middle, put soldiers on the sides, and so we marched along. There weren't enough horses so we were using oxen, and at night they'd bellow—a real give away. Only no use giving them one with your rifle butt; they'd bellow still worse. As long as the bread held out, you could stick a chunk in their jaws and they'd shut up, but then it got worse.

"Once we were supposed to march all night. The scouts reported everything clear: 'It's all right,' they said, 'you can go on.' We got ready and marched off, the transports and the oxen in the middle. Those nights in the mountains—anyone that's been there'll tell you what it was like. Nothing could be worse. Nights black as pitch—you couldn't see a thing. We marched along without making any noise, only the pebbles would go rattling down, clear to the bottom. When you go along at night, what only don't you see! There seem to be people under the bushes all round you, waiting. People seem to be sitting in the trees. There's a big stone, and in the dark it also looks like a man. No matter how damned brave you are, you'll begin to shiver. It's terrible at night, and it's that way because you can't see where to shoot, and you don't know where to run to, as though you were encircled. Command? How can you command when you can't see anything! Just sit there until somebody knocks you over the head. It's different when you yourself attack—you kick up a racket, and then scoot back. But in the mountains, when you don't know anything, then what?

"So we marched and marched, and then someone up in front thought he saw the enemy. He fired, but nobody fired back. He fired again, and then things began to happen all by themselves—and worse and worse. It was narrow there and we were going single file. There was firing in front and firing behind, too. Then everybody began to run back down the mountain because chaps began to fall down dead, and you couldn't tell where the bullets were coming from. They began to run back and there were the transports and the oxen were stampeded and went galloping back down the mountain, too, smashing everything in their way. There was such a jam, you couldn't get by on horse or on foot. There was no other way, and so we began to climb over men and waggons. Those lower down the mountain thought it was the enemy coming down and opened up on them. They began running back and firing. They'd turn round and look up, and fire again. My God, the people that were killed! And what was the cause of it all? Nothing but panic—real panic that was. Whenever anybody says anything to you, whenever you see anything—you look close and make sure, don't begin shouting 'the enemy's coming!' "

"Why shout? Of course you mustn't shout," Shmarin chimed in, as though he didn't understand that this was meant for him. "It all comes from shouting."

"It's from shouting, all right," Chapayev muttered in an aside, puzzled at this manoeuvre of Shmarin's.

"I think there are situations," Fyodor interposed, "where it's impossible to stop a panic, simply impossible. No matter who you are, or what you do, you can't stop it. In the case you were telling about, for example."

"Yes, that was a real disaster," Chapayev agreed.

"A disaster. And we ourselves create these disasters," Fyodor developed his thought. "What we have to do is not to fight against panic after it comes, but before. We have to prevent panic. But how can you do it? The devil knows. Every case is something special. There in the Carpathians, it seems to me that special picked soldiers should have been sent ahead—and the reconnaissance should have been picked men, too; least apt to get scared at night. Then the number of shots and signals should have been agreed upon. And the men should have been told to fire only at an agreed signal, and not just when somebody took it into his head."

"It wasn't a case of signals, at all," Chapayev interrupted. "Signals—how are signals going to help you when the horses have stampeded, and the oxen? They shouldn't have been put in the middle. You can't do that at night. And then, in general, the march shouldn't have been made at night, at all."

"Why not? It could have been done very easily, if it had been organized."

"Oh, they organized it, all right," Shmarin laughed. "Couldn't have been better, the way they organized it."

His strange laughter and his ambiguous words put an end to the conversation. No one wanted to sleep or to sit there, and there was no need to stay any longer. It was just beginning to get light, but the night chill still made itself felt. It was quiet. The village had calmed down and gone back to sleep after the night alarm. Chapayev was waiting beside the porch while his horse was saddled. Fyodor saddled his own horse. In a few minutes they were riding back the way they had come the day before.

XII

FORWARD

Chapayev's Division was to by-pass Belebei to the north; other forces were assigned the task of taking the town. But it is a weakness of all commanders to head for the bigger places, and they are sure to talk about the part they played in capturing them.

In the Civil War, the destruction of enemy manpower was not always the immediate aim—more often the object was to take territory and particularly important, well-known towns. This, by the way, did not spring from purely military, but also from political motives. Every big centre, every big city, was at the same time the political centre of a more or less extensive territory around it, and its being occupied by the Whites or the Reds was by no means without influence on the political morale of the given territory. Inasmuch as politics was the prime mover in the Civil War, each side tried to capture the central points as quickly as possible.

Belebei was not a very important centre, but still it had some significance as a consolidating factor. The brigade forming the right flank of the Chapayev Division approached the town just at the time of the decisive attack, took part in it, and entered the town along with the neighbouring division. This caused a lot of loud talk and protests and arguments as to who had actually taken the town, had entered first and had manifested resourcefulness, heroism, ability, etc. There is never any end to such quarrels once two army units have simultaneously occupied some point. Chapayev took no part in the arguments; he left this to Potapov, the Brigade Commander, who fairly outdid himself in the art of diplomacy.

The regiments took up their positions to the north, along the Usen River, and waited. Here were the Reds, and across the river were the Whites. It was that way for several days. The units rested, recovered their strength, and prepared for the next attack. Chapayev cursed; he cursed continually, and in general was loud in his dissatisfaction, considering this halt along the Usen as criminal.

"Why this rest?" he shouted. "What fool tries to rest at the front? Who needs this rest? Maybe it's the staffs that need it," he jeered, hinting at possible treachery, at a deliberate slowing down of the swift and victorious advance of the Red troops. Actually, they were not advancing at a particularly rapid pace. What with halts and breathing-spells and preparations for regrouping, it came to around eight or ten versts a day on the average. There were people who got pleasure out of reckoning it up, and they gave Chapayev figures that made him rage.

"I'm not tired!" he would thunder, striking his fist on the table. "When I ask for a rest, then give it. But now we've got to advance. The enemy's on the run, and we've got to keep right on his tail, and not camp along the river."

"Well, but Vasily Ivanovich," they told him, "you're only talking about your own division. You're funny—what about the other divisions? We've got to even them up, relieve the men, bring up reinforcements; there's always lots of things that have to be done at the front. You can't just take your one division, and think that it'll do the whole business."

"Oh, won't it, though!" Chapayev exclaimed, his eyes flashing. "What kind of help is it I get from the side? As though anyone ever helped even the least bit. Like hell, they'll help. I'll take Ufa with one division, only don't interfere. Don't stick your nose in!"

"Who is it that isn't to stick his nose in?"

"Don't let anybody stick their nose in. I'll do the job myself," he answered, modifying his tone a little as though he realized that he had said too much.

Such quarrels, big and little, were frequent. All the way to Ufa, Chapayev was dissatisfied with the way the operation was going, although his division won victory after victory. It always seemed to him that he wasn't given sufficient scope for action, that his initiative was being pared down, that his advice was not listened to, and his opinion not taken into consideration.

"What can they see there—just a map," he would bluster within his own circle. "Well, we're fighting on the ground and not on a map. It's the ground we're fighting on, the devil take it!" he would shout, getting more and more incensed. "We see everything here and know everything ourselves. No need to tell us anything, only give us help."

"Again you've got it all wrong, Vasily Ivanovich," Klichkov tried to reason with him. "All the actions have got to be co-ordinated, got to be united."

"Unite them, then," Chapayev interrupted. "Who's stopping you? But I say don't interfere. We ought to be advancing on the double, and here we are celebrating some kind of a holiday on the Usen."

"Holiday! You don't know what you're saying," Fyodor retorted. "You've got into enough trouble by being in too much of a hurry. Experience has shown, that—"

"—that you have to sit down and wait, is that it?" Chapayev interrupted. "Along all the rivers, eh? When Kolchak is running for all he's worth? Well, you can fight that way if you like, but I'm not used to it. They thought up this idea of relieving the division—is this the moment, I ask you?" he grumbled. "Have the soldiers been complaining, been asking to be relieved? To hell with everything! I'll drop the whole thing and go back to commanding a detachment. There, when you plan something it's all yours, but here—" and he spat with feeling.

"So you're against being relieved," Klichkov kept trying to make him see reason. "You're a funny chap. You ought to understand that there are reasons for it—it wasn't for nothing they decided to do some reshuffling at such a time. Maybe the men are really worn out—at the end of their strength."

"Bah," and Chapayev made a gesture of disgust. "Nobody's tired. Yesterday I met a Red Army man in the woods. He was hobbling along alone, all bandaged up, a little chap, thin as a herring. 'What's this,' I asked, 'where are you off to?' 'Why, I'm going back to my unit.' 'Why are you limping?' 'I've been hit in the leg.' 'Why don't you let it heal up?' 'No time for that, Comrade,' he answered. 'No time now for resting, we've got to fight.' 'If they kill me,' he said, 'then I'll lie down in my grave—nothing to do there and my wound'll have time to heal.' And he was laughing all the time. When I looked at him, I thought, what the devil, that's a real hero.

I took the watch off my wrist and gave it to him. 'Here,' I said, 'wear it and remember Chapayev.' Evidently he hadn't recognized me right away. He perked up but wouldn't take the watch—kept waving it aside. Finally, he took it. I went my way. When I looked back he was still watching me. There's tired men for you. With tired men like that I'll lick the hell out of all Kolchak's troops."

"Yes, there are lots of them like that," Fyodor agreed. "Maybe even most of them, but just the same, even they can get worn out."

But to make Chapayev agree with this was extremely difficult. It didn't even help to refer to Frunze for whom Chapayev had the greatest respect.

"Well, but orders aren't given without Frunze knowing about it, are they? It isn't just the generals that sign them!"

"And if it's only them?" Chapayev protested somewhat enigmatically and in a low voice.

"How could that be?"

"Why, this way—Kolchak knows our orders before we do—that's how it is."

"Now, where did you get that from?" asked Fyodor in amazement. "Well, once in a while an order may get to Kolchak, but you can't make such sweeping conclusions, Vasily Ivanovich."

But it was useless to argue with him. Chapayev stuck to his opinion. When it came to "staffs" it was impossible to change his ideas—he mistrusted them to the end of his life.

Early one morning, Fyodor and Chapayev set out through greenwoods for Davlekanovo. They rode uphill and down, crossed crystal clear, spring-fed brooks, cantered through fragrant lanes of bird cherry. The road was sunny and peaceful, and full of the scents and sounds of a spring morning. From the woods, they rode out to the brigades and regiments of hungry, dirty, worn-out, lousy and badly clothed Red Army men.

The closer the Red Army got to Ufa, the more desperate was the resistance of the enemy troops. They clung to every convenient position, especially in the hills, concentrated handfuls of shock-troops and made counter-attacks. They were careful of their transports, sending them back before them in good time, and guarded with large detachments. Evidently they had no desire to furnish the Red Army with supplies.

Each day, it became more difficult to move forward. Wide-spread espionage was discovered. Kolchak had his agents working for him, and he had the kulaks and often Tatars, many of whom had been deceived by the story alleging that the Bolsheviks were fighting with the sole aim of taking away their Allah and destroying the mosques. There were instances when Red regiments were fired on from the windows when they entered Tatar villages. The firing was done not by the rich villagers but by the downright poverty-stricken. They were caught. What was done with them? It depended on the circumstances. Some were shot on the spot—no standing on ceremony in war-time. Some were turned over to the Tatars among the Red Army men to be "talked to." The Red Tatars soon explained to their fellow tribesmen what they were fighting for, and there were frequent cases when, after a short talk, the prisoner himself enlisted as a volunteer in the Red Army.

Spies were often caught.

At Davlekanovo, the Red Army men told Fyodor that there was some girl in the regimental baggage train, whom they had picked up along the road. She was asking to be taken nearer Ufa, and wanted to enter the city along with the Red Army. She said her mother and sister were in Ufa, and her kinfolk.

"Bring her to me," Klichkov ordered.

The girl was brought in. She was about nineteen, and walked with a limp. She said she had recently finished school. She was poorly dressed. She talked a lot about Ufa, and wanted to get there as quickly as possible. Nothing at all suspicious about her. Still, Fyodor felt instinctively that something was wrong though he had no reasons for it, no facts whatever to go on. He decided to test her, thinking. "If I'm mistaken, I risk nothing—I'll let her go and that's the end of it."

He talked with her for quite a while about various trifles and then suddenly rapped out:

"Were you wounded very long ago?"

"A long time ago—that is, no. What makes you think that I was wounded?"

"Because you limp," Fyodor said firmly and stared hard into her eyes.

Comrade Trallin, Head of the Army Political Department was sitting beside Fyodor silently observing this original interrogation.

"Well, yes," she said in confusion. "My leg was—but that was a long time ago—a very long time ago—"

Fyodor realized that he must ask his questions quickly and without stopping—stun her—not give her time to think out her answers and wriggle out of it.

"Where were you wounded, when?"

"I was carrying a paper to Headquarters."

"Was the fighting close?"

"Close."

"You worked in their Intelligence Service?"

"No, I didn't. I was a typist."

"You're lying!" he suddenly shouted. "See here—I know everything. D'you understand? Everything. Our agents have told me everything about you. Give me your identification paper, this minute. The one on the little thin paper, you know."

"On what paper?" she asked fearfully.

"Real thin paper—something like tissue paper—you know what I mean. Come on, now. Hurry up with it! Our agents know it was written for you. Hand it over!"

Fyodor's eyes bored into hers, and he himself was surprised at the unexpected effect. The girl was completely overcome with confusion when she heard about the little paper. It was known that all agents were given identification certificates on bits of the thinnest paper, to be hidden in the seams of their clothes, in hollowed-out heels, in their ears—in the most unimaginable places.

The girl pulled out a cigarette holder, unscrewed it three times and fished out a little paper rolled up and stuck to the barrel. The paper gave her surname, Christian name and patronymic.

It was a remarkable success. The girl was given an official questioning, first at Regimental and then at Army Headquarters. She was also questioned by Comrade Frunze who happened to be there at the time. The girl gave much valuable evidence, and declared, among other things, that certain Red agents were also working in the White Intelligence Service at one and the same time. The double-dealers were quickly eliminated. She gave much information that proved to be very useful.

There were several such incidents, though not as lucky and revealing ones. On one occasion, when a colonel's wife, suspected of espionage had been shut up in a bath-house (for want of a better place to keep her in), a clever Communist disguised as a White officer was shoved in, and the foolish woman blurted out a lot of valuable information.

The Red regiments were marching on Chishma. It was clear that they would have to pay a dear price for this important point which was the junction of two railway lines—Samara-Zlatoust and Volga-Bugulma. A dozen versts from the town, the trenches began—deep, even, and neatly finished; there were excellent dug-outs and secret passages into the valley, and detours around the hill. Whole groves of trees had been chopped down and places cleared off for cavalry ambushes. There were barbed wire entanglements intertwined like tropical lianas in front of the trenches. Nothing like this had been seen either at Buguruslan or at Belebei. Such substantial and well-dug trenches, in particular, had not been encountered for a long time. It was evident that the enemy had made thorough preparations.

It was Sizov's brigade that was advancing on Chishma—the Stepan Razin, Domashkin and Pugachov regiments. The last versts had been marked with uninterrupted fighting, which kept increasing in intensity. The nearer they got to Chishma, the more bitter were the engagements. Their attacks were repulsed and the enemy also made frequent counter-attacks.

Still, a feeling of doom was to be felt on the part of the enemy. Even his fiercest attacks lacked confidence in his strength, a striving to develop successes achieved, which alone ensures victory. It was as though the enemy was only trying to beat off attacks, and had no hope of coming out the victor.

Have you ever watched some wretched little dog tearing down the street, while hot on its tail comes a larger dog, more powerful and more confident, snapping at it and worrying it? The dog that is running away has lost all thought of really fighting—it can only try to beat off the larger dog. It bites, and even bites hard, but it can't put up a real fight. The little dog is running away and will be shamefully defeated. It was just such an impression of a little dog trying to beat off a larger one that the Kolchak forces gave already here at Chishma. The enemy made counter-attacks, but only, it seemed, to give the main forces and the transports time to withdraw. It was as though only rear-guards were in action. Actually, this was not the case.

The enemy's main forces were engaged. But they had lost the initiative at Buguruslan, and could not regain it now no matter how hard they tried.

Demoralization spread at an ever-increasing pace and proved fatal for the Kolchak army. No measures whatever—neither favours nor reprisals—could check this inevitable historical process. Apart from the general causes of decay which affected all the White armies more or less quickly, there were, in the case of the Kolchak army, special factors which greatly accelerated the process. In the first place, Kolchak carried out his mobilization of the population without the least discrimination, having regard for numbers rather than quality. In the second place, in his attempt to unite and cement this enormous mass of mobilized troops with a handful of loyal officers, he had no choice but to give these officers a free hand in meting out repressions against their own army. All the old abuses in the treatment of soldiers were resurrected in the Kolchak army, probably to a greater extent than in any other White army. The heterogeneity of the troops, and the brutality of the officers were the two causes which particularly hastened the decomposition within the Kolchak army.

After one battle, a whole heap of enemy documents fell into Klichkov's hands. Among them were telegrams, orders, instructions, and enquiries from the Kolchak command. For example: "All badly-trained troops are to be collected as soon as possible at one point, to be sent off by railway. *An officer* is to be assigned to accompany them, without fail." The italicized words are most eloquent; they indicate a mortal fear of their own "Christian troops."

But Kolchak's position was even more serious, still more tragic. It seemed that it was impossible to depend unreservedly on the officers either—at any moment they might sell out to the Red command. Here is an instance: Ten Red cavalrymen or so ran square into an enemy skirmish line—a hundred and twenty men and two officers, with one machine-gun. What could be easier, it would seem, than to take them prisoner or shoot them off their horses with one volley? However, what happened was this. The officers shouted to their men, "Don't you dare fire!" and ran out to meet the Red cavalrymen. They declared that they wanted to go over to the Reds with all their men. Note that this was in spite of all the stories about "Red atrocities" and Red Army ruthlessness towards White officers. These two officers were not afraid: they had made up their minds to go over, and did so. The cavalrymen, for their part, pleaded eloquently with their commanders for these officers, as if people who surrendered to the Reds of their own free will were in any particular danger.

One of the officers, it seemed, had been a clerk, the other a school teacher. They had much to tell about the "discipline" in the Kolchak army. Officers were shot for the slightest informality in speaking to soldiers. The observance of etiquette and caste distinctions was demanded, and enforced with the most brutal severity. Fear of their troops had deprived the High Command of all reason, and they saw deliberate and vicious "agitation" in the simplest and most natural conversation between an officer and a soldier. A process of fermentation was in progress among the lower ranking officers; the gulf between them and the senior officers was apparent and was widening every day.

The stories told by these officers were unquestionably true. Fyodor was convinced of this by what he had read in the documents mentioned above. "Lieutenant Vlasov is to be kept under observation," one of the orders of a division commander read. "The officers Markov, Zhuk and Lizentsov, who have been trying to talk with the soldiers, are to be kept under the strictest surveillance," so read another of his orders. There were also enquiries and statements concerning certain officers—all of the nature of espionage.

It was obvious that things were not going well with Kolchak if discipline was deteriorating even among the officers. A number of telegrams told of insubordination and disregard of orders. In order to maintain the army's "morale," the senior officers resorted to measures of very doubtful merit. They were beginning to appropriate the victories of the Red forces, and, in their orders and leaflets, to enumerate, as their own, points over which the Red Flag had been flying for a week at least. Their troops, of course, found out the truth and lost all belief in their reports—even when they were unquestionably veracious.

In a word, there was no doubt that the Kolchak army was falling to pieces. The Red troops did everything possible to speed up this process. Cart loads of propaganda literature were hauled to the enemy rear; millions of appeals and open letters and leaflets of all kinds were distributed by the population, or dropped from aeroplanes, or scattered by Red agitators. These last penetrated into the very thick of the White soldiery and there, fearlessly and quite openly carried on their heroic work.

Nevertheless, in spite of all this, the fighting was so bitter and fierce at times as to belie all assumptions that decay had set in within the White army. It was the most steadfast of the White regiments that fought in these stubborn battles. There were but few of them in relation to the general mass of the army, but they fought magnificently, and they were magnificently equipped.

At the approaches to Chishma, the fighting was so heavy that in some of the companies of the Red regiments, only thirty or forty men were left. The Red troops fought desperately, with frenzy, with inspiration. Armed only with hand grenades, they threw themselves on armoured trains until the track was carpeted with their dead. They ran after the monsters shouting "Hurrah!" and pelting them with their deadly missiles. When armoured cars approached, the skirmish lines threw themselves flat on the ground and lay there without raising their heads. They saved themselves by following the axiom that "an armoured car can't hit a person who's lying down!" The armoured car would plough through their lines, cruise about in their rear, fire at everything in sight, but with little effect, and then, as it turned to make off, they would run after it, the same as after the armoured trains, and shower it with hand grenades. Their heroism bordered on madness. Many were the Red warriors laid low at Chishma by the machine-guns of the armoured trains and the armoured cars.

And twenty minutes after the battle was finally over, when the smoke still hung over the battle-field, and the air was filled with the groans of the wounded, both friend and foe, as they were carried away, Chishma awoke to the life usual in such cases. The peasants, who had been terrified by the shooting, came crawling out of basements and cellars, sheds and barns, ovens and hearths, from under the floors and from under the roofs, and began fussing about the exhausted Red Army men. The peasant women began to bustle about with their buckets knocking together, and their cups and spoons and dishes and pots clattering; the samovars began to sing. From the huts came the hum of conversation. The Red Army men were telling about how things had been going with them, recounting what they had seen, heard or experienced, what they had got out of it and what they were hoping for. When they had had something to eat and had drunk their tea, some of them began to play leap-frog, and one might have thought that these lads had got together not

after a battle, but from neighbouring villages for the feast day of their patron saint.

In the evening, the choir of the Stepan Razin Regiment gathered together to sing. There were about twenty-five men in it. Many had excellent voices, but what with the marching and the fighting, they never had time to rehearse. However, they were so fond of singing that at every halt, if there was the least chance of a breathing space, the singers at once gathered in a knot about their leader, and the singing would begin. Others who wanted to sing too would come up and surrounded the chorus until almost half the regiment was there. Now it was impossible for the choir to sing alone. They struck up a song which everyone knew, and then all began to sing together. They sang all kinds of songs, but mostly about Stepan Razin and Yermak. There were also lively dance songs. Someone singing a fanciful falsetto, winking slily and arching his brows coquettishly, would lead off in the highest possible pitch:

Oh, you Dunyushka, Dunya!
Oh, you Dunyushka, Dunya!

Then the chorus joined in a mighty wave of sound:

Oh, you Dunya, Dunya, Dunya,
Dunya, Dunyushka, Dunyasha.

They clapped in time with the song, and stamped their heels, but this was just the beginning. At the second verse, they couldn't contain themselves any longer, and as soon as the chorus blared out:

Oh, you Dunya, Dunya, Dunya—

two or three dancers would jump into the middle and begin to stamp it out for all they were worth. They danced until they were giddy and almost fainting. After them others, and still others.

Singing was not enough; an accordion would appear. Often, the dancing and the accordion crowded out the chorus, but this was mostly because the singers had sung themselves hoarse.

The regimental "intelligentsia"—the commissaries, the quartermaster-sergeants, and the clerks—danced with particular frenzy, but the battalion and company commanders were not to be outdone. They, too, were brave dancers.

They changed over from singing to dancing, and then back to singing, at frequent intervals. They would sing until they could sing no more, and then begin to dance. They would dance till they were exhausted, and then begin to sing again. And this went on as long as their legs and their throats held out.

During the last few months, two new songs had become popular, particularly the refrains, and they were sung with the greatest animation and enthusiasm. The tunes were old but the words were new. The new words to the refrain of the first song went this way:

> *So louder, music, and we'll sing of vict'ry,*
> *We've won and the foe's on the run, the run, the run.*
> *For the Council of People's Commissars,*
> *We'll give a loud Hurrah, Hurrah, Hurrah!*

The refrain of the second song was a favourite with the whole Red Army:

Bravely to battle we'll go for the Soviet power,
And as one we'll lay down our lives for the cause.

The words of the verses were of no particular significance and not much attention was paid to them; a really good song had still to make its appearance, but as to the refrain—why, the way the refrain was sung was magnificent.

"Now let's have 'Eternal memory,' " someone in the crowd proposed.

The singers exchanged significant glances.

"Shall we?"

"Why not?"

"Somebody start off the chant!"

A very tall, stoop-shouldered, pock-marked fellow pushed his way forward. He took his stand in the middle, and without any further preliminaries began to intone hoarsely in a deep bass:

"A prosperous and peaceful life, health, salvation and success in all our undertakings, confusion and destruction of our enemies, give us, O God!"

He stopped and looked around, as though saying, "Well, now it's your turn," and those standing around whined out the response:

"Go-o-o-d ha-a-a-a-ve mer-r-rcy."

"To the All-Russian Socialist Red Army, with its leader and comrade Lenin," he chanted on in his booming voice; "to the valiant command of the Twenty-Fifth Infantry Division, and to all the Two Hundred and Eighteenth Regiment named after Stepan Razin, lo-o-o-n-n-ng year-r-r-r-r-s!"

"Long years," the chorus thundered after him.

"To the artillerymen, cavalrymen, telephonists, motor cyclists, machine-gunners, mortar-men, hand-grenademen, aeroplane pilots, scouts, infantrymen, orderlies, cooks, butchers and all the transport men, lo-o-o-n-n-ng year-r-r-r-r-s!"

Again they came in with "long years"—in unison, jolly and loud. Their faces were all gay and wreathed in smiles; their eyes proudly and triumphantly proclaimed: "We didn't get this song from somewhere; we made it up ourselves in our own regiment!"

The chap leading the chant dragged out in a lower and still more solemn tone:

"Eternal peace in blessed sleep bestow, O God, on the Siberian supreme ruler, and oppressor of all the toilers, His High Excellency, the White admiral, Kolchak, and all his God-fearing flock—Jesuit metropolitans, bishops and archbishops, bandits, spies, and agents, officials, and gold shoulder-strappers, and all his worshippers, White Kolchakites, deceived lads, and hangers-on and toad-eaters, the Czechoslovak gentlemen, eter-r-r-nal-l-l peac-c-ce!"

The chorus struck up a funeral hymn—nasal and off pitch. It was enough to make one sick, as though it really smelled of something dead.

"To all counter-revolutionaries," the leader interrupted, as he began the last verse, "to the imperialists, capitalists, White Socialists of all kinds, careerists, monarchists and other adventurists, traitors and distillers, speculators and wreckers, marauders, deserters, and big-bellied bankers, to all such sons-of-bitches, eter-r-r-nal peac-c-c-ce!"

The chorus and all standing round chimed in with "eternal peace" after him. When they had finished, they stood a few minutes silent and motionless, as though waiting for applause. The regiment was extremely proud of this canticle, and liked to sing it. Sometimes it was performed three or four times at a stretch.

They kept up their singing and dancing until late at night, even though the next day they would have to be on the march when it was hardly light. It meant nothing that they had slept little: their stride was as quick and as light as ever.

Chishma was considered the key to Ufa. Now the road was open. There was every reason to believe that the enemy would withdraw across the Belaya River, and that the strongest resistance would be met with on the far bank.

The Red troops pressed on still faster, still more stubbornly in pursuit of the retreating Kolchak army.

"Now we'll capture Ufa sure," said Chapayev, "if only the right side doesn't let us down." He had in mind the division operating on the right flank.

"Why are you so sure?" the others asked him.

"Why, there's no place for Kolchak to get a foothold, he'll have to retreat to Siberia."

"Well, we hung on at Samara," they objected, "and how we did run!"

"We hung on," he agreed. "What of it?" He hesitated, not knowing how this was to be explained, trying to think of an explanation, but couldn't. Then he added: "We hung on—that's another thing—he's not going to. We're going to take Ufa."

This confidence in victory was common to the majority, and particularly to the rank-and-file Red Army men. Whenever the question of immediate possibilities and military prospects happened to be discussed in the regiments, only days and hours came into consideration. Nothing was ever said about man-power, about the enemy's equipment, the training of the enemy troops, and their powers of resistance. They calculated in this fashion:

"Tuesday morning, we'll be at that village, and by evening, we'll get to the river. If the bridge hasn't been blown up, we'll cross that night; otherwise we'll be held up till morning. By Wednesday evening we should get to such and such a place, and by Thursday, etc., etc."

It was as though they were on the march with no enemy before them, so nicely did they calculate the days and hours when the various points should be reached. It was seldom that they were mistaken in their calculations; they usually arrived before the time set. Ufa itself was taken before the date indicated in their time-table.

The rapidity of the advance and the endurance of the Red Army men were at times astounding. They recognized no limits and refused to admit that anything could check them. The fight at Chishma, when the Red Army men threw themselves on the armoured trains with their hand grenades, demonstrated that next to nothing could bar their way.

Decorations, sent in for the victory at Chishma, were to be distributed among the regiments. But complications arose: one of the valiant regiments that had especially distinguished itself in the fighting refused to accept the decorations. The Red Army men and the commanders who had been awarded decorations declared that all of them, the whole regiment, had in equal measure honestly and bravely defended the Soviet Republic, and that there were neither good nor bad among them, let alone cowards, since the lads themselves would have made short work of such. "We don't want any decorations," they declared, "in our regiment we'll all be equals." In those days such incidents were a very common occurrence. The transports of feeling, the heights of enthusiasm, were truly something to marvel at. The Red Army men looked on the matter of decorations quite simply, naïvely, and absolutely unselfishly.

"Why should I stand out? I'd rather be like everybody else. In what way is my mate worse or better than I? If he's worse, let's pull him up till he's even, if he's better, then pull me up, that's all."

In the Pugachov Regiment, some three hundred of the men had organized an original "commune" in 1918. Everything was owned in common—clothes and shoes and all other property. Each put on what he needed most at the moment. Their pay and everything received from home was also pooled. In battle, this group was distinguished by its solidarity. By now, of course, the group had all been killed or wounded, because its bravery had been something extraordinary.

The refusal of one of the regiments to accept decorations was simply a more striking manifestation of the scorn for distinction which was characteristic of the whole division, including the commanders and political workers, large and small. On the same day, the comrades in the Political Department got together and asked Klichkov, who was in complete agreement with them, to send a protest to the Central Committee of the Party against the system of awarding decorations, and to lay down their views on this question. After some discussion, the following letter was drafted and sent:

"Dear Comrades,
"When we began to distribute decorations among one of our valiant regiments, the men began to protest, and refused to accept the decorations, declaring that they had all fought with equal bravery for the Soviet power and would continue to do so. Therefore they wanted no marks of distinction but desired to remain on the same level with the other men in their regiment This great scrupulousness has forced us Communists to think seriously about the whole system of awarding decorations which has been instituted in the Red Army. It is never possible to select the most deserving, since it is impossible to set up one single criterion of merit. One man may display great initiative; another, great foresight, so saving hundreds of lives; a third, courage, cool-headedness and tenacity; a fourth, reckless bravery; a fifth, a capacity for systematic, painstaking work towards raising the efficiency of the units; etc., etc. Can any such enumeration be complete?
"To tell the truth, decorations are often awarded without proper discrimination. There have been cases when they were distributed by drawing lots; there have been cases of fighting and bloody clashes because of them. In our opinion, decorations have a most pernicious and destructive effect. They arouse envy, even hatred, among the best Red Army men, and give food for every sort of suspicion, shallow gossip, and idle discussion to the effect that we're going back to the old ways, and so on.
"Decorations incline the weak to abasement, flattery, and servile attempts to ingratiate themselves. We have not heard one person who has been decorated say that he was overjoyed by it, or that he valued or esteemed it highly. Quite the contrary. All the commanders and men with whom we have spoken have been indig-

nant and have protested against the awarding of decorations. It goes without saying that if decorations continue to be sent, they will be distributed, but if the whole system is done away with, believe us, no one will regret it, but will rejoice and will breathe more freely."

That was the letter sent to the Central Committee of the Party. No answer was ever received.

The letter contains much that is naïve and much that is incorrect. The approach to the question is not statesman-like; the feeling and kindness expressed are somewhat mawkish, but still it is all sincere, open-hearted, and very much in the spirit of the times.

In a few days, another letter was sent to the Central Committee, and after that, a third, but we'll speak of this last letter a little later.

The second letter was couched in the same terms as the first, and dealt with the new rates of pay. The fact was that during the march on Ufa, the general situation in respect to food supplies was fairly good, except for brief periods of shortage, since in cases of extreme need, food could be got from the population. The army went hungry only when something went wrong with the supplies, and the regiments were advancing rapidly through territory that had been devastated, where everything had been burned or otherwise destroyed. There, it was hard going indeed.

It often happened at the front that there was absolutely nothing to spend money on, and it was simply a burden to those who had no special thirst for hoarding. In those months and years of great spiritual uplift and most profound moral sensibility, there was a high degree of scrupulousness even among people occupying the highest posts and even in respect to the most trivial matters and occasions.

A commissar would dress simply, like ordinary Red Army men; he ate from the same kettle as they did, rubbed elbows with them on the march, and always tried to be the first to lay down his life in battle. It was thus that the best ones deported themselves. Knaves that appeared in the army by chance—people out for their own interests, cowards, and people unfit in general for such an exceptional situation—why, they quickly disappeared. They were driven out, or were transferred, or simply deserted, legally or otherwise. The great prestige of the Communists in the army was not won easily. In the most difficult situations, in the most critical operations, it was the Communists that went first and that were committed most often. We know of cases when of the fifteen or twenty people killed or wounded in some brush with the enemy, one-half or three-fourths were Communists.

And so we repeat: at that time there was a great trend towards "leveling," one might even say it was the general rule. There were frequent instances when commanders or commissars refused to accept special rates of pay, and turned over the difference to the regimental fund, being content to receive only what the rank-and-file Red Army men did. This desire for "levelling" was so great that one day Fyodor and Chapayev quite seriously discussed the question of finding a way to force the whole division to go over to the Russian familiar form of address. What led to this discussion was the following.

The higher-ups almost always used the familiar form when addressing Red Army men. This was not from any feeling of contempt, but because they, naturally enough, looked on the formal manner of address as a piece of fashionable etiquette, entirely superfluous in the stern and harsh atmosphere of battle. At such times "polite" conversation seemed even ridiculous in a way; in those days, at least, it was out of place. The commanders and the commissars were themselves either workers or peasants; they talked with the Red Army men as simply as they had been accustomed all their lives to talk to their mates at the factory or in their village. What drawing-room politeness had there ever been there? They talked to the men simply and were answered in kind.

In the regiment, in general, almost all the people were accustomed to using the familiar form in addressing one another. But at levels higher than the regimental, the picture was different. There, the familiar form was used when speaking to the men, but the men themselves were a little hesitant when it came to answering in the same way. So it was on the question of "levelling" that Fyodor and Chapayev had a talk. They discussed and cogitated and made assumptions, but could not arrive at any final decision.

Imagine now what happened when it became known in the division that the pay of everyone except the rank-and-file had been raised. The first to protest were the political workers themselves. They protested because they really did not want to be distinguished from the men, and because reproaches and suspicions were usually showered on them more than on anyone else. In such cases they were told: "Look how it goes: in words, equality and fraternity, but in deeds, what?"

These remarks, primitive as they were and of such common occurrence, should not have disconcerted them, it would seem; they should have got used to them; but actually, this was not the case. The political workers, themselves the same Red Army men as all the others, were indignant, and frequently not only tried to soothe the regiments in such cases, but took it upon themselves to "communicate" with the authorities—to "protest," and so on.

When the new pay rates became known, all the regiments were in a turmoil. At the Political Department, protests began to pour in. During his trips to the various units of the division, Fyodor never heard the end of these "exorbitant pay rates." Only it is not to be thought that the rise was by any means large; on the contrary, it was the merest crumb, but in those days, crumbs seemed whole loaves.

At that time, a division Party Conference was called for a short and speedy discussion of a number of questions arising from their approaching Ufa. At this conference, Klichkov was again asked to send a protest to the Central Committee, and learning that the majority of the commanders were of the same opinion, he sent another epistle:

"Dear Comrades,

"I am writing to you on behalf of the political workers of our division and the more conscientious commanders. We are highly displeased and indignant over the new pay rates which have been instituted. They are exorbitant—incredibly high. What do we need money for? In our circumstances, it leads to nothing but corruption Leaving out of consideration the fall in the purchasing power of the ruble and the rapid rise in prices of food and other things, we ourselves are being taught to swagger and play the gentleman and throw money around, or to hoard up big sums, and to become misers. At the same time, not a kopek has been added to the men's pay. Does the Party know about this? Are alien elements trying to sow discord between the Red Army men and us? The indignant murmur of the Red Army is becoming more and more audible. Perhaps high salaries are needed on the Petrograd Front, and the other fronts where there is famine, but why do we need them here, where bread and butter is to be had almost for the asking? Perhaps it would be better to divide the front into belts. We are even striving to level the pay of all political workers with that of the Red Army men, and here we are being given new increases. A wolf, to paraphrase a Russian proverb, will never be satisfied no matter how much you feed him, but as to us, no extra feeding is necessary—no one could make us stop fighting even if we were hungry."

This letter also creates an impression more of warm sincerity than of serious thought, and in places the colours are laid on too thick. For example, the phrases about "swaggering and playing the gentleman." What swaggering could there be at the front, what playing the gentleman on the march and in battle?

The rise in pay was only enough to effect a very slight improvement in the position of the political workers and commanders over the men, and these "phrases" are of course to be understood only as "eloquence." And then, as to the Central Committee. Why, after all, should the enquiry have been sent directly there and not to the Army, not to the institutions of the Front, not to the central organs of the Red Army? Why, because it was considered that this was obviously a general question, and not one concerning only the division or the Army. And then, belief in the Central Committee was most profound—reverential, one might say, and they were so convinced of the successful outcome of their message that they even expected an immediate answer.

An example of their naïveté, by the way, was the postscript to their letter to the Central Committee, which gives the impression of something tacked on without rhyme or reason. This postscript spoke of the meagre resources at their disposal for putting on plays and performances in the army. It concluded with these words:

"It is necessary to bring pressure to bear in the proper quarter to have collections of fresh plays, valiant songs, and genuinely artistic works in prose and verse created—to get them born. If such collections have already been published, we haven't seen any Rush them to the front as quickly as possible."

Here, we have not only belief in the omnipotence of the Central Committee, but also complete despair of getting anything from the higher organs of the army. How naïve they were at the front then not to realize that it was impossible to order literary collections to be "created"—they must be conceived, have time to come to completion and be born in the regular order, and at the normal time. But there was neither time nor patience to wait for the normal "birth" of literary collections. Not seeing any other way out, people raised all manner of questions wherever they could see a chance of getting results. Much of the time there was no co-ordination in the work; there was much wrangling, unnecessary interference, and unnecessary taking of offence, frequent threats and reprisals.

Take, for example, the "woman question" in the Red Army. What only wasn't said, or written in connection with this question; what only orders weren't issued, and what came of it all? Actually, in all cases it always boiled down to the same "use your judgment." Instructions had been issued, though not always officially and openly, to remove from the army all wives, and women in general. There were serious reasons for this "purge." It was not only commanders and commissars that had wives—whole flocks of them followed the regiments of Red Army men, many of them with their household goods, others with children. All this enormous "army of the rear" was carried by government vehicles. Only think what an array of peasant waggons were constantly employed in the most unproductive work! Then, there were other considerations. As might have been expected, the women were in one way or another the cause of various rows, serious and trivial. In the army this was absolutely inevitable. How could it be otherwise when for months and years the army was forced to live its own peculiar, isolated life, shut off from much that was absolutely necessary? Then, too, it was often women, and in particular wives, that were responsible for the fact that men devoted much of their time to personal matters having nothing to do with the life of an army on the march. Finally, it was among women that spies and agents were often found. In a word, there were many reasons for the issuing of special orders and instructions concerning women.

But what a hornet's nest was stirred up when these instructions began to be carried out! First of all, the regiments were thrown into an uproar, especially when they heard that the women at Division Headquarters were to be left where they were. Finally, they were more or less calmed down. Then the purge of the various organs was begun, but it was discovered there that to eliminate the women workers was something entirely different from removing several hundred Red Army men's wives. How could women workers that were needed be removed, especially when there was really no one to take their place? How, and why, should the women medical orderlies be removed from the regiments, or the heroic Red Army women who fought shoulder to shoulder with the men and died with them in battle? Why remove the women political workers, the nurses and doctor's assistants, who were so few and so necessary? But orders were often issued categorically, and they were understood literally and enforced to the letter.

One day, several Red Army women, former weavers, ran up to Fyodor all out of breath, and begged him to intervene on their behalf because they were being turned out of their regiment. They hurriedly told him that there had been four "shameless" ones among them, but the others had refused to have anything to do with them and had driven them out of the regiment. Klichkov had to ride to Regimental Headquarters himself and explain that the women should not be expelled. It can well be imagined what a vexed question it was when even the division authorities were often in a quandary as to how to act.

Sizov's brigade took Chishma by a sudden, swift blow, seizing it from under the nose of Potapov's brigade which had been entrusted with the operation. Potapov's regiments had been marching past Lake Leli-Kul, steadily advancing up the Dyoma River, and when Chishma fell, he was quite near.

At the front, it often happens that a small victory filched from another is the cause of a great catastrophe. Some commander is carried away with himself, and striving for the effect of a sudden strong blow, appropriates part of the task assigned to another, so mixing up everything with his victory. It would have been better if he had not won it. A victory does not always mean success, and may have serious consequences.

Say that a deep flanking operation is planned with the idea of encircling and capturing an entire enemy grouping. If some hothead makes a frontal attack on the enemy and frightens him, he will throw everything out of gear and through his partial victory will inevitably do harm to the entire operation which, being on a greater scale, is of far more significance. This might have been the result now, when Sizov burst into Chishma leaving enemy regiments in his rear along the Dyoma River. They could have mauled him thoroughly if Potapov had not come up with his brigade in time. Mutual assistance was the order of the day in the Chapayev Division, and every unit quickly and resolutely came to the aid of any other unit which had got into difficulties. However, this was not always and the case; sometimes the reverse was observed, which inevitably led to grave consequences.

As soon as Potapov understood the situation, he immediately attacked, and engrossed the enemy's entire attention; taking advantage of the confusion in the enemy's ranks, he kept pressing him back towards the river. The artillery duel was so intense that three guns were put out of action. The enemy was driven back across the Dyoma. On retreating he blew up all the bridges, evidently having no hopes of returning, and tore off, forced march, for the Belaya River.* There were no halts of any consequence; Chishma was the last point that the enemy

---

* The river on which Ufa is situated —*Ed.*

had had any hopes of holding this side of Ufa. From now on, it was apparent that the enemy's mood had changed radically and for good—from now on, there was only an orderly retreat. He made no more attempts on this bank of the Belaya to achieve the "turning-point" for which he had been hoping, just as the Red Command had once hoped for the turning-point at Buzuluk and Buguruslan.

XIII

UFA

The enemy regiments and army corps retreated across the Belaya to the Ufa side, blowing up all the bridges, and took up positions along the high bank, which was soon bristling with their bayonets, the muzzles of guns and the barrels of machine-guns. Big forces were concentrated there. Kolchak did not want to lose the Ufa sector, and from the heights along the right bank of the Belaya, he commanded the positions of the Red divisions advancing from various directions.

The Red Command had planned to take Ufa by encirclement. The divisions on the right flank were assigned the task of advancing to the Arkhangelsky Works in the enemy's rear, but difficulties with transport prevented them from putting even a single Red Army man across the Belaya before the other divisions had advanced to the very bank.

The Chapayev Division took up its position opposite Ufa. Its right flank, formed of Potapov's brigade, rested on the enormous bridge flung high over the river straight to the city. The left flank curved around to Krasny Yar, a small village some twenty-five versts down the Belaya, which had been reached by Shmarin's and Sizov's brigades.

When the regiments at Krasny Yar crossed the river and advanced on the city, they were to be supported by

Potapov's brigade which was to cross at the bridge. The enormous iron bridge was still intact, but no one believed that the enemy had left it untouched. He was sure to have mined it, and therefore the crossing must not be made by it. The railway line leading down from a high embankment and across the bridge had been taken apart in places, and waggons loaded with gravel and rubbish had been shunted on to the middle of the bridge. At first, there was absolutely no way of getting across the river here; it was only later that the Red Army men got together a few boats from somewhere or other and dragged up beams and boards, which were tied together to form makeshift, portable rafts.

However, it was planned to deliver the main blow from Krasny Yar. When Vikhor's cavalry darted out on to the bank not far from Krasny Yar, a tug and two small steamers were proceeding calmly up the Belaya. The people on board were of the most motley types, though the majority, of course, were army men, some thirty of them officers. Their unconcern was amazing, incomprehensible. It was as though they were completely ignorant of the fact that the Red regiments were so close, and had no idea of the possibility of an attack from the bank. The Red cavalrymen simply gaped when they saw the "gentlemen" with shoulder straps on board. At first, the officers did not realize what was up, either. They must have taken the cavalry for their own.

"Halt!" came the command from the bank.

"Why halt?" was shouted back from the steamboats.

"Stop the boats, or we'll open fire! Pull up to shore!" shouted the cavalrymen. But those on board realized what had happened and tried to increase their speed, hoping to get to some swamps where the cavalry could not approach the bank. As soon as the cavalrymen saw this, they roared threateningly:

"Halt! Halt!"

The boats steamed on. The first shots rang out from their decks. The cavalrymen returned the fire. An unequal battle began. A machine-gun was rushed up and began its rat-tat-tat. People on the boats began to scream, and rush headlong below deck, hiding wherever they could. The boats were brought to the bank. The officers did not want to be taken alive—most of them shot themselves or threw themselves into the water. These little river boats were a real windfall; later they were an enormous help in ferrying the Red regiments across the river, and at once eased the difficulties in which the Red Command found themselves. The steamers were hidden to keep the enemy from discovering that such a treasure had fallen into the hands of the Reds.

Two days before the attack was launched, Frunze, Chapayev and Fyodor arrived by motor car, and at once called a council of the commanders and commissars in order to get a clear, detailed picture of the situation, to weigh and take into account all eventualities, and again, and once again weigh their forces and their chances of success.

Frunze had an original method that was of great help to him in unravelling the most confused and complicated matters. He would call an informal council of all those concerned and would face them with the most vital questions, deferring for the time being consideration of secondary matters. He would bring their various interests into collision, arouse discussion and direct it along the desired channel. When the council was over, it only remained for Frunze to assess the chances revealed, sum them up, co-ordinate them, and so come to the logical conclusion. This would seem to be a very simple method, but it is not everyone who can apply it. However, Frunze was a master hand at it.

When the division heads now gathered at Krasny Yar, it was necessary to take into consideration not only the equipment and the number of effectives in the various regiments, but their fighting qualities, especially with reference to the present exceptional situation. The choice fell on the Ivanovo-Voznesensk weavers regiment in Shmarin's brigade. There was good reason for this choice. The regiments in Sizov's brigade had covered themselves with immortal glory. In a purely military respect they occupied one of the first places in the division, but at the present moment class consciousness was extremely important, as selfless daring alone might prove insufficient. The Red weavers came up to this requirement.

The council was over. They jumped on their horses and galloped towards the river to the place where the crossing was to commence. They left their horses half a verst from the bank, and went down the sandy slope on foot. They looked towards the opposite bank, expecting the enemy to open fire at any minute, but all was quiet. They climbed on to a hill, and from there examined the other bank through their field-glasses. They selected the exact spot for the crossing, and came to final agreement on all details. Then they rode back. Soon the two little steamboats were sent to the place where it was planned to cross—the tug had run aground. They began to load fuel and to knock together landing-stages.

The attack had been held up for a day, but now the decisive hour was near. Before they parted, it was decided that Chapayev himself would be in command of the crossing at Krasny Yar, while Fyodor would go back to the bridge where Potapov's brigade had taken up positions, and would direct operations there until the city was captured.

Since evening fell there had been great activity on the river-bank at Krasny Yar, but the absence of all noise was unusual for such occasions. People hurried to and fro like shadows; groups formed, then melted away and disappeared, again formed and again disappeared. This was the Ivanovo-Voznesensk Regiment preparing for the crossing. The little steamers were packed so full that there was no room to move. The steamers would carry one load across and come back for others; they would carry these across, and again return for more. In this way, the whole regiment was silently ferried across the river in the inky darkness. It was now long after midnight, and dawn was approaching.

The Red batteries at Krasny Yar opened fire. They began to shell the enemy's front-line trenches, which closed the loop formed here by the course of the river. Several dozen guns were firing at once. The range had been determined beforehand, and the results of the shelling were soon apparent. It was senseless to remain in the trenches under such fire, and the enemy troops began to waver, and then to run in disorder for the second line of trenches. As soon as this was reported, the artillery ceased firing and the men of the Ivanovo-Voznesensk Regiment, who had come up by now, charged, and drove the enemy back as far as the settlement of Noviye Turbasli. The enemy was retreating in panic, unable to hold on anywhere.

The Ivanovo-Voznesensk lads entered Noviye Turbasli on the heels of the fleeing Whites. There they had to wait until reinforcements were ferried across the river. It was extremely dangerous for a single regiment to push on. They consolidated their positions in the settlement. Meanwhile the Pugachov Regiment was advancing along the shore towards Alexandrovka.

The Stepan Razin and Domashkin regiments were being loaded on to the boats. They were immediately to go to the assistance of the regiments that had gone before them. Four armoured cars were ferried across, but three of them immediately overturned, and lay stranded on the

highway. Later, they were raised by the cavalrymen, and put on their feet and sent into action.

By this time, the enemy, who had been driven uphill had recovered, and began to attack the Ivanovo-Voznesensk Regiment. It was already seven or eight o'clock in the morning. In driving the enemy beyond Noviye Turbasli, and in holding their positions in the settlement and beating off sham attacks, the Ivanovo-Voznesensk men had shot off all their cartridges, and now they were left almost with empty hands and without any hope of having any ammunition brought up soon. They recalled the order given by Sizov, who commanded the entire group that had been thrown across the river:

"Don't retreat. Remember, there's only your bayonets in reserve!"

It was a fact that nothing was left to the weavers now but their bayonets. And now, when instead of sham attacks, the enemy launched a genuine, all-out attack, the lines wavered, and unable to withstand the charge, began to fall back. At this time, the regiment was commanded by Burov who had been transferred here from his post as commissar. His commissar was Nikita Lopar. They galloped along the flanks, shouting for the men to stop retreating, because there was no place to retreat to. Behind them was the river, and it was impossible to take them across. They must stop, hold firm, beat off the attack. And the Red Army men who had begun to waver were pulled up short. At this moment, several horsemen galloped up to the skirmish lines and sprang to the ground. It was Frunze, and with him, Trallin, head of the Army Political Department, and several of their close associates. Frunze seized a rifle, and ran forward shouting, "Hurrah! Hurrah! Comrades, forward!!!" All the men standing close by recognized him. The news ran down the lines like lightning. The men were seized with wild enthusiasm, and threw themselves forward in a furious charge. It was an unforgettable moment. They charged the advancing mass with only their bayonets, shooting very rarely, because there was little ammunition. And so great is the power of heroic enthusiasm that now the enemy lines began to waver, and then turned and fled.

Sizov had told his orderlies to keep close to Frunze, ordering them: "If he's killed, bring his body away whatever you do. Bring it here to the crossing, to the boat!"

Carts of ammunition were being rushed up from the river. As soon as the skirmish lines lay down beyond Noviye Turbasli, carriers crawling on their bellies got the cartridges to the men.

When Trallin ran forward with the others, a bullet struck him in the breast. He was lifted up and helped off the field. Now, the Order of the Red Banner glows on his breast over the spot where once was the tiny wound that might well have proved fatal.

They had turned the tide, and recovered their positions. Frunze left the regiment and rode off with Sizov to the Pugachov Regiment. They climbed on to hillocks and ridges, and studied the surrounding country. They discussed how best to develop the operation, again and again referred to their maps, comparing every dot with what they saw here in reality. The Pugachov Regiment continued to advance along the shore. The Stepan Razin and Domashkin regiments began to come up, and took up positions along the highway. At noon, the order was given for a general attack. The Pugachov Regiment was to continue up the bank; the Stepan Razin and Domashkin regiments were to advance in the centre, while the Ivanovo-Voznesensk Regiment was to advance from the extreme left flank. It had by this time occupied Stariye Turbasli, and had halted there, resting. Just then what appeared to be columns of enemy troops came into view. They were moving from the north across the front of the Ivanovo-Voznesensk Regiment, threatening a blow against the centre of the group which was preparing to attack.

"It might be a herd of cattle," some of the men surmised.

"What kind of a herd is it, when you can see the bayonets flashing?" others objected.

It is impossible to say whether or not they could see bayonets flashing, but all finally agreed that it was enemy regiments advancing, and that very much depended on the ensuing battle. Frunze wanted to take part in this action also, but Sizov prevailed on him to go to the crossing to speed up the work of ferrying across the regiments of another division. Everybody agreed that that would be better and Frunze galloped off to the crossing. Soon his horse was killed under him, and he himself was severely shell-shocked by a detonation close by. But he did not leave the work there on the river-bank. He supervised it and hurried things up.

Part of the artillery was sent across. The first battery to go into action was that of Khrebtov, who took up his position behind the skirmish lines of the Ivanovo-Voznesensk Regiment. During the first enemy attack, when the men froze in a condition of almost crazed, paralyzed expectation, Khrebtov's guns opened fire. The men, hearing their own battery, took heart, and charged the enemy.

It proved impossible to develop the attack. The whole weight of the enemy masses moving from the north was hurled against the Stepan Razin and Domashkin regiments. The enemy's numerical superiority was too great for the Red Army men to beat off this onslaught. The Razin men wavered and began to fall back. One battalion was thrown into disorder. Here there were few seasoned fighters; most of the men were green new-comers. This battalion abandoned its position and ran headlong for the river-bank, followed by some of the men in the other battalions. The others slowly retreated, fighting, hard-pressed by the enemy. The Ivanovo-Voznesensk Regiment had halted at Turbasli. Now, part of the enemy formations were turned against them. Sizov galloped up to Khrebtov.

"The Stepan Razin Regiment is retreating—got to help them! Turn your guns round and shell the Whites that are chasing them! To the right there!"

Khrebtov shifted his fire. The sure eye, resourcefulness, and skill of the battle-hardened gunner worked wonders. Shell after shell fell in the very thick of the enemy columns. The White soldiers were thrown into confusion. They stopped their pursuit, halted for a space where they were, and then began to retreat while the fire kept increasing in intensity. The shells fell faster and faster, ploughing up the enemy ranks. The charge was stopped. The Stepan Razin lads pulled up short and took fresh heart.

At this time, Mikhailov was on the other side of the river, helping Chapayev to get more forces across. When he looked across the river and saw that a mass of Red Army men had run back to the opposite bank and realized that things were going badly, he ran up to Chapayev to tell him about it. Chapayev, however, already knew everything: he had just talked with Sizov over the telephone. Mikhailov opened his mouth to tell Chapayev what he had seen, when the latter began giving him orders:

"Listen, Mikhailov! We've just loaded another battalion. They've got to have more forces. But that's not all. We've got to drive our men back from the shore, there. D'you understand? They're spoiling everything. Go across, and lead them back to the lines. D'you understand?"

Mikhailov was on the other side in no time.

He didn't waste words—the situation didn't permit it. He held up those running away, some with his riding whip, some with his revolver.

"Stop running, damn you!" he shouted. "Where are you running to? Halt! Your only hope is to advance. After me! Not a word! The first man that runs gets a bullet in his head! If the man next to you runs, you shoot him. Forward, Comrades!"

This timely interference put an end to the panic. Those running, halted, and stopped dashing about on the riverbank. They huddled together and looked at Mikhailov fearfully and in bewilderment, but with hope: "Maybe he'll manage to save us?"

He did save them. At such a moment the only effective means were revolver bullets or a whip. He rallied the men and led them after him. He got them into formation, and the mob again became organized troops. Now when he led them back to meet the main body of their regiments, which were making an orderly retreat, the latter were beside themselves with joy, and shouted:

"Reinforcements! Reinforcements are coming!"

To have explained their mistake at such a moment would have been a crime. They were assured that it really was reinforcements. The battalions turned round and began to attack. But victory was not secured here. It was with difficulty that they managed to beat off the enemy, but in doing so they turned his main forces against the Ivanovo-Voznesensk Regiment. The weavers came under heavy pressure but withstood four successive assaults by several enemy regiments at once. They displayed exceptional heroism and staunchness. They beat off all the attacks and stood their ground without wavering until their own regiments came to their assistance and eased the situation.

It was necessary to pull back the Pugachov Regiment which was advancing up the river, to keep it from getting separated from the others. When the Pugachov men received the order and began to withdraw, the enemy, who had up till now been silent, evidently waiting for them to walk into a trap, made heavy attacks one after the other. The Pugachov Regiment retreated with losses. The men closed with the enemy and repulsed his attacks, but did not make any counter-attacks, intent on getting back in line with the other regiments as quickly as possible.

When all the units were again drawn up along the highway, the news came that Chapayev had been wounded in the head and that the command of the division had been turned over to Sizov. The disheartening news flew rapidly from one regiment to another, filling the men with deep dejection. They hadn't seen Chapayev during the fighting but they had felt that he was with them; they knew that all the attacks, the advances and retreats, had been made with his knowledge. And no matter how difficult the situation was, they always believed that a way out would be found, that the situation would be saved. Such commanders as Chapayev and Sizov would never lead them to destruction.

When the men heard about Chapayev's being wounded, everything seemed to become hushed and mournful. By this time the advance had stopped and the twilight had put an end to the firing. Silence descended on the regiments. Outposts had been stationed everywhere, and patrols sent out in all directions. The regiments settled down to rest. A general attack had been ordered for the next morning before sunrise.

While Chapayev was at the crossing, he had talked over the telephone every ten minutes, now with Sizov, now with the commanders of the regiments. Communications had been excellently organized; without this the operation would not have proceeded so successfully. At all times, Chapayev knew the exact situation beyond the river. When the men there began to get anxious about the shortage of shells or ammunition, Chapayev already knew what it was they needed, and sent over what was required by the next boat. He kept asking about the morale of the regiments, and about the enemy's activity, his capacity for resistance, the approximate amount of his artillery, whether there were many officers, and what sort of troops he had in general. Every detail interested him. He weighed and took everything into account. At all times, he held the threads controlling operations. His brief concise instructions over the telephone, and the orders he sent by orderlies—all this showed how distinctly he saw the situation at each moment. For a time, he was bothered by the enemy aeroplanes, but he was angry, not confused. Our fliers had no petrol, and could not take the air to meet the enemy. Breathing thunder and lightning, however, was of no avail, and our machines remained grounded. All the work on the river-bank had to be done while bombs were falling and the place was being strafed by machine-guns. But there was nothing that could be done. True, our artillery fire soon forced the enemy planes to climb higher, but it couldn't drive them away. Their bombing and strafing inflicted appreciable losses. It was on the river-bank that Chapayev was wounded. A bullet struck him in the head, lodging in the bone. The instruments slipped six times while they were removing the bullet. Chapayev sat there, silent. He endured the pain without uttering a sound. The wound was bandaged, and Chapayev was taken to Avdon, a little place about twenty versts from Ufa. That was on the evening of the eighth, and the general attack was scheduled for the morning of the ninth.

The persevering work on the river-bank, the exceptional performance of the artillery, the excellent communications, the rapid and untiring ferrying across of men and supplies on the steamboats—all this spoke of the co-ordination, the splendid organization, and the harmonious persistence with which the whole operation was carried out. This was not a case of one person's services but a manifestation of the collective will to victory. This will to victory shone through every order and through the execution of every order; it was revealed in every step and every action of the commanders, commissars and rank-and-file Red Army men.

Late in the evening, a worker who had come over from the Whites was brought to Sizov. He maintained that in the morning an attack was to be made by two battalions of officers, and the Kappel Regiment. They were to advance against the Pugachov Regiment, make a breach, cut off the other regiments, and surround and destroy them, with the support of other White regiments holding positions to the north. The worker swore that he was from the Ufa factory, that he sympathized with the Soviet power, and had come to warn the Reds at the risk of his life of the danger. He said he had got the information quite by chance when he had been working in the house where a council was held. He swore that he was telling the truth, and was ready to prove it any way they liked. They didn't know whether to believe him or not. At any rate, Sizov postponed his attack one hour. The patrols were strengthened. Scores of machine-guns were made ready so as to give the enemy a warm reception. The worker was put under guard, and told that he would be shot if his information proved false and the Whites did not attack.

The anxious night dragged on. Hardly any of the commanders slept in spite of their extreme fatigue after the arduous day. Everyone had been informed of what the worker had said, and all were ready to meet the enemy. And, at last the hour had come.

The officer battalions and the Kappel Regiment advanced in noiseless black columns. Not a word was spoken. There was no rattle of arms. They were flung far across the field, encompassing a wide area. It was evidently their plan to creep up noiselessly to the sleepy, exhausted skirmish lines, and then with a sudden charge to shoot or bayonet the men, sow panic, and destroy them all.

The Red battalions allowed the enemy to approach within short range, and then, at a command, opened fire all at once with the dozens of waiting machine-guns. It was a ghastly carnage. The machine-guns mowed the enemy down. Rank after rank was laid low. The Red Army men sprang out of their trenches and rifle-pits and rushed forward. The officer battalions lay cut down, whole lines of them, while the men of the Kappel Regiment were running away in panic. They were pursued several versts. This unexpected success filled the Red regiments with the rosiest hopes.

The worker was released from arrest and sent off with every honour to Division Headquarters, and from there, to the Army.

Later, Sizov gave Fyodor, who had been at the bridge with Potapov's brigade, a detailed account of the whole incident, and told him that after this success the units had advanced victoriously and without a halt. By the evening of the ninth, they were already close to Ufa itself.

Leaving Chapayev, Fyodor rode off with a few comrades in the direction of Potapov's brigade. From Avdon, the sandy Ufa Hill was visible twenty versts away. The houses on its slope showed as black specks, and the watch-tower looked like a tall pillar. The gold domes of the churches gleamed in the sun. They went at a quick gallop, and came out on to a wide meadow which lay in full view of the enemy and was within range of his guns. As soon as any movement was noticed, the enemy batteries opened fire. The riders strung out, single file, seventy paces apart, and galloped quickly in the direction of Brigade Headquarters. They crossed the railway where many burned-out, smashed and crippled waggons lay on either side of the tracks or stood on them. From somewhere behind a hill, the Red artillery was shelling Ufa, and beyond the wood came the rattle of machine-guns.

They arrived at Headquarters, set up by Potapov at a tiny railway station two or three versts from the river. A council of the commanders happened to be in progress— they were discussing the best way to cross the river. It was decided that forcing the river should be completely subordinated to the progress of the other two brigades, and that they would not yield to any rash impulse, would not, for example, rush across the bridge, which it was almost unanimously agreed the enemy had mined. The question of other means of getting across the river arose —there seemed to be none. A painstaking search for such means was begun, and some means were actually found.

On the very bank of the Belaya, there were two small huts. Cables were stretched to these huts, and telephones and telegraph apparatuses set up. The regiments lay down in the grass along the bank on either side of the bridge. The batteries took up positions to the rear behind the wood. It was decided to feel out the enemy that very night, and to find out once and for all whether the bridge had really been mined or not. (The brigade had received information that the Ufa workers would not let the Whites blow up the bridge or even make preparations for doing so). At eleven o'clock, when it got completely dark, an advance party of workers were due to arrive. They had volunteered to clear the bridge, which had been blocked up with goods waggons, and to repair the track, which had been dismantled. Eleven o'clock came, and twelve, and one but the workers did not appear. They didn't come till after two o'clock, when the night was already getting lighter.

As soon as it was reported that the workers were approaching, the artillery behind the wood began to clear the way for them to do their work. All the batteries began to shell the river-bank simultaneously, trying to drive the enemy out of his first line of trenches. They hoped to create a panic, and draw his attention away from the repair gang. But as soon as the barrage began, the enemy came back with a counter-battery fire that was still more intense, and the first blow of a hammer on the rails was the signal for the heavy guns along the opposite bank to begin to boom. The enemy had the range down to a nicety. While waiting for their Red visitors, the Whites must have done a lot of practising and made thorough preparations to give them a warm welcome. The first two shells fell near the stone column at the near end of the bridge as though feeling their way and with their fiery signals showing the next shell where to land. Their instructions were exact. The third shell landed right on the sleepers in the first span. The rails were torn apart with a crash, and chunks of sleepers were hurled in all directions. The workers scampered back without managing to reach the waggons, which loomed up black on the bridge ahead of them. They had no sooner jumped back than a hurried but accurate shelling of the target began. The shells were all falling on the bridge, on the sleepers and rails, and the track was soon torn up completely. The repair gang was drawn back behind the hut. Later it was sent back to the bridge, and though there were constant interruptions in the work, still it went forward.

When the firing was shifted beyond the bridge, Fyodor, Zoya Pavlovna, two women medical orderlies and some twenty Red Army men began to climb the stairs, hugging close to the steps or flattening themselves against the side of the embankment. Suddenly, a shell burst over their heads with a deafening explosion, and they all rolled head over heels to the bottom. They scrambled to their feet and instinctively rushed for the hut, hiding behind it, their backs pressed tight against the wall. This time they got off lucky, only two people were wounded. The medical orderlies bandaged them on the spot, and they stayed there with the others. The shells groaned and snarled and screamed as they hurtled past their heads. When shrapnel exploded, the fragments showered the hut, hammering on the roof, puncturing it or ricochetting off and slapping into the ground at their feet. At first, they stood more dead than alive, not saying a word. The shells from their own batteries behind the wood also tore by over their very heads. They all listened greedily to their screeching and whistling, but they listened even more keenly when an enemy shell was approaching.

"Will it land here or fly over?" this terrible thought drilled into the brain of each of them. . . . And the whine of the shell gets nearer and louder, becoming a horribly shrill, grating noise, as though enormous iron plates are being ground together faster and faster, and there is an excruciating squealing and groaning and rasping.

"Will it explode over us or fly past?"

Suddenly the scream of the shell is directly over their heads. It pierces the brain, curdles in the ears, rushes through the blood, the nerves and the muscles like a hurricane, setting them quivering. They all draw in their heads with a quick involuntary motion, lean over, and huddle closer together. They cover their faces with their hands as though that could save them from the fiery, hurtling shell. A deafening explosion. Everyone starts, and then stands frozen to the spot a whole minute, not moving a limb, as though waiting for the detonation to be followed up by something even more terrible. The fragments beat against the roof; they fly through the trees, setting the leaves rustling, and breaking branches; they smack into the ground, raising a whirl of dust. Several seconds of bated breath and death-like silence, and then someone moves, and tries to joke in a strained voice:

"It's gone over. Light up, lads!"

It is an amazing thing that after these awful moments, the first words are almost always uttered jokingly, rarely otherwise. Then they again stand there without a word, waiting for the next explosion.

This went on for several hours, until sunrise. Several times, Potapov ran over from the other hut, and several times Fyodor ran over to him, and then back again to his watch. They had not abandoned the daring idea of bursting into the town if only they could ascertain that the bridge was not mined. The suddenness of the raid would make it possible to create panic among the enemy with only a regiment, and thereby assist the brigades advancing from Krasny Yar.

As soon as it got light, the firing ceased. They all went back to the little railway station where Headquarters had been set up. Exhausted by the strenuous night, they were soon asleep. Then, in the evening twilight, they were again at the bridge and again probing, trying to find out whether or not the bridge was mined. The scouts had already got to the middle of the bridge, when they were discovered and came under machine-gun fire. Then Fyodor and the regimental commissar made their way towards the waggons on the bridge. They pushed on two hundred paces and began to sing the *Internationale*. This must have aroused a strange emotion among the Kolchak soldiers: they did not fire. Fyodor shouted from the bridge at the top of his voice:

"Comrades!"

As soon as he shouted, the machine-guns again began to bark. They threw themselves on the rails and crawled back. There were no casualties. They reached the last span, climbed the stairs and went down to the hut. They walked along the river-bank beside the skirmish lines. The Red Army men were lying in the grass on all sides; some had crawled off into the wood, and there, clustered together in small groups, were having a smoke. Others made their way down to the water on their bellies, filled their canteens with water, and then crawled back. The men were munching bread and washing it down with cold water; the canteens were passed from one man to another and were soon emptied. Then others would crawl down the bank, their heads hidden in the tall, sharp-leaved sedge, and then they would wriggle back, the brimming canteens splashing in front of their noses.

This night was just like the preceding one. Reports came in that the two brigades from Krasny Yar were already pressing forward on the other bank, which meant that decisive developments could be expected here. The scouts made repeated attempts to penetrate to the other side of the bridge or at least to the waggons blocking it, but the enemy kept a keen watch on all cracks and crannies which it was at all possible to squeeze through. The night was pitch dark. On the other bank there were only a few dim lights, and it was impossible to make out what the enemy was up to. About two o'clock, the artillery ceased firing, and a strange stillness set in. Then came the first hint of dawn.

Suddenly the bridge was blown up with a frightful crash. Giant slabs of iron were hurled into the water, and a bright blaze played over the waves. For a second it became as light as day. Everyone standing near the hut scrambled up on to the embankment and gazed across the river, consumed with a desire to know what was happening at the enemy positions. Why was it now, at this hour, that he had destroyed the iron giant? Something must have gone wrong. Perhaps he was already retreating. Perhaps the brigades were already approaching Ufa.

Everyone was seized with feverish impatience. The hours dragged by. As soon as it became known that the brigades were actually approaching the town, the order to force the river was given. Small boats appeared from somewhere, and little rafts made of logs tied together were dragged out of the grass, and launched; some of the men rolled logs into the water, straddled them and pushed off.

The enemy immediately came to life, but the firing though intense, was disorderly. It was evident that he was greatly disturbed, perhaps in a panic. The Red artillery intensified its fire, shelling the enemy trenches along the river-bank. Singly, in two's and in little groups, the Red Army men paddled across under the enemy fire. As they landed on the other bank, they at once threw up little mounds of sand to protect their heads. Lying there on the bank they themselves opened fire.

The midday sun beat down. It was broiling hot. The sweat ran off the men in streams. They were tormented by thirst.

The Red skirmish line kept getting thicker and stretching out further and further. Its firing became more persistent, breaking down the enemy's resistance and finally demoralizing him. With a "Hurrah!" the men jumped up and dashed forward. They took the first line of trenches. Some of the Whites escaped, and some were taken prisoner. Again the men lay down, and alongside them lay their prisoners disarmed, bewildered, filled with mortal terror. Then another rush and another, further and further from the river, deeper and deeper into the city.

The Red troops were entering the city from various directions. Everywhere were enormous crowds of shouting workers mad with joy. Shouts of delight, cheers for the gallant regiments, laughter, and happy, unrestrained tears. People ran up to the Red Army men, seized them by their tunics—the men were strangers to them but very near and dear. They pounded them on the back, shook them enthusiastically by the hand. A scene stirring beyond description!

... Workmen in their stained blouses line the streets. They stand in front of the rest of the crowd. This happy victory is their victory! And on the pavement, behind the blouses and workmen's shirts, and in the alleys, on the fences, at the open windows of the houses, on the roofs, in the trees, and on the telegraph poles, are many other citizens of liberated Ufa, and they, too, are overjoyed to welcome the Red Army. Those who are greatly displeased have run away in the wake of Kolchak. The Red troops march past, regiment after regiment. Their bayonets flashing proudly, they march past in perfect order, calm and conscious of their invincibility. The marble, majestic calm that has settled on their dusty, exhausted faces can never be forgotten.

First thing—to the prison, without delay. Has one at least been left alive? Can it really be that the Whites have shot them all? The heavy prison doors swing open, with a grating of rusty hinges. They run along the corridors to the common cells and to the places of solitary confinement. Here's one man, and another, and another. "Hurry up, Comrades! Out of the prison!" Touching scenes! The prisoners throw themselves on the necks of their liberators; the weaker, and those who have been tortured the most, break down completely, and sob hysterically. Here, just as outside the prison walls, there is laughter and tears of joy. The gloomy surroundings impart a peculiar, profound power to this meeting, a hidden and symbolic meaning.

In their flight before the Red regiments, the White generals had not had time to shoot the last few prisoners. But just the last few. Only the black nights that hung over Ufa, only Kolchak's White gendarmes can say where those comrades lie, who were led away every night in mournful parties no one knew where, and never to return. Those left in the prison later related the agonizing torment they had gone through—living in the foul air of brutal torture, of shameless and stupid baiting by the officer riff-raff, and of waiting every twilight for their turn to be led away into the night.

As soon as the prisoners had been liberated, guards were posted everywhere: patrols in the town itself, permanent posts on the outskirts. There was no pillaging, no violence, no outrages or brawls. It was the Red Army that had taken over the city, an army welded by discipline, and permeated with the consciousness of its revolutionary duty.

This first day, one after the other, there came deputations from the workers, from the employees of various institutions. Some greeted the Red Army, some expressed their gratitude for the tranquillity and quiet, for the order that had been established in the town. A deputation came from the Jewish Socialist Party, and told of the horrors that the Jewish population had lived through during the Kolchak regime. There had been no limit to the White brutality. People were thrown into jail without the slightest pretext. For some gold-braided scoundrel to beat up a Jew in the street was the greatest fun, and it went unpunished.

"If you retreat," said the spokesman of the Jewish Socialist Party, "we will all go with you, to the last man. Better bare and starving Moscow than this hellish nightmare in well-dressed and well-fed Ufa."

That very day, the Jewish youth began to organize a volunteer detachment, which joined the Red Army.

The Political Department of the division immediately launched extensive work. First of all, an enormous number of leaflets explaining the situation, were immediately distributed. Wall-newspapers were posted in the town, and the next morning the daily division newspaper began to appear regularly. Short informal meetings were held all over the town. The population gave the speakers an enthusiastic reception; many of them were tossed high into the air, right at the meetings, and carried on the shoulders of the crowd—not for any exceptional oratorical ability on their part, but simply from the crowd's overflowing joy, from an excess of feeling. The big opera-house was taken over by the division's troupe of actors. Here, all the work was done by the indefatigable Zoya Pavlovna—she fussed with the scenery, hunted up costumes in the town, directed the performances and acted in them herself. The theatre was always packed tight with Red Army men. A few days later, when the wounded Chapayev arrived in the town and came to the theatre, he mounted the stage and presented Zoya Pavlovna with a bouquet, thanking her on behalf of the Red Army men. The crowded hall resounded with loud shouts and frenzied hand-clapping. This was Zoya Pavlovna's best and never-forgotten reward from the Red soldiers.

The town immediately took on a brighter look, and life began anew. This was particularly noted by those who had had a grim and difficult time of it during the White regime of "freedom."

Beyond Ufa, it was other regiments that drove Kolchak onward, while the Twenty-Fifth remained behind for a rest. For over a fortnight, the division was stationed in the Ufa sector. No time was wasted. The units put themselves in order after their long and arduous campaign. The various staffs and departments gradually began to straighten out all the business that had piled up during the strenuous campaign. The Political Department worked tirelessly. In place of Rizhikov, it was now headed by Suvorov, a Petrograd workman, quiet and shy in appearance, but an excellent, untiring worker. He put in very long hours at the Political Department, and could be found there at all times. Evidently, he slept there. Krainyukov, Fyodor's assistant, became close friends with Suvorov, and whenever he had a spare minute he spent it at the Political Department. It was these two who actually performed the enormous amount of political work that was done during this two weeks' halt. Klichkov only assisted them with his advice, and took part in various conferences. His time was spent in the other divisional organs, which he and Chapayev had come into contact with for the first time since Belebei.

Soon alarming reports began to come in from the Uralsk front. The Cossacks were scoring one success after another. They had besieged Uralsk, but hadn't managed to break into it yet. Information was obtained from the newspapers, from Army despatches and telegrams, and especially from letters. The Red Army men learned that savage Cossack bands were tearing through their native villages like fiery whirlwinds, destroying their farms, and torturing or killing those whose sons, husbands or brothers had entered the Red Army. The regiments grew anxious and alarmed, and asked to be sent to the Ural steppes. They pledged themselves to fight there with redoubled energy against the Cossacks, who had run completely amuck.

Fyodor and Chapayev often talked about this. They saw that it was necessary to transfer the division, and that this would be useful, unless some exceptional circumstances prevented it. They talked about this with the Centre many times, and explained to Frunze the mood that had seized the soldiers, and how disadvantageous it would be to send them to any other than the Uralsk front. And now, individual refugees began to arrive from those parts, or simply volunteers who did not want to serve anywhere except in their "own" division. The mood of the men worsened. The Centre considered the situation and soon ordered the division to be transferred to the Uralsk front. There was no end to the rejoicing of the regiments. They made their preparations for the campaign as though for some happy holiday outing. Chapayev was also satisfied, no less so than the men. He was going to the steppes, those steppes where he had fought so long, where everything was so much a part of him and so understandable—not like it was here among the Tatar villages. Preparations were completed in the shortest possible order, and the division set off.

XIV

THE RELIEF OF URALSK

For a long time Uralsk had been enclosed in a Cossack ring—right up to the arrival of the Chapayev Division which liberated it. The heroic defence of the city will go down as a brilliant chapter in the history of the Civil War. Cut off from the whole world, the defenders of Uralsk withstood the Cossack siege with honour; time and again, they beat off attacks with great valour, and themselves made sorties, harassing the enemy on every side. The exhausted garrison, reinforced by the Uralsk workers who had volunteered en masse, never complained of fatigue or hunger. They never had the least thought of surrendering to the exultant foe. The battle was to the death. All realized that there could be no compromise, that capture by the Cossacks meant torture and the firing squad. Conspiracies were discovered within the city itself. The local whiteguards managed to get in touch with the Cossacks despite the vigilance of the garrison; they received instructions from the Cossacks, and themselves informed the Cossack command of everything that took place in the city. Ammunition was running low and food was coming to an end. The heroic Red defenders might soon have to fight with their bayonets alone, but even this did not daunt them. They were cheerful and confident. When the news reached them that the Chapayev Division was coming to their rescue, they grew even more resolute and beat off the last enemy attacks with still greater staunchness and heroism.

There were no big battles on the way to Uralsk, although not a day passed without skirmishes. The Cossacks, who had reason to remember the Chapayev regiments since the fighting in 1918, did not exhibit any great desire for an all-out battle with them, but preferred to retreat, inflicting pin-pricks here and there whenever they could. On the road to the Cossack village of Sobolevskaya, the Cossacks attacked the Ivanovo-Voznesensk Regiment with two armoured cars, supported by cavalry on the flanks. They hoped that the fire of the armoured cars would make the Red Army men waver and run, and then the cavalry would get to work. Actually, it all turned out very simple, even tame. The Red skirmish lines lay as though dead. They made way for the armoured cars, letting them penetrate to their rear, while they themselves fired at the faint-hearted enemy cavalry. Meanwhile, the Red battery was landing its shells nearer and nearer to the death-dealing machines. The monsters were forced to turn back without accomplishing anything. This enemy thrust was met and neutralized so simply and calmly, and in such an organized way, that there weren't even any casualties.

But at a place not far from this same Sobolevskaya, the Cossacks surrounded a company of Red soldiers who had got separated from the main body, and practically annihilated them. Another company was sent to the rescue, and it also suffered heavy losses. A third company was sent, and its fate was the same. Only then did they grasp the fact that it was impossible to render effective assistance with such tiny reinforcements, that this meant a useless loss of men and matériel. They sent a regiment, and it did what was necessary with amazing quickness. When Chapayev heard about this, he was in a towering rage, and cursed and threatened:

"You're no commander, you're a damned fool! You've got to get it into your head once and for all that Cossacks don't know how to fight; they only know how to mop up small units. And you let them, sending one company after another, you blockhead! Ought to give you one where you need it!"

In spite of the unceasing daily skirmishes with the Cossacks, the regiments made rapid progress, covering up to fifty versts a day on foot. The Red soldiers were met as liberators in the Cossack and peasant villages; the villagers received them hospitably, helped them in whatever way they could, and shared their supplies with them.

Chapayev himself was accorded an especially warm welcome. He was the "hero of the day" in the full sense of the word.

"Tell us just one thing, friend," the peasants would beg him, "will the Cossacks come again, or have you driven them away for good?"

Chapayev, pleased and in a good humour, would give a knowing twist to his moustache, and answer good-naturedly:

"You get together and help us—then they won't come back. But if all you do is cling to the women's skirts, then who's going to protect you?"

"But what can we do?"

"Why, the same as we," Chapayev would answer, pointing to the men around him.

Then he would begin to explain to the peasants the source of the Red Army's strength, how necessary it was to Soviet Russia, and what the attitude of the toiling peasantry should be towards it.

There were a dozen or so infallible and indisputable formulas which had stuck in Chapayev's head. Some of them he had read somewhere or other, but for the greater part, he had picked them up in talks. For example, there was the formula about the class composition of our army; then the one to the effect that for the time being the majority of the Cossacks were our enemies, not by chance but inevitably; and the one about the necessity of immediately assisting the famine-stricken centre from the abundant stores in the outlying regions, and so forth and so on. His clear, keen mind had grasped these simple, convincing formulas, and retained them once and for all, irrevocably. He was proud of knowing them and of remembering them, and was always sure to try to drag them into the conversation, no matter whether they were relevant or quite the contrary.

Chapayev got particular pleasure out of elaborating these ideas in his talks with the peasants, who always listened to him with the greatest attention. At times he would talk the worst rot, but the general result was always excellent. For example, it was with great difficulty that he could picture to himself large-scale collective farming, and he had the vaguest conceptions of the organization of labour on such farms, as well as of the relations between their members, etc. He often slipped into such notions as "property division," "self-support," and the like. So far as these questions were concerned, he found no satisfactory explanation for anything, but even these talks of his had constructive results. He appealed for industriousness, and protested against greed and selfishness, against darkness and ignorance; he fought for new and advanced labour methods in the peasant economy. In one village, he painted such a vivid picture of the famine among the factory workers and so bitterly upbraided the peasants for completely forgetting their brothers, while they themselves had plenty to eat, that the peasants at once passed a decision to collect grain in the village to be sent to Moscow. At this very meeting, people were elected to organize the matter, and they swore to Chapayev that everything they could scrape up would be sent off to Moscow, and that they would let him know about it at the front. Nobody knows whether the grain was sent, or whether it was even collected. They were unable to inform Chapayev about it—soon after, his life came to a tragic end.

And so, warmly welcomed at every step, the Red regiments advanced to the walls of Uralsk. One last battle and the Cossacks fled, lifting the siege. Accompanied by a squadron of cavalry and a brass band, the leaders of the besieged garrison rode out ten versts to meet Chapayev and his division. They met with joyous shouts, and the band struck up the *Internationale*. They embraced with tears of joy. And there was much they wanted to tell one another, and all at once, but their emotion overwhelmed them.

"Fyodor!" someone shouted beside the motor car in which Klichkov was riding. He turned and saw Andreyev on a tall black horse. They kissed each other like the old friends they were. In Andreyev's fine clear eyes, there was something new, something which Fyodor had never noticed before—his glance was cold, stern and mistrustful. It looked as if he were not even glad to meet Fyodor, but this was at once belied by his hearty greeting. The furrow across his forehead had got deeper, and there was a sharp groove above the bridge of his nose that never smoothed out.

They began talking, and Fyodor found out what an active part Andreyev had played in the struggle against the webs of treachery and conspiracy that had threatened to enmesh the besieged Uralsk. To make short work of scoundrels, decisive, ruthless measures had been necessary. The fight was a bitter one, and it had left its stamp on his youthful face—a grim, deep and ineffaceable stamp. Soon, circumstances brought Andreyev into the regiment. In the ensuing fighting, his unit was surrounded, and after a desperate battle, he was hacked to pieces by the infuriated enemy.

The streets of Uralsk were so jammed with workers and soldiers that it was impossible to pass. The entire population had turned out.

"Long live Chapayev! Long live our hero! Long live the Chapayev Division! Long live Chapayev, our Red leader!" These shouts resounded throughout the liberated Uralsk. It was hard for the motor car Chapayev and Fyodor were in to nose its way through the dense crowds that thronged the streets. The people gazed at Chapayev with adoration. They cheered him; they threw their caps in the air; they sang songs of victory. The city was red with flags, and everywhere speakers' stands had been put up and meetings opened. When Chapayev stood up to speak, the general ecstasy passed all bounds; the crowd went mad; it rocked and roared like the sea in a storm. His first word brought a dead silence, and his last broke loose a new wave of mad enthusiasm. Before he could get into his car, he was seized by dozens of workers' hands and tossed. Then, when the car drove off, they all ran after it as though they wanted again, and yet again, to tell him how grateful they were, to express their sincere admiration.

The Red Army men were also accorded great honour. The people of Uralsk did their best to surround them with care and affectionate attention; they saw to their food, collecting and turning over to them all they possibly could; they organized entertainments of all kinds; they cheered them at parades.

The celebrations lasted for several days—celebrations while the shrapnel was bursting over their heads! One shell landed on the roof of the theatre while a performance was under way, but such incidents in no way detracted from the general holiday mood.

The Cossacks had retreated across the river; they had to be driven still farther away without loss of time, to prevent them from gathering their forces, and to eliminate the threat to Uralsk. More ground must be placed between them and the city, which was such a strong magnet.

For Chapayev there could be no better reward than fresh victories at the front, and therefore, as soon as the first wild enthusiasm in the city had abated a little, he was again flying from regiment to regiment, and keeping an eye on the work at the crossings. A bridge was being built across the river, but there were already two Red regiments on the other side which had crossed on anything they had been able to find. The work had to be speeded up so that the artillery could be sent across; without it the regiments felt helpless, and the most alarming reports had begun to come in from the commanders.

It was on the second or third day after his arrival in Uralsk that Chapayev set out early in the morning to check up on what had been done during the night, and to see how the work was progressing in general. Fyodor went with him. Everywhere on the green slope, Red Army men were bustling about, hauling enormous logs down to the bank. There were forty men clustered around every log, jostling one another and getting in each other's way. It would seem that nothing could be easier than to

hoist a log on to a pair of waggon wheels, but again there was such a crowd that nothing could be done.

"Where's your chief?" Chapayev asked.

"Over there on the bridge."

They went up to the bridge. There, on a pile of logs, calmly smoking, sat the engineer to whom the whole job had been entrusted. When he saw Chapayev, he marched out to the middle of the bridge and stood there looking around as though nothing at all had happened and he had been watching the work from there all the time, not smoking unconcernedly on the bank. At such times, Chapayev was violent in the extreme. Still fresh in his ears were the tearful requests that were coming from across the river. They were continually in his mind, and he was sick at heart for fear that the regiments there might be destroyed any minute. Every hour was dear. Superhuman efforts were needed to speed things up. He had deliberately put such a number of men to work here, even turning over half the commandant's detachment. He was consumed with worry about the bridge, and had been expecting it to be finished almost any minute, and here, all of a sudden, he found complete disorganization —some people bustling about to no purpose whatsoever, while others were calmly smoking.

He rushed up to the engineer like an infuriated beast, and without a word, drew back and struck him a fierce blow in the face! The engineer swayed on the logs, and almost fell into the water; he was pale and trembled with fear, knowing that he might be shot on the spot. Chapayev did actually reach for his holster, but Fyodor, stunned by the unexpectedness of it, prevented him from making short shrift of the engineer. Beside himself with rage, Chapayev cursed the trembling engineer with his most biting, his choicest invectives:

"Wreckers! Sons-of-bitches! I know you don't care a damn about my soldiers. You're ready to let them all be killed, you dirty riff-raff. U-u-ugh, you swine! Have that bridge ready by dinner! D'you understand? If it's not ready, I'll shoot you like a dog!"

The engineer began to run about on the bank. Where forty men had been hanging on to one log, three or four were left, and the rest were assigned other jobs. The Red Army men worked with a will, and things began to move. The result was that the bridge, which in two days and nights had only advanced to about the quarter-way stage, was finished by dinner-time.

Chapayev knew how to make people work, but the measures he took were exceptionally severe. The times were such that, in certain cases, any measures could be considered justifiable. Even the most severe, the worst of these methods, that of giving a man "a punch in the jaw," was excused. There were cases when a commander had to lash his own men with his riding whip, and *this saved the whole unit.*

Whether what happened at the bridge was avoidable or not, it is impossible to say. In any case, there can be no doubt that the building of the bridge was a most urgent matter, and that Chapayev had called in the engineer several times and himself had been to the site, had given orders, tried to hurry things up, cursed and threatened, but the work had gone forward as slowly as before. Who can say whether this was premeditated sabotage or whether it was all a matter of chance? But that morning, Chapayev had come to the end of his patience. The inevitable happened. And by dinner-time the bridge was ready. Such is the stern, inexorable, iron logic of war!

There were instances when Chapayev exhibited a morose pigheadedness, an unusual naïveté, a failure, almost, to understand the most elementary things. During their stay in Uralsk, about a week or a week and a half after their arrival, the division veterinary surgeon and his commissar came running in one day to see Fyodor. There were tears in the surgeon's eyes. Both were shaking and flustered, and nothing could be made out of what they were trying to say. (Veterinary commissars are a delicate folk in general.)

"What's the trouble?"

"Chapayev—he's shouting and cursing—swears he'll shoot—"

"Who is he cursing? Who does he want to shoot?"

"Us. Both of us. Either I'll clap you in jail, he says, or I'll shoot you."

"What for?"

Fyodor sat them down, and when he had got them calm, they told him a strange, almost unbelievable story. A peasant whom Chapayev knew had come to him from the village; he was a well-known "horse-doctor," who had been working at this trade for nine or ten years and obviously knew his business. And so Chapayev had called in the division veterinary surgeon and the commissar, and sat them down at the table. The peasant was also there. Chapayev "ordered" the surgeon to examine the "horse-doctor" in his presence and give him a certificate that he was also qualified to be a "veterinary doctor". To make the paper stronger, the commissar should also sign it. They were to examine the peasant, strictly, but there must be no sabotage. "I know you sons-of-bitches," he said. "You won't let a single muzhik get to be a doctor."

"We tried to explain to him that we couldn't examine the man," the veterinary said, "and that we didn't have the right to issue documents. Then he jumped up and pounded on the table. 'Shut up!' he shouted. 'Examine him here, this minute, or to the lock-up with you, you swine! I'll shoot you!' Then the commissar mentioned you. 'Let's go,' he said, 'and ask him how to hold the examination, let's ask his advice.' When he heard your name, he cooled off a bit. Gave us five minutes—he's waiting. How can we go back to him? He'll shoot us."

The two of them looked at Klichkov beseechingly. Klichkov kept them in his office, telling them not to go anywhere. He knew that Chapayev would appear himself. And sure enough, in ten minutes, Chapayev barged in—angry, menacing, with flashing eyes. He went straight up to Fyodor.

"What are you up to?"

"And what are you up to?" Fyodor smiled at his menacing tone.

"You're with them too, are you?" Chapayev thundered.

"In what?" Again Fyodor smiled.

"You're all swine! Intelligentsia! Examine him this very minute in my office. Quick march!" he shouted at the trembling veterinary. "Quick march to the examination!"

Fyodor saw that things were taking a serious turn, and decided to try to subdue Chapayev with his usual tactics, that is, by remaining perfectly calm. When Chapayev began to shout and to shake his fists under Fyodor's nose, threatening to beat him up or to shoot him, he tried to reason with him; he tried to show him what a ridiculous thing it would be to issue such a certificate. But on this occasion, Fyodor seemed to make no headway with his arguments, and so he had to seek a compromise.

"D'you know what?" he said. "We can't decide this question ourselves. Let's send a telegram to Frunze and ask him what to do. Whatever he answers, that's the way it'll be. D'you agree?"

Frunze's name always had a soothing effect on Chapayev. This time also he stopped kicking up a row, calmed down and tacitly agreed to the proposal. They dismissed the surgeon and the commissar, and wrote and signed a telegram, but Fyodor refrained from sending it. In five minutes, they were having a friendly glass of tea, and now in a quiet talk, Fyodor finally succeeded in convincing Chapayev that the telegram should be burned, and not shown to anyone, otherwise people would be laughing at him. Chapayev didn't say anything, but it was evident that he agreed. The telegram was never sent.

There was no end to these absurdities of Chapayev's. It was said that in 1918 he had given one "high-ranking" personage a flogging with his riding whip. Another, he had given a good "cussing" over the telegraph. A third had had such an "endorsement" put on an order or an appeal that it was enough to make one's ears wilt just to read it. A most eccentric figure! There was much that he still did not understand, much that he had not digested, but there were also fine and rational things to which he aspired consciously, and not only instinctively. In two or three years, some of the things that he had just begun to grow out of, he would have grown out of entirely; he would have gained much that had just begun to interest him, had only begun to fill out his personality and attract him irresistibly. But it was to be otherwise....

XV

FINALE

The division was marching on Lbishchensk, which is over a hundred versts from Uralsk. Steppe—nothing but steppe in all directions. Here the Cossacks were "at home." They found sympathy and support everywhere and received every assistance. The Red regiments were given a hostile reception. Where part of the population remained behind in the Cossack villages, not a good word was to be heard, no assistance was offered. In the majority of cases, these Cossack settlements were completely deserted by the time the Red units appeared, or at most there might be a feeble old woman or so, forgotten by everyone. The retreating Cossacks frightened the population with their tales of the "Bolshevik cut-throats," and the villagers loaded all their belongings on to their waggons, leaving only the grain in their barns, and even this was for the most part burned or mixed with sand or shovelled together with mud to make a foul swill. The wells were almost all poisoned or filled up half way with dirt; not a single bucket had been left behind. Everything that could be spoiled, was spoiled thoroughly. All the constructions of military value were torn down or burned. It all gave the impression that the Cossacks had left never to return. Here, around Lbishchensk, they gave constant battle as they retreated; they fought fiercely, and beat off attacks doggedly and skilfully.

The Chapayev Division had its Headquarters at Uralsk while the advance units were dozens of versts ahead. There was a shortage of ammunition, uniforms and bread. The hungry Red Army men were marching through wheat country; they found mountains of unthreshed wheat in the Cossack villages but were without food. Their need at that time was extreme. Even mouldy, half-rotten bread sometimes didn't get to the front for weeks at a time, and the Red Army men were literally starving. What unbearably rigorous days those were!

Almost every day, Chapayev and Fyodor went by motor car to one brigade or another. The roads here were wide and even, and one could travel very fast. When their car broke down—how often that happened!—they rode horseback, and covered up to one hundred and fifty versts a day, leaving Uralsk at dawn and getting back by nightfall. Chapayev could find his way in the steppe with the greatest ease, and could always locate villages, hamlets, roads and paths to a nicety, but once even he lost his way. Fyodor wrote about this wandering around in the steppe in his diary under the heading of "Nocturnal Lights." We are giving his account, but it should be remembered that it doesn't convey one-tenth of the queer and novel sensations this Chapayev party experienced that night they lost their way in the steppe. Much of the "nocturnal," Fyodor was unable to describe adequately, and then, in general, things "nocturnal" are extremely difficult to depict.

NOCTURNAL LIGHTS

We had to see Sizov. No time was wasted in getting ready: we saddled our horses and galloped off, accompanied by twelve reliable men. We passed Chagan, and avoiding the road which was strewn with horses' carcasses, set out straight across the steppe for the lake. We rode through standing grain, high grass, and bright, flower-covered meadows, till we came to this shallow lake, or puddle, as you like. We rode to the top of the ridge, dismounted and led our horses down to the water. The horses drank greedily, but we drank even more greedily. It was already five or six o'clock in the afternoon. For the next thirty versts we didn't see a single hamlet. We began to look into every gully, hunting for water, but they were all dry, and we were tormented by intolerable thirst. In the distance, on the tops of little hills, we now and again saw horsemen—very likely Cossack scouts or pickets. Any minute, the Cossacks might suddenly charge out of some gully. That was their favourite trick—to wait somewhere in ambush, let the enemy get a few paces ahead, and then hurl themselves on him like a hurricane, whooping and whistling, brandishing their spears, their naked swords flashing; they would fly on the enemy, slashing and thrusting so swiftly that a man would have no time to unsling his rifle. So as we rode we were constantly on the alert, examining every depression, and ready for anything.

The smoky wisps of cloud suddenly thickened into black rain clouds and hung low over the earth. The twilight came on with a rush. The wind picked up and scudded across the steppe, packing still tighter together the pile of dark and lowering clouds. The first drops began to fall, and then it came on harder and harder. A real steppe downpour, heavy and deafening. All of us were soon drenched. As luck would have it, I had on only a very thin shirt, and I was wet to the skin even before the others. I was frozen to the marrow; my hands were shaking and my teeth chattering. I was hot and cold by turns. To one side, we saw some half-ruined clay huts, the remains of an old settlement. There seemed to be some people moving about.

We rode up and found it was two of our transport men. The unlucky fellows were quite helpless. They had fallen behind their regiment and then had had an accident—a wheel had broken, their nag had fallen, and they couldn't get it on its feet no matter how they tried. They decided to leave everything at the well and push on to overtake the regiment before they fell into the hands of the Cossacks. We got a three-litre bottle from them, tied the end of the reins around it, weighted it with a stone and lowered it into the well. Although we knew that the Cossacks often poisoned the wells, we drove away the sinister thought, so great was our thirst. We had to wait a long time for the water to fill the narrow-necked bottle, and by the time we had drunk our fill it was almost dark. We could hardly make out the track in the grass, but we knew exactly the general direction to take, and so we set out confidently. We rode about four versts and decided to turn aside and ride straight through the steppe towards a light that shone in the distance. We calculated that it must be some ten or fifteen versts away and that we should reach it in an hour and a half. As to the light itself, there were various conjectures, but we finally decided that it must be a camp-fire where our men were bivouacked. It might not be our men, but we decided to push on—we couldn't miss our own lines; we'd be sure to run into them somewhere. We rode on in silence. Before the rain, when we were dry, we had been singing songs and shouting and whooping, but now everybody was quiet. Although, when making guesses about the camp-fire, we had said that we couldn't miss our own lines, still there was a different thought at the back of each of our minds: "What if we're mistaken and are riding right into the hands of the Cossacks?"

Such thoughts preyed on our minds, and every sort of nonsense began to creep into our heads. It was no use for Chapayev to strike match after match, pushing his finger across the map and gluing his nose to the compass—nothing came of it and we rode blindly, at hazard. The light ahead of us would flare up and then die away, winking and becoming pale and dim and endlessly far away; now there was something queer and mysterious about it as though it were not a light at all but a spectre making sport of us in the murky night. We had thought at first that the light must be ten or fifteen versts away but we had already gone a good ten versts, and there it was still calmly winking away, now getting stronger, now disappearing somewhere very far away. We began to wonder if it really was a camp-fire. Maybe it was a lantern on a tall pole at a great distance. Then why did it seem to be moving away from us all the time?

We decided to pursue it no farther. We had lost the track long ago. The horses were moving through the wet grass, lush and high; it crunched under their hoofs and tore apart with a sound like breaking strings. To the right, another light appeared, and again it seemed quite close, but when we had ridden about a verst towards it, we again saw that something was wrong. Suddenly there was a second light, and then a third, and a fourth. There was something sinister in the black steppe empty and silent as the grave. The rain would stop, and then again begin beating through our thin clothes already sopping wet. Brrr! How cold it was! How unpleasant the trickles of cold rain running down my back, and down my neck on to my chest, like so many little snakes crawling across my body. How good it would have been to be in a dry hut next to a hot stove, and to warm up a little. And before us was the whole night—cold, rainy, and miserable. Our spirits sank to the lowest ebb.

We rode on and on—but where were we going? At times we seemed to have turned round, seemed to be riding past places where we had been before, as though we were circling round one enchanted spot. If there was a rustle somewhere, our heads turned quickly and our eyes bored into the darkness—was it a Cossack patrol? Maybe they had discovered us, and were following at our heels; maybe they had crept up on us, and this very minute— one—two—three! The devil knows what sort of power it is that the black night has over a person! It makes even the most courageous helpless, timid and uncertain.

There, off to one side, loomed something long and black, sprawling, clumsy. We sent out two of our horsemen. They trotted cautiously towards it in such a way as to approach from two sides. They came back and reported that it was stacks of unthreshed grain. It was decided to halt here beside the stacks and wait for sunrise. The horses were not unsaddled, not even hobbled. Some of the men were to watch all night, relieving one another every two hours.

Our rifles were loaded and ready to hand. We dug small caves in the straw and squeezed ourselves in. The rain didn't stop for a minute. I thought I had made myself a fairly comfortable seat, with plenty of straw below, but in a few moments, I felt that I was sitting in a puddle. The oozy muck was unbearably cold and clammy. Chapayev was sitting beside me, his face thrust in among the wet straw, and suddenly—calmly and cheerfully—he began to sing his favourite song softly to himself: "Behind the iron grating in a dungeon's foul air—" It was so eery, so unexpected, that I couldn't believe my ears for a minute—I thought he might be muttering to himself. But Chapayev was actually singing.

"Vasily Ivanovich, how can you sing now?"

"Why can't I?" he answered in a muffled voice.

"What if a patrol comes by? They'll hear you."

"They won't hear me. I'm just singing to myself. It's so damned cold and miserable sitting here in the water."

Just to hear this homely, human remark made me feel better.

"You know, Fyodor, this reminds me of something I heard once," Chapayev went on. "Two people had lost their way in the desert—same as we have, only there was only two of them. Whether they had been left there or had got behind some way or other, I don't remember, but there they were sitting on the sand and nowhere to go. For us, it's just because it's night—when the sun comes up we'll find our way. But what could they do? Day and night was all the same—just sand all round them, and nothing else. Each of them had a canteen of water but they didn't drink. They didn't want to die, and they knew they'd die when they had drunk all the water. Water was all that kept them alive. For three days they wandered around but couldn't find any path—there was no end to the sand. On the fourth day, one of them flopped down, and said: 'I'm dying, but you lie down beside me; we've been together all the time—let's die together.' He fell down on the sand and that was the end of him.

The one that was left alive sat there beside his friend. He saw that his eyes were wide open and glassy looking, and his lips drawn back showing his teeth. It was terrible for him there alone in the desert. He'd go away from the place and then he'd be sorry. He'd walk a little way off and then come back again so as not to lose the place — he was afraid to be alone. Although the other one was dead, still there seemed to be two of them. And now listen what happened. Some camels stumbled on him — seems there was a caravan going by, and so he was saved. Yes — he buried his friend in the sand. So there you are! To be lost in the desert that way — that's hard, all right. Where can you go if there's only sand for thousands of versts?"

"What's that?" Chapayev quickly poked his head out and jumped to his feet. I jumped up, too, and after me, Petka. We grabbed our rifles, and froze there, waiting. In a few seconds, the figure of one of our orderlies loomed up out of the dark, and behind him, champing and snuffling, the horses. Again we lay down among the hard, prickly sheaves.

"Why did you tell that story?" I asked Chapayev.

"I just remembered it. Whenever I'm in a fix, I always try to remember times when people were in worse fixes. Then I begin to think that they got through it, so why shouldn't I. Once I heard about a ship that was wrecked at sea and a sailor caught hold of a beam and floated around that way for two days till he was picked up. Just think what it was like for him with his legs in the water and him expecting every minute to be there himself. And still he got through."

Listening to him talk, we had huddled closer together. Petka was listening with all his ears. When he had to cough, he'd cover his mouth with his hand, and burrow still deeper in the straw and let out a muffled snort. In the dark, his black eyes shone like a cat's. As soon as

Chapayev finished, Petka glanced quickly at him, and began to fidget. You could see that he was burning to tell something himself.

"And what happened to me—can I?" he asked Chapayev.

The other didn't answer but silently smoothed his moustache.

"What happened to me, for instance, in 1918 on the Don," Petka began. "The Cossacks locked up about twenty of us in a little shed. In the morning, they said, they'd find out which of us were Bolsheviks. And if we didn't tell, then we'd all be shot for Bolsheviks. It was all up for us. We knew the swine would shoot us. We began to shove on one of the boards, real soft like. It gave a little. We shoved again and it slid clean away. I was the smallest of the bunch, so they told me to climb out first, and if I got caught, not to give them away. I was to say I'd climbed out all by myself. They told me to kill the sentry with a stone—at one blow, maybe, but I'd see what to do. And so I got ready to crawl out. It was the same kind of a night as now—it was raining and pitch dark. I stuck one leg through without making any noise—nothing happened. I bent over and shoved my shoulder through, and then my head and one arm, and then my other leg. I saw I was on the ground beside the shed, and at the corner, sure enough, was the sentry. I laid down on my belly. I thought I'd better crawl up first to make sure whether he was sitting there or standing on his feet. So I wriggled along in the mud like a worm, and the chaps stuck out their heads and watched. He was sitting on a chunk of wood and his head was bent down—I thought maybe he was asleep. I took a brick—they handed me one out of the shed—and crawled up close to him, and let him have it right in the temple. He keeled right over on to the ground, poor chap—didn't have time to let out a squeak. I hit him again three or four times and the blood spattered all over me. Then the whole gang of us climbed out.

"The shed was at the edge of the village, and we kept crawling until we got clean away, without being noticed. We knew where our unit was that we'd got separated from, and found it. E-hh! That was a good scare, too."

"It was a scare, all right, but still you're alive," Chapayev remarked somewhat enigmatically.

"Alive!" Petka echoed, bucked up and flattered by his attention. "All alive—the whole gang crawled away, honest to goodness."

"I believe you," Chapayev smiled.

Petka again covered his mouth with his hand and coughed into the straw.

"Look at them all asleep," said Chapayev, pointing to the others lying around us. "And I never can go to sleep if there's anything wrong."

Still our tiredness got the better of us. When we stopped talking and again burrowed into the straw, we fell into a light, nervous sleep, waking up now and then at the slightest rustle. We dozed that way the rest of the night, but at the first hint of grey in the sky, we got to our feet, tired, wet through, shaking with the cold and worn out by our sleepless night. We decided to get warm by riding fast. As soon as Chapayev could make sense out of the map and pick out which way to go, we galloped to the nearest hill, and there in a few minutes we did begin to feel better. When the sun began to rise, we were quite cheery. From the hill, we saw a transport and started riding towards it, but as soon as they saw our party of mounted men, they whipped up their horses to a gallop. Petka set off after them to find out at least if it was our transport or not. The rest of us trotted behind. The transport turned out to be ours, from the very brigade we were going to. In half an hour, we rode up to the little hut where Sizov had stopped with his flying staff. The hamlet was called Usikha.

. . . .

It was not yet six o'clock but Chapayev and his party found Sizov and his commissar already up and about. They had climbed up on to the flat roof of their clay hut and were scanning the distance through their field-glasses, and discussing something. When they saw Chapayev's party riding up, they climbed down and led them into the dark, filthy hut. Both of them looked absolutely wretched. Their faces were a cadaverous green, and their eyes burned feverishly. They were exhausted to the last degree, and there was a sort of hopelessness in their gaze. Both had taken off their tunics and were in their undershirts—it was so stuffy and hot in the hovel that it was impossible to work fully dressed. Sizov was barefoot. From the dirt caked on his feet, one would say that the last time he had had a bath must have been several months ago. His hands were shaking from the sleepless night he had spent, and from the severe strain, and when he began to talk fast his voice broke and he began to stumble over the words, while his Adam's apple jerked nervously. His pale, dry lips were cracked. He couldn't say a single word calmly. He kept shouting in a high, protesting falsetto, waving his hands in time with his speech, and beating his chest with his fists, trying to prove what was plain without any proof: that it was impossible to fight without ammunition. It was flat country all around, and Sizov could easily see the Cossack positions through his field-glasses.

"What about ammunition, Comrade Chapayev?" he asked, his voice cracking. He stared into Chapayev's face, striving to read his expression, to catch his first word.

"It'll be brought up. The order's been given."

"What d'you mean, the order's been given? I can't keep it up any longer!"

"Well, wait a little. Where can I get ammunition for you? I haven't brought it with me," Chapayev tried to reason with him. "I tell you they're bringing it—they should get here soon."

"Do you know," Sizov began, turning his burning, half-crazed glance on everyone around, "the commissar and I don't climb down from the roof all day long. There's no other place here to watch from. And the swine make four attacks a day—four attacks! We can see how they get ready, and how they come galloping along for the charge—we can see everything from here. And we can't do a thing—no ammunition. Yesterday, I told every third man to fire. and then every fifth. Now every tenth man is firing. We let them come up to within ten paces. Hand grenades are all we have to save ourselves with. We can't do anything. Just think—four attacks a day! You can see the place yourself—flat as a table."

"Have you got the order for tomorrow?" asked Chapayev, and glanced around the room.

"I got it. That's all right—these are all our lads," Sizov said, reassuring him. "But what can I do without ammunition—I can't do anything with bare hands."

"I know all that," said Chapayev, beginning to get angry. "Why waste time talking about it? It'll be easier for you right away. Shmarin's starting already. He'll draw off their forces, and you—"

"That's plain," Sizov agreed. "Only there's one thing—cartridges."

"And how are you for shells?" Chapayev asked.

"Just the same—well, with them we can still get along somehow or other. Now, bread—no bread at all! Can't offer you anything to eat—not even a crust of bread, so help me God! Only water. There, in the teakettle."

"The lorries are bringing bread, too," Chapayev explained. "Right now we've got to go on to Shmarin—we can't wait. Well, good-bye."

They rode from Sizov with a feeling of depression. They had fifteen versts to go. Their horses were hungry and so were they, too, but they knew that supplies should have got to Shmarin the day before. As soon as they arrived, breakfast was got ready for them. Shmarin was sweating over the division order. His brigade was to open the attack the next morning. Shmarin's task was a very hard one; everything had to be weighed very carefully, but he had practically no one whom he could ask for advice. He called in Chief-of-Staff, but what could be expected of him? Not much of a personage. It seems he had been some kind of a clerk in the brigade before that, and there had been no one to make Chief-of-Staff, so they had stuck him in. He did understand a few things —he turned out to be a sensible chap—but of staff lore he knew nothing, had never even heard about it. Chapayev, Shmarin and the others discussed the situation over tea, and cleared up all the details—where there were villages and how far away, the strength of the enemy forces and the reliability of the information gathered, and whether there had been any indications that the enemy was also going to try something. All this was cleared up in an informal talk, but as soon as they had had something to eat, they sat down to study the map, and Chapayev began to explain to Shmarin, in the greatest detail, just how to conduct the operation from the very first moment till the last. One could go into raptures over Chapayev's foresight and the exactness of the calculations he made. The ability to take the smallest things into account was a peculiar faculty of his.

"If you begin that way, then this will be the result.... By that time, Sizov will be holding this position, and Potapov, across the river, will have reached this point."

He took into consideration the speed at which the exhausted, sick and almost barefoot Red Army men could march; the amount of ammunition and bread needed, and the time required to bring them up; the absence of water; the presence of the local population or their complete evacuation; the amount and quality of the reconnaissance work done; the readiness of the Cossacks to meet an attack; the amount of assistance that could be expected from Sizov's brigade; the deviations in the roads and the speed of marching straight across the meadows. Chapayev weighed and adjusted absolutely everything. He began by making three or four assumptions as to the unfolding of events, and then tried to substantiate them by summing up all the existing, accompanying or preceding facts and circumstances. Then he chose the most likely of these assumptions and concentrated his attention on it, only warning the others not to lose sight of the alternative assumptions, and to remember what should be done, and when and how.

The council lasted two hours. When it was over, and Chapayev and Fyodor had already got ready to ride back to Division Headquarters, some people appeared from the reserve regiment of the brigade which was stationed about two versts from the positions, and invited them, of all things, to a theatrical performance. This was something unusual. On the morrow, a serious operation was planned, the enemy trenches were almost alongside, and now all of a sudden, a performance!

"It's always that way," smiled Shmarin. "When the actors get here, it seems the lads are already waiting for them, and even if a battle is soon to begin, they must have something put on—there never were such theatregoers!"

"But the enemy's so close."

"What do they care? It has happened sometimes that when everything was quiet, half of the men would crawl out of the trenches—they would see one act out, and then come back and the other half would go. That way they'd all see it to the last man."

"They put the show on alongside the trenches?"

"Yes. When it comes to that, Zoya Pavlovna isn't afraid of anything. She travels around everywhere with them herself. If the men somewhere hear that she's on the way with her troupe, they can't wait for her to get there. They begin to get everything ready themselves. Sometimes when she comes, the stage has already been knocked together. They tear up the fences in the villages, the rascals."

Chapayev and Fyodor knew that during the last few weeks, Zoya Pavlovna had organized a travelling theatre, but they had no idea that she was putting on performances so close to the trenches. She herself had kept quiet about it, biding her time; she would only say she was giving performances in the brigade. They had not questioned her more closely. When they visited the brigade, they only had time to discuss military matters. And now, from this conversation, it turned out that once when she was travelling across the steppe with her nomad troupe they had come under fire. The brigade was attacking, and the regiment where the theatre happened to find itself was already leaving its positions and beginning to advance. Without thinking twice the actors left a driver for each van, grabbed up rifles and went forward with the soldiers. Zoya Pavlovna was always on horseback. She rode up to the regimental commissar and in ten minutes was galloping away with him and five Red Army men to reconnoitre. These were amazing times! Actor, organizer, political worker, agitator or commissar—they were above all, soldiers. The division troupe was particularly popular because the Red Army men saw that the actors were soldiers like themselves—saw that they were always with them, and when necessary fought beside them.

The Red Army men waited for their troupe with the greatest impatience, and usually knew exactly in which brigade it was playing, whether it would stay there long, and whether it would come to them next or go to another brigade. The moment the news that the theatre was coming reached them, their spirits rose, and the glad tidings were quickly passed from one man to another. Preparations were at once begun, and when the troupe appeared the men were often able to give its members a good treat, even out of their scant supplies. The stage was usually put up ahead of time, and if they were on the march in the open steppe, where they knew they wouldn't find boards, and the troupe was due to appear any minute, they carted a pile of lumber along with them.

What excitement there was; what a gala occasion when the stage was set up! There were so many inquisitive people that they had to be shooed away in a friendly manner to keep them from crowding around and hindering the troupe in setting up the scenery, preparing the costumes, making up the actors. It might happen that some particularly persistent Red Army man would keep standing in front of an open trunk of costumes, admiring the dress-coats and the frock-coats, and then, when everyone's back was turned, would pull out some brightly coloured waistcoat, climb into it with the seams cracking, and then bellow to the others, his face one broad grin:

"Hey, chaps, look at the king!"

Well, of course, the "king" was at once laid hold of and his royal attire pulled off, and sometimes he might get a friendly punch or two, but he'd still stick around the back of the stage, on the look-out to see if he couldn't grab something there to put on for a good laugh.

This getting ready for a play was almost more fun than the performance itself. The actors would begin to dress. Where could they hide from the audience so as to make them gape with the unexpectedness of it all later?

They would try one place and then another, but nothing would come of it. They had either to let all who came along see everything, or else pick out a small party and let them look their fill on conditions that they would keep away the others. Of the two evils they chose the lesser: forty or fifty men would be selected and the actors would let them watch while they put on their costumes, tried on their wigs and put on their make-up. The amount of charcoal wasted on make-up was something amazing. It's not hard to imagine what kind of resources the theatre had in 1919 when a crust of stale black bread was considered a fortune! What thought could there be of expensive grease paints! If anything valuable in this line came along, it was not wasted but was saved for special occasions, for example, a big victory, or the arrival of new uniforms, or an increase in rations—there were plenty of occasions for special celebration in the division!

The acting was nothing wonderful, but still it created quite an impression. In justice to Zoya Pavlovna it must be said that she knew how to choose the best for the times from the scanty repertoire at her disposal. She acted herself, and she understood the Red Army men. She knew that what they needed was a simple, understandable, stirring, topical play. Such plays were found. Some of them were even written by men in the division, at times, not without a certain talent. The majority were clumsy and could not be called literature, but still they had a kind of inexplicable originality and strength, they had the right angle on things, the right idea, and a strong emotional appeal, though at times this was accompanied by complete inability to embody these thoughts and feelings in an artistic form. The troupe's repertoire was rather weak, but not particularly so for the times. In other places it was worse, weaker, and at times, the plays performed were actually harmful.

It required Zoya Pavlovna's exceptional love for her work to create out of nothing and in such circumstances a travelling theatre so popular with the Red Army men. That amateur theatres have been born under other, more favourable, conditions is not surprising, but in this case, when there was nothing at hand, when the division was constantly engaged in bitter fighting, to create such a theatre was truly a great achievement. At times the actors would go plodding along over the steppe behind a string of two or three camels with all the props packed nicely on the camels' humps. When possible, they got horses and rode in waggons from regiment to regiment, where the men would have been eagerly looking forward to their coming for a long while.

When Chapayev and those with him received the invitation to "honour" the theatre with their presence, it seemed that everything was ready and waiting, and that the curtain could be raised at once, as one of the Red Army men who had come to invite them announced. They decided to go—why not? The place was quite near, and they would have to change horses at Shmarin's brigade anyway.

The crowd of spectators were expecting them, and when they rode up, they all turned round, and a whispered "Chapayev!" "Chapayev!" flew from mouth to mouth. It was a remarkable scene. On the ground right in front of the stage, the first rows of the audience were lying flat on their stomachs; the people behind them were sitting normally; behind these again were more rows on their knees, as though at prayers on Holy Thursday; farther back, people were standing upright (these formed the majority); then came a score of waggons with people sitting in them; and finally, this most originally seated audience was closed up by a swarm of cavalrymen, mounted and fully armed. In this way, several hundred people were accommodated in an absolutely flat glade, and all could see and hear everything.

Way was made for Chapayev, Fyodor and Petka to go down and occupy seats in the "stalls," that is, to sit on the ground.

That day, they put on a short three-act play that had been written by someone in the division. It was on a serious theme and it was not badly written. The play showed how the Cossack women received the Red Army women as they passed through the Cossack villages with their regiments—how they shunned and cursed them at first, and finally came to understand them.

The play opened with a regiment marching into a village. The Red Army women, the majority of them Communists, are dressed in men's clothes—shirts, pants, jack-boots, half-boots, or bast shoes, Red Army helmets or caps on their heads, their hair clipped short or shaved off completely. When the Cossack women meet them, they turn away, curse them, and spit, and some begin to scoff and ridicule them:

"You fool woman, you, why've you put pants on? What are you going to do with them?"

"Hey, soldier!" a Cossack woman calls to one of the Red Army women, "What do you need a fly in your pants for?"

"It's all on account of you, you damned bitches," the village women at another place begin cursing, "it's on account of you that we're losing everything. They've ruined the whole district, the swine. They've got you whores in the army, couldn't find anything better for you to do! What have you sluts got to lose? Nothing, of course, and that's why you're loafing about. Who wouldn't eat someone else's bread?"

"You've got it all wrong," the women Communists try to object. "We're not what you think, not that kind at all. We're working women. We work just the same as you do, only we work at factories instead of doing farm work."

"You're swine, that's what you are!"

"Why do you call us swine? We have families at home, too, and children."

"We know all about your children, we do!" the village women begin to cackle. "We know what kind of babies you have—bastards they are."

The women Communists try to convince the Cossack women that they are not "sluts", but honest working women who have been forced by circumstances to leave their work and their families and go to the front.

"It's the same here for you as it is there," the Cossack women shout in reply. "You can find men anywhere because you're that kind. You're loose. If you weren't, you wouldn't be here, you wouldn't."

"But do you women know why we've joined the Red Army?"

"What's there to know? Of course we know," the others say, trying to avoid answering.

"Oh, no, you don't."

"And we don't want to know!" The village women turn their backs on them. "Whatever you say is a pack of lies."

"What kind of an answer is that? Come right out with it!" And the Red Army women begin to press them to the wall. "Give a plain answer: do you know? or don't you? Because if you don't know, we'll tell you."

"Oh, you'll tell us, will you?" the village women scoff, "there's nothing to tell, it's only bawdy talk."

"It's not bawdy talk at all. Listen to this..." and in a tone of good-natured reproach, "Just look at you now. Let's put it this way: we're women and you're women. Isn't that right?"

"Well, yes and no...."

The woman Communist who's been leading the talking seems puzzled.

"What's that you say? But still you *are* women, aren't you?"

"Well, women, then."

"And you wash your clothes, don't you?"

"What's it to you who does our washing? Are you wanting to steal something, that you're asking?"

"I daresay you've got children," the persistent, sly siege continues, "they've got to be taken care of."

"As if we didn't have children. Doesn't everybody have children? It's your brats that are left in gullies and under fences."

But the women Communists refuse to take offence—nothing can shake these persevering agitators.

"You take care of the cow—sweat over the stove. Is there any end—"

"You talk to the point, if you want to say something," the Cossack woman interrupts the persistent Red Army woman. "I know about all that better than you do."

"So you do everything," came the answer. "D'you understand? You work a lot, woman, but do you see the light of day? Do you see the light of day or not, I ask you? Do you live an easy life, woman? a happy life? Huh?"

"Oh, it's happy, all right!" The resistance of the village woman begins to weaken. But the attack becomes more and more persistent.

"Yes, and your Cossack beats you—why not admit it? Your husband beats you, doesn't he?"

"Go to the devil!" shouted the Cossack woman waving her off. "What business is it of yours?"

"So yours is quite the gallant, is he?" and the agitator laughs. "So he's never beaten you, not even once? You can lie to other people, woman, but not to me. I know better. I had a husband myself, but he's dead now. What a swine he was—bad luck to him. When he was drunk, he used to fight and bite me like a dog on a chain. Do you think I'm sorry to have lost him? I'm better off a lot alone—I get up when I like and I go to bed when I like."

"You're talking rubbish, girl," the Cossack woman protests.

"All right, we'll say he doesn't beat you," the other concedes. "Even if you haven't been beaten, still your life has never been happy, and it never will be, because who's going to give it to you? Nobody! You've got to make it yourself! You could make it yourself, but you're like a stump—you can't be moved from where you're rooted down, and you don't want to even listen to friendly advice. Who can get you out of your rut after that?"

"What d'you mean, get me out of a rut?" asks the Cossack woman in bewilderment. "I've been got out enough already." Here all the rest of the village women begin to buzz.

"It's got to be done!" the Red Army woman tries to convince them. "You've got to come out on to the open road—it's only now that a real life is beginning. You don't understand that, you women!"

"It's beginning," the Cossack woman grumbles. "With you, it's always beginning, but you can't seem to finish anything."

"We haven't been able to, woman, but oh, how we'd like to finish it all, and the quicker the better!" the woman Communist exclaims warmly with unfeigned regret. "That's why we've put on pants—so as to finish it more quickly, and you don't understand that and laugh."

"We laugh because it's funny," someone in the crowd answers, but the laughing has stopped long ago. After every word, the resistance becomes weaker, quieter, more helpless.

"You'd better try to understand, than just laugh," the Red Army women try to reason with the village women. "Laughing won't make you any wiser."

"Just look how wise you are!"

And so the talk goes on—easy, animated, natural. The acting is done with great enthusiasm. The way the Cossack women begin to give way under the irresistible influence of plain, simple and convincing words is well depicted. These talks are repeated. While the regiment is stationed in the village, the Red Army women help the Cossack women; they help with the children, and with the cattle, and with other work around the yard.

And now, when the regiment is marching away, the picture has changed. The Cossack women have baked pies for their "teachers," and buns, and have come out to say good-bye to them with bows and kisses and tears and with grateful words—new words of good-will. From now on there are two camps in the village, and the Cossack women who have listened to the women Communists are called "Bolsheviks" by the others, and are fiercely persecuted.

The regiment has gone, and the Cossack village has been left to itself. Many of the women begin to weaken. It is only a few who remain true to the new principles they have been taught, but the recollection of the Red soldier women brings a smile to the faces of all of them, and warmth to their hearts. Then, they believe that they will not spend their whole life in a cow-shed, that there will surely come a different life, though they don't know when it will come or who will bring it to them.

. . . .

The play was over. The curtain had been lowered. The audience had been ordered not to shout and not to do any applauding, but nothing could restrain the men's enthusiasm for their beloved troupe and they clapped wildly. What did the Cossacks at their positions think when they heard this uproar? Did they realize that here on the stage their wives were being converted to the "Communist faith"?

After the play there was a surprise. It seemed that when the village had been occupied, a poem had been found in one of the huts. It had been written and signed by the whiteguard poet P. Astrov, and was dedicated to Chapayev. It had been carefully copied, and was now read from the stage. Later, it was given to Chapayev as a souvenir.

Here is the poem:

> *On old Uralsk, from the Volga,*
> *Bringing death to man and beast,*
> *Came the Bolsheviks' huge armies,*
> *Quickly marching to the East.*
>
>> *And they had much ammunition,*
>> *Many a mortar, gun and spear,*
>> *And there led them, arms akimbo,*
>> *Grim Chapayev, mutineer.*
>
> *He'd have liked the Ural stormy,*
> *To subdue and take in hand;*
> *And the villages were burning,*
> *Bitter wailing filled the land.*
>
>> *All the shooting, rape and pillage,*
>> *Can it ever, then, be told?*
>> *So the villagers held council,*
>> *All the men both young and old.*
>
> *"There'll be sorrow, there'll be trouble,*
> *"In the land we all adore,*
> *"Oh, you Cossacks, take up lances,*
> *"For the happy days of yore!*
>
>> *"Send the Bolshevik invaders,*
>> *"And their Commissars to Hell,*
>> *"'Fore they came to stir up trouble,*
>> *"Russian Cossacks lived full well.*

"Rise you eagles of the steppe land,
"For there's jolly work that's toward,
"From the wall take down your rifle,
"Sharpen well your trusty sword!"

All the Cossacks leaped to saddle,
Gave the horses, then, their heads,
And in solid mass formation,
Hurled themselves against the Reds.

While behind them Old Man Ural,
Watched the charge with smiling face,
As the Reds ran back in terror,
In the depths of their disgrace.

The reading of this poem from the stage was a surprise for almost everyone. Whose idea it was, never became known, though as a matter of fact, no one ever tried particularly to find out. In any case, it need not have been read publicly, but could merely have been handed over to Chapayev. However, when the reading began, no one wanted to stop it in the middle, and the verses were read to the end. When the last lines were read, everyone was puzzled, and faces fell. Fyodor nudged Chapayev: "Go up there and say something to them—tell them how the Cossacks 'beat' you."

The suggestion was all that was needed. Chapayev's pride had been touched to the quick. He mounted the platform and made a short but most colourful speech, full of episodes from his campaigns. When he finished, he was seen off with the greatest enthusiasm. Everybody was in a festive mood.

... On the morrow, many of these spectators were left dead in the steppe, their bodies mangled and trampled, others were carted away maimed to the villages and to Uralsk.

That was the last trip that Chapayev and Fyodor made together. Within a few days, Fyodor was called away for other, more responsible work, and his place as commissar was taken by Baturin, a man whom Fyodor had known in Moscow. We shall not stop now to tell about where Fyodor went or what he did—that's an entirely different story. It was in vain that Chapayev sent tearful telegrams begging the Commander-in-Chief not to take Fyodor away from him, as the question had already been decided. Chapayev well realized what a friend he was losing when Klichkov went away—Klichkov, who had understood him and loved him so well, who had always defended him against attacks by others, and taken such a calm and sensible view of his outbursts and his frequent abuse of the people "on top," the "damned staffs" and the "Chekas." Klichkov had forgiven Chapayev his abuse of commissars and "political authorities" of all kinds; he had not tattled to the Revolutionary Council about these outbursts, and had not taken offence himself, realizing that they were fits of temper and nothing more. There had been a time when Fyodor had been ready to put Chapayev in the same category as Grigoryev and Makhno,* but then he had discovered his error, had realized that he had formed his opinion in too much of a hurry, and had done it in a temper. Chapayev was incapable of ever betraying the Soviet power, but his behaviour and his abuse when certain ticklish questions came up might have raised doubts in the mind of anyone who did not know him well. It might be mentioned that once when the division was somewhere near Ufa, an "important personage" had arrived from Moscow, and this "personage," who had only once heard Chapayev speak, but had heard a lot of rubbish about him, made approximately this

* Chiefs of anarchist bandit groups which fought the Soviet power in the Ukraine during the Civil War.

remark to Fyodor: "If he's just a little *that* way, we'll have him tied hand and foot in a jiffy."

At the time, Fyodor had been highly indignant, and had even made a number of impertinent remarks to the "personage" and so come into disfavour with him. But what was there surprising in this "personage's" doubts? They were quite legitimate, since Chapayev had behaved towards him on the first day in exactly the same way as he did towards Fyodor on the two hundred and first. However that may be, after Fyodor had been with Chapayev for over half a year, he carried away with him never-to-be-forgotten memories. This separation was as hard for him as it was for Chapayev. He did not know that it was to save him from sure death—that within two weeks Pavel Stepanovich Baturin, who replaced him, was to die *for him and at his post.*

Later, Fyodor began to cogitate and to wonder: in what way was Chapayev a hero, in what did his exploits consist, and in general, are there such things as heroes and heroic exploits? Chapayev and he had been so long inseparable, day after day, hour after hour. The time had been turbulent, and spent in continual marches and battles. Fyodor was aware of Chapayev's every move, and saw and understood them all; he knew and understood, in most cases, even the hidden factors and considerations behind his moves. Now he went over in his mind, day by day, the time between his first meeting with Chapayev at Alexandrov-Gai to the last day here in Uralsk. The Battle of Slomikhinskaya: the speed with which Chapayev travelled from one place to another, his ability for lightning-like calculations, his enormous capacity for work, and the rapidity with which he worked. The march on Ufa. The Battle of Pilyugino. The Battle of Ufa. Again here in Uralsk. But where were the truly heroic deeds? Chapayev's fame was wide-spread, and, it was true, his fame was better deserved than that of anyone else. The Chapayev Division had never known defeat, and this was to a great extent thanks to Chapayev himself. It was indeed heroism to have fused this division into a single solid unit with one burning desire, to have made it believe in its invincibility, and to have taught it to bear the hardships and privations of the march with patience, and even with contempt. He had given the division its commanders; he had selected and tempered them, and he had instilled into them his own impetuous will; he had rallied them round him and concentrated their thoughts on one aim—victory, and again and again, victory. That was indeed heroism, but not the heroism that legend linked with the name of Chapayev. Legend would have it that Chapayev always galloped before the skirmish lines, brandishing his naked sword, that he killed the enemy with his own hands, and that he hurled himself into the hottest fighting and himself decided the outcome. This was not entirely the case. Chapayev was a good organizer, a keen organizer, for the times, for the circumstances and the environment that had produced him—the environment which had given birth to him and which exalted him. If the times had been but a little different, if the people had not been what they were, no one would ever have heard of Vasily Ivanovich Chapayev, the popular hero. His fame was borne across the steppes, and beyond the steppes, like a wisp of down, by hundreds and thousands of Red Army men who themselves had heard of his deeds from others, but who believed what they had heard and were in raptures over it, had further embellished it with the fruits of their own invention and carried it further. If these singers of Chapayev's praises were to be questioned, however, it would be revealed that the majority knew none of his deeds at first hand, nor Chapayev himself personally. They did not know one authentic fact.

That is how legends about heroes are created, and that is how the legends about Chapayev came into being. His name will go down as a shining star in the history of the Civil War. And there are grounds for it—such men as he were few.

We have come to the drama which brings these notes to their conclusion. We have already said that Chapayev's request that Fyodor Klichkov be left with him came to nothing; he was recalled categorically and even peremptorily. Looking back to what he had been six months before, Klichkov could not recognize himself, so greatly had he developed, so much stronger had he become spiritually, and so tempered had he been by the ordeals he had undergone. Now he proceeded simply and confidently to solve the most diverse problems, which before his experience at the front would have seemed infinitely difficult. It was only now that he felt the mighty effect that army life had had upon him, the great educational significance of life at the front.

Pavel Stepanovich Baturin arrived and put up with Fyodor at his quarters. They had a pleasant talk about old times in Moscow. Then they switched over to the division, and Fyodor began to tell him about the situation in which he would be working. Pavel Stepanovich, who had been gloomy, taciturn, and dejected for some reason, immediately brightened up when he learned in what unusual surroundings he would find himself.

That day there was a division Party Conference. It was the last Fyodor would be presiding over, and he took the occasion to introduce his successor to everyone. Fyodor's comrades took leave of him with the warmest and most sincere feelings. His going was a matter of real regret for them. They had come to love and appreciate him during this half year. They especially valued him for his ability to hold in check Chapayev and *Chapayevism*, that is, all those unpleasant and at times simply dangerous attacks on political workers, the Cheka, and the staffs.

That evening, after the conference, Fyodor invited all the commanders and commissars to his quarters to bid them farewell. Pavel Stepanovich was there too, but he was in a strange mood. He at once sat down in a corner and stayed there almost motionless, not saying a word to anyone all the hours that Fyodor's friends were having their last talk with him, recalling their army life together and expressing their regret that they had to part with their good, true comrade.

In the morning, they kissed one another good-bye, and set out in different directions—Fyodor to Samara, and Chapayev and Baturin to the positions, to inspect the brigades and regiments.

The offensive was developing successfully. Shmarin's brigade, reinforced by a brigade from another division, was marching along the highway down the River Ural. Potapov's brigade was advancing towards the Bukhara country, as the land beyond the Ural was called. Sizov had executed a manoeuvre with his regiments near Usikha where Chapayev and Fyodor had arrived after the night spent in chasing the lights in the steppe. The results of this manoeuvre had been disappointing and did not justify the heavy losses sustained. Chapayev, who was so keen and flexible, who so quickly adjusted himself to any change in the situation, realized that here in the steppes it was impossible to fight against the Cossacks in the same way as against peasants forcibly mobilized into the Kolchak army. The Cossacks were not to be frightened or disconcerted by the loss of territory. The wide open steppe was Cossack territory; they could gallop back and forth across it from one end to the other, and everywhere they would be welcomed by the Cossack population. They would live in your rear, impossible to catch, infinitely treacherous, and genuinely dangerous. The aim should be not to drive the Cossacks, not to wait until dissolution of their army set in, and not to capture their villages, one after the other—this, to be sure, was very important, but it was not the most important thing. The principal thing was to destroy their man-power, to smash the Cossack regiments. It had been possible to find replacements for the depleted ranks of the Red Army from among the Kolchak prisoners, but this could not be done with Cossack prisoners. The Cossack was an inveterate enemy, or at least he wouldn't become your friend and ally very quickly. The destruction of the enemy forces was the task that Chapayev set himself. The further the Red regiments advanced, the deeper they got into the steppe, the harder this would be to accomplish. Their needs would increase, exhaustion, hunger and thirst would take their toll, and their isolation from the centre would make itself painfully felt.

It would be hard for the Cossacks, but still harder for the Red Army men. This meant that they must hurry, whatever the cost, must be prepared to sacrifice men and matériel—to give up much to avoid losing more by allowing themselves to be drawn deep into the steppe. So Chapayev was feeling out ways that would lead to the desired goal. The Usikha manoeuvre had not been what was needed, by no means so. Accordingly, forces were concentrated, and Lbishchensk, the second Urals capital, was captured by a frontal attack. Losses?—yes, there had been losses, but the results had been better. Five such blows and the campaign would be over!

After Lbishchensk, they passed Goryachensky and took up positions before Mergenyovsky. The retreating Cossacks well realized their position and saw what awaited them in the barren sands around the lower reaches of the river. They must repulse the Red forces somewhere here before everything was lost. So they strengthened the defence of their villages to the utmost. They put up stiff resistance at Lbishchensk, hanging on stubbornly for a long time, but the Reds' powerful frontal attack was evidently something they hadn't expected. They had assumed that Chapayev placed all his hopes on manoeuvres, that he still believed only in encirclement. They had been mistaken. But they learned something from this mistake, and now fortified Mergenyovsky with all the means at their disposal. They made use of the deep trenches that had been left from the spring fighting, concentrated their artillery, and placed machine-guns behind every corner, and in every opening, besides hiding them in the trenches. The Red regiments made a frontal attack against Mergenyovsky and took the town in spite of everything. Many Cossacks were killed, but the Red Army losses were still heavier. The victory cost them dear. The Cossacks caught on to Chapayev's tactics and countered his every move. When Chapayev became convinced as a result of the Mergenyovsky battle that frontal attacks must be put aside for the time being, he gave Sizov orders to advance along the highway, while he sent Shmarin to the Kushum Valley against the Kzil-Ubin settlement, so that by cutting back at Sakharnaya he should make it easier for Sizov to capture this Cossack village.

At the time, Cossack regiments were moving in this direction from the Slomikhinskaya sector, and happened on a hamlet where the transport of the Ivanovo-Voznesensk Regiment had been detained. There was a frightful massacre. Only three Red Army men managed to escape. They reported what had happened, causing consternation in the brigade—the Cossacks had not been expected from that direction. The regiment was sent back to the hamlet to save the transport, but they were only partially successful—the Cossacks had seized all the best and carried it away with them as they retreated, fighting, from the hamlet.

It was a ghastly picture that met the eyes of the Red Army men. The bodies of two girls lay on the ground, their breasts cut off, and beside them, soldiers with smashed skulls, their faces cut to ribbons, their arms chopped off. The bloody body of a skinny Red Army man lay on its back, the penis cut off and stuck into the mouth—a revolting and terrible sight.

Besides satisfying their thirst for revenge, the Cossacks evidently thought to terrorize the Red Army men, to make them shudder at the thought of being taken prisoner—at the very idea of being here in the steppe—and cause them to desert. If so, the results were the opposite to what had been expected. Fearing torture by the Cossacks, the Red soldiers were not to be taken alive; they fought with amazing stubbornness, literally "to the last drop of their blood." The news of what had happened at the hamlet flew from company to company, from regiment to regiment. The men cursed the savage butchers and swore to conquer or to die in battle.

Sizov fought his way down to Karshinsky and there halted waiting for news of Shmarin's approach, but Shmarin and his regiments had got lost in the steppe and couldn't establish contact with Sizov for several days. He sent out messengers but they were captured by the Cossack patrols who were on guard everywhere. The Cossacks wormed various information out of them, seized their letters and documents, and then chopped off their heads, as they were loth to waste bullets, and there was nothing to hang them on. No matter how many messengers were sent out, their fate was the same. The situation could not have been worse. There were no Cossack villages here, only bare steppe on all sides, with here and there a little hamlet. They had eaten their bread to the last crumb, and were now slaughtering their cattle. Meat was all they had to eat, and they roasted it over their camp-fires. There was an increase of sicknesses of all kinds; jaundice in particular incapacitated many. There were no doctors and no medicines. There was no water. Men galloped to the Kushum River but at that point it had dried up. Instead of water, they found only a greenish-brown muck like that in old stagnant ponds. They filled tins and pails with this filth, pressed out the mud, and drank what was left. They brought back a pailful for each regiment. A fight began—who was to have the first drink?

They happened to run on to a well. Cossack wells never have much water in them. In all, they dipped out fifteen bucketfuls. They had to set up a machine-gun at the well mouth where the bucket was sent down, and station a big guard all round. The water was divided evenly among the regiments, and at each pail there was a queue of a thousand yellow-faced hollow-cheeked exhausted soldiers waiting their turn. Each came up and looked into the cold water with crazed burning eyes as though he would throw himself on the pail, seize it with both hands, lower his burning face to the water, and drink with greedy lips—drink and drink and drink; you could beat him, try to tear him away, try to chase him away, shoot him—he wouldn't stop drinking! It might have happened that way if there had not been guards around, and if the mug had not passed to him through other hands. The poor fellow would come up, and they would give him the mug. He would look and look at the thin layer of water running around on the bottom of it.

"Just a little bit more, mate," he would say to the man at the pail, his eyes pleading, sorrowful, and suffering.

"Can't do it. Everybody gets the same."

"Just a drop."

"Not even a drop," he is told.

He looks once more at the bottom of the mug and then slowly raises it to his lips, reluctant to drink; then he drinks it down and sucks and sucks at the empty mug as though it contains not water but thick, sweet, luscious honey, full to the brim, and no matter how he tries, he just can't drink it all.

They found wells filled with earth, halfway to the top. They dug them out, but at the bottom they found only mud. They found two wells filled up with the rotting carcasses of cows and horses. The stench filled the air for a great way off. Even these wells were cleaned out. The carcasses were hauled out, and the stinking, chocolate-coloured liquid they got from the bottom of the well was strained and drunk.

That was what Shmarin's brigade went through until they established contact with Sizov's regiments, which had by that time captured Sakharnaya. They had not stopped to wait for support from Shmarin, but had pressed on.

Grim, beside himself with wrath, Chapayev had Shmarin court-martialled for not carrying out orders; he himself demanded that Shmarin should be shot! However, Sizov, who was chairman of the commission appointed to investigate the case, insisted that Shmarin should be demoted to the command of a regiment. In this, he was supported by Baturin, and the next morning, Shmarin was removed from the post of Brigade Commander. The regiments were already preparing to march on—through Kalmikov to Guryev on the Caspian Sea. But it was now that a tragedy occurred which can never, never be forgotten.

Division Headquarters was at Lbishchensk. From there, Chapayev and Baturin continued to make the rounds of the various brigades by motor car almost every day. The cold autumn weather was approaching. Bracing fresh days were quickly followed by twilight and black, silent autumn nights. The position of the retreating Cossack forces was becoming more and more hopeless: before them was barren steppe, feather-grass and hunger —an alien land. If they were to resist, it could only be now—soon it would be too late. So the Cossacks decided to make a final desperate effort: to lull the watchfulness of their triumphant adversary and strike him a blow straight to the heart. They decided to make a deep raid from beyond Sakharnaya, through the Kushum Valley, and past the Chizh swamps, past the very places where in the spring Chapayev had beaten them in the Battle of Slomikhinskaya—to penetrate unnoticed to the rear of the Red forces, and with a sudden blow, to destroy everyone and everything that had been concentrated at Lbishchensk. At that time there were not only numerous personnel in Lbishchensk, but also the various divisional departments, and even extensive military supplies—ammunition and uniforms, which had just been received. It had been planned to outfit the division with shoes and clothes in view of the fact that whole companies and even battalions were down with typhus due to the filth, hunger and the privations of the march.

During the arduous march from Uralsk to Guryev, more Red Army men were put out of action by typhus than by the fighting. The village huts, the regimental baggage waggons, and sometimes even the ditches at the side of the roads were filled to overflowing with the sick. One batch of sick men had hardly been carried away before others fell ill, and there was no way of moving them. They were left in the empty huts of deserted Cossack villages, or on the grass, in the ditches, or on the road. There were no medicines, and half the medical staff had died or were ill.

The Cossacks were little better off, but they had the advantage of being the first to reach the villages, and there they took everything. They drove the cattle away with them and carried away everything else they could. Whatever they couldn't carry away, they burned, destroyed, poisoned. They did their utmost to make everything unfit for use. The Red regiments moved through places that had been plundered and devastated, and they were in greater and greater need of bread and water, cartridges and shells, waggons and horses. The farther they went, the worse their plight became. The Cossacks knew this, and placed big hopes on it in planning their indisputably talented raid. They thought that when Division Headquarters had been destroyed, and communications dislocated, the regiments which had advanced a hundred versts down the river would be left empty-handed, and they would be glad to surrender, seeing the complete hopelessness of further resistance. They thought that the invincible Chapayev Division would be defeated, and its destruction would mean that the Ural steppes would be freed of the Red invaders. They pinned great hopes on this operation, and accordingly, their most experienced military leaders were put in command. Black clouds were gathering over Lbishchensk, and the town was unaware of the terrible catastrophe imminent.

That day, Chapayev was more gloomy than usual. Early in the morning he sped away to the front by motor car, but he didn't stay long, and at midday returned to Lbishchensk. The advance was slowing down. Typhus was ruthlessly mowing down the men in countless numbers, and the transports were not able to bring up necessary supplies in time. He saw all this, and realized that it was impossible to "jerk somebody up" for it—you can't lift yourself by your boot-straps. The brigades were working to exhaustion, but the situation was too much even for their heroic, selfless exertion. Chapayev was in a black mood. He went in to see Baturin for a minute to discuss the uncertainties that were worrying him, and then went back to his own room. He kept pacing up and down the room in the big Cossack hut. He wanted to think out something, but nothing came of it—he couldn't find the answer he wanted. Petka watched from behind the door, but didn't say anything; he was only waiting in case Vasily Ivanovich should give him some order.

Chekov came up, but Petka stopped him in the passage and advised him not to go in. "He hasn't got time for you now, mate," he said to Chekov, and the latter snorted in his thick, bushy moustache, and turned away without saying anything. Ilya Tyotkin also looked in. He wanted to tell Chapayev something "very important," but on hearing what kind of a mood Chapayev was in, went away. It was with a heavy heart that Petka admitted Chief-of-Staff Novikov. Novikov wanted to make his report, and Petka didn't dare try to dissuade him.

Novikov was a young man, twenty-three years old, a former tsarist officer, one of the very few whom Chapayev trusted. He even loved Novikov, who entering the Red Army in 1918 had proved his loyalty to the common cause time and again. It was said that he had been wounded. Novikov knew all the commanders personally, understood them perfectly—in a word, was one of them. They, in their turn, loved and respected him and accepted him as one of themselves. How greatly Chapayev respected him was evident from the fact that during all their service together, he had never cursed him or threatened him with all the torments of hell, and there was hardly another man so lucky.

Novikov entered the room but stopped in the open doorway holding a stack of papers under his arm.

"Come in! Why are you standing there?" Chapayev said, looking up.

"Very good." Novikov came in, and seeing that Chapayev had sat down at the table, bent over and began his report. While talking he pointed to the map to show the line occupied by the division according to latest information. Chapayev asked him questions, in particular about the reports received from the brigade that had crossed the Ural into the Bukhara country, and which, almost cut off and receiving very few supplies, was fighting under extremely difficult conditions. But when he heard that a telegram had been received from there confirming the arrival of the latest transport sent, he brightened up, became kindlier and spoke more quietly and calmly.

"As you know," Novikov went on, "an attack was made yesterday on one of our transports not far from here—fifteen versts or so."

"I know."

"An investigation has been made. There are killed and wounded. The Cossack patrol following them came up close to the village, but then galloped away nobody knows where."

"Did they chase them?" asked Chapayev.

"Our men were too late and didn't even see where they'd gone to. The transport men that were left alive don't know where they went either."

"Don't you think, Novikov, that close by here somewhere, there are bigger detachments?"

"Can't say. According to your orders, we sent out patrols in all directions early this morning, and two aeroplanes also flew out."

"Nobody back yet?"

"The fliers report that they have seen no movement anywhere."

"D'you know what?" said Chapayev, "tonight, put the Division School on guard."

"Very good."

A few more questions, and Chapayev dismissed Novikov. Presently Pavel Stepanovich came in. He had just talked to the men in the patrols who had by now returned—they also had discovered nothing anywhere.

Who it was that took the Division School off their posts that fatal night is still a matter for wonder. It has never been cleared up. Chapayev never gave anyone such an order. Novikov is beyond all suspicion—he fought heroically and suffered greatly the night of the Lbishchensk massacre.

There can be no doubt that the Cossacks were in communication with people in the village. It is a fact that there were ambushes in some of the huts—people began firing from them with rifles and machine-guns. The depots and departments of the division were hunted out very quickly. Thorough investigations had been carried out, and all preparations made beforehand.

While Baturin was talking with Chapayev, some well-wishing Cossack woman whose son was an employee in Uralsk burst in upon them in spite of Petka's attempts to keep her out. In great haste she tried to tell them something, tried to make them understand that danger was threatening because "people were riding in the steppe," but her warning went absolutely unheeded. Chapayev and Baturin only laughed, thinking that the woman was talking about the patrol that had attacked the transport. Petka told about this "fool woman" to Tyotkin, who had again appeared. When Tyotkin heard that Chapayev was busy with the commissar, he again meekly turned round and left.

It was long past midnight, and the first hint of dawn was in the sky, but the village was still sleeping peacefully. The advance Cossack patrols silently stole up to the outskirts and removed the pickets. Others began to ride up, and the groups flowed together, swelling every moment. When enough had gathered they rode forward in a black mass.

The first warning shots of the sentries rang out, but the danger had been discovered too late. The Cossacks had already spread out through the streets of the village. Blind, disorderly firing began. Nobody knew where to fire or at whom. The Red Army men jumped up and began running in all directions with nothing on but their underclothes. Complete disorganization was evident, as well as complete unpreparedness. Little isolated groups of people formed spontaneously, and those that had had time to seize rifles stopped anywhere they could find cover, and opened fire down the streets. Then they made off and ran on towards the river. The general direction taken by the retreating men was towards the bank of the Ural. At the edge of the village, the Cossacks galloped after the fleeing Red Army men, hewing them down, capturing them, driving them off somewhere. Here there was practically no resistance, but the Cossacks couldn't penetrate to the middle of the village. At one place several dozen men had gathered around Chapayev, and soon they lay down on the ground in a skirmish line. Chapayev himself had also run out in his underclothes, a rifle in his right hand, a revolver in his left. It had got quite light by now, and everything could be made out easily. There were two or three minutes of agonizing suspense, and then the men in the skirmish line saw a solid mass of Cossacks galloping down on them. They fired a volley, a second and a third. A machine-gun that had been dragged up began to chatter, and the Cossacks swept back.

In the neighbouring street, where the Political Department had its headquarters, some eighty men had gathered around Baturin. Among them were Novikov, Krainyukov, and Suvorov and almost all the workers in the Political Department. Seeing that the Cossack attacks were becoming more frequent and more stubborn, Baturin himself led his tiny detachment in a charge. The attack was so sudden that the Cossack machine-gunners, who were riding in waggons in front, jumped off and scattered, leaving two machine-guns in Baturin's hands. The machine-guns were at once turned on the enemy. At that moment, Novikov was severely wounded in the leg. He was dragged a little to one side, but the others didn't know what to do with him and left him there. He crawled to a hut, dragged himself in and hid under a bench. Baturin's group held out longer than any of the others, but surrounded on all sides, they believed till the very end that they were only a handful cut off from the main fighting and the main forces, which were somewhere near, most likely where Chapayev was. They perished in this belief. The various groups were isolated, and for that reason the success of one was entirely paralyzed by the mishaps of its neighbours. Nobody knew what was happening around him or what he should do himself. Seeing that they couldn't hope for quick victory by frontal attacks, part of the Cossacks dismounted, and making their way through gardens and back-yards, began to penetrate to the rear of the defenders.

When firing began in their rear, and the masses of Cossacks in front bore down on them, one charge after another, Baturin's group cracked and began to retreat and fall to pieces. Men dashed away, each intent on hiding wherever he could. Of course, not one of them saved himself. The inhabitants gave them all away, to the last man. The only people who saved themselves were those that ran to the Ural and succeeded in swimming across. Baturin ran into a hut and hid there somewhere under the stove, but the housewife gave him away immediately, telling the Cossacks that "this must be the commissar himself." The cursed woman evidently remembered the meeting when Pavel Stepanovich had made a speech to the villagers. When the infuriated Cossacks found out that the "commissar himself" had fallen into their hands, they didn't even think to try and learn something from him by questioning and torturing him. They were consumed with a brutal lust to get bloody revenge on him as quickly as possible. They dragged him outdoors. Each wanted to be the first to sink his sabre into the prisoner's chest. They brandished their rifles over his head, their swords crossed and rang together, as they waited with fiendish faces for him to be thrown to the ground. And as soon as he was thrown down, swords and bayonets were plunged into his stomach and throat and face. A bloody orgy began. But this was not enough. They seized him by the legs, and whirling his body over their heads brought it down with such a blow that his skull was cracked open and the brains dashed out. Then they ripped and tore and jabbed and cut his clothes. They kicked the lump of bloody flesh, each one trying to kick what had been the face. Several Red Army men who had been taken prisoner were standing nearby; they looked with horror at the remains of their fine commissar, Pavel Stepanovich Baturin. Hapless men! Almost every one of them died in a few minutes under the sabres of the Cossacks.

But where was Chapayev?

It had been impossible to remain in the trenches very long. The Cossacks penetrated these positions, too, from along the river. A retreat followed to the steep bank, which here rose high above the water. To climb the ridge meant making a target of themselves, but there was nothing else they could do. Cossack machine-guns had been placed at both sides, and they were keeping the river under fire, killing the swimmers that sought to save themselves by getting to the Bukhara side. Chapayev was hit in the arm. When he wiped his face, he left bloody stripes on his cheek and on his forehead. Petka was standing beside him all the time.

"Vasily Ivanovich, let me bind up your head," he shouted.

"That's all right—nothing wrong with my head."

"Your forehead's bleeding," Petka insisted in a choking voice.

"Leave off. It's all the same."

Step by step, they retreated to the steep bank. There was almost no hope. There were very few that succeeded in escaping across the rapid Ural, but they were determined that Chapayev should be saved.

"Help him down to the water!" shouted Petka.

Everybody understood who it was that was to be helped down. Four of the men standing close by helped Chapayev down the sandy slope, carefully supporting his bleeding arm. Chapayev and three others ran into the water and swam off. Two were killed at once, but two swam on. They were already at the other bank when a cruel bullet struck Chapayev in the head. When his companion, who had crawled out into the sedge, looked round, there was no one there. Chapayev had disappeared in the swift waters of the Ural.

Petka stayed on the bank till the end, when he had no more cartridges for his rifle. He then shot six bullets from his revolver into the advancing line of Cossacks, and the seventh into his own heart. The Cossacks glutted their insane rage on the dead body of this rank-and-file soldier, so small, but so noble and brave. It was only with great difficulty that his comrades later identified his body—a piece of bloody human flesh crushed into the sand.

Two months after this tragedy, the Revolutionary Military Council of the Republic awarded the gallant fighter Pyotr Isayev the Order of the Red Banner for his heroism. The award was two months late.

Along with Isayev, Chekov had retreated with the others to the very bank of the river. He was killed on the

sand before he could reach the water—a bullet hit him in the head. Now there was no more resistance anywhere. The Cossacks pursued the fleeing Red Army men. They overtook and caught them and chopped them to pieces on the spot.

"Yids, commissars and Communists—step out!"

And the Communists came forward, not wanting the other men to be killed. But this did not always save the others. They stepped out before the ranks of their comrades—so proud, so splendid in their silent bravery, with quivering lips and eyes burning with anger, with curses for the Cossack whips, and died under the Cossack blades and bullets. Others were led off to the field and mowed down with machine-guns. Three enormous pits left from brick-making outside the village were filled to the top with the bodies of those that had been shot.

... The brigades were holding positions at Sakharnaya and at Cossack villages farther up the river when the terrible news flew round: Headquarters had been destroyed and with it the Division Command and the Political Department; communications had been cut; the depots had been captured and there would be no ammunition, uniforms, boots, bread. The situation was catastrophic. The Red Army men were worn out with fighting, and weakened to the last degree by hunger; whole companies were ill and dying of typhus. Cut off, surrounded by the Cossacks, their commanders gone—what could they do?

Sizov assumed command of the division—nobody appointed him, nobody confirmed him—he took command himself because there was no time to wait. With sorrow and horror, the soldiers passed the tragic news from one to another until soon all of them down to the last man knew what had happened at Lbishchensk.

"Shall we go forward or back?" they asked one another, not knowing that the new commander of the orphaned division had himself not yet decided this agonizing question: forward or back?

To continue their advance was senseless. To go back meant they would have to break through the Cossack masses at Lbishchensk with their bare hands. But in the second alternative there was at least a glimmer of hope. In the first, there was not even this hope of success—nothing but destruction, quick and sure. It was decided to retreat immediately, evacuating their positions unnoticed, endeavouring to confuse the enemy so as to get the better of his watchfulness.

The first brigade was to leave Mergenyovsky, to be followed soon after by the second brigade, which was stationed at Sakharnaya. It was decided to set off at night, and so quietly that the enemy would never guess that the Red regiments were retreating. A solid ring was thrown round the transports and artillery, and the division cavalry was left as rear-guard. Slowly, quietly, the brigade moved off into the darkness. Fires were left burning in the village—let the Cossacks think that the Red soldiers were still peacefully warming themselves at them.

The Red soldiers were moving farther and farther into the steppe. Commands were whispered and passed on from mouth to mouth down the invisible lines and columns. A wheel might creak, someone's foot might be crushed and he would groan involuntarily, someone might smother a dull cough in his fist—then again silence, silence all round. They did not march, but seemed to fly on wings. The settlement of Karshinsky had been left behind, and Mergenyovsky was in sight. At that moment, from afar came the muffled thunder of an explosion. The division cavalry covering the retreat had blown up the last of the shells that had been left in Sakharnaya because there was no way of carrying them away. As soon as the shells had been destroyed the cavalry set off at a trot to catch up with the units that had long gone before them.

They marched for almost two days and nights without any rest. They might sink to the ground for a moment and then on again—there was no time to stop—every minute was dear. The second night they got to Lbishchensk. The Cossacks had left the place the day before the first brigade arrived from Mergenyovsky, and had marched up the river towards Uralsk. They were also hurrying, and banked on the suddenness and unexpectedness of their blow. They considered the Red brigades that had been cut off as doomed—they would be finished off from Sakharnaya! But they themselves—on to Uralsk as quickly as possible! But it all turned out differently, quite differently! The "doomed" men remained alive and whole.

Now the second brigade was passing through the sinister, bloody Lbishchensk. The village was still a frightful place—dead and deserted. The dead Red Army men still lay in the streets, their bodies run through with bayonets, slashed with sabres, riddled with bullets. The first brigade had not stopped here but had pushed towards Kozhekharov. The men of the second brigade gathered up the dead bodies, carried them away and buried them. They went out into the fields and there, in common graves, buried those who had been shot down by the hundreds, by the Cossack machine-guns. There were no words of farewell, there was no funeral march. The soldiers knelt on the ground, their heads bared, motionless and speechless over the precious graves, their hearts heavy with sorrow, their minds filled with stern thoughts.

They did not halt in Lbishchensk long, but again set out. Here, they were overtaken by the Cossack units that had been pursuing them from Sakharnaya, and a battle began—a battle to the death. The Cossacks could not believe that these exhausted men could resist, and launched furious attacks against them in their haste to finish what they had neglected to do before. But the Red regiments, seemingly doomed to destruction, broke away from the iron embrace of death, forced their way through, beat off attacks, and showed again and again what the regiments of the Chapayev Division were capable of.

They got to the hamlet of Yanaisky at night. They were completely worn out, couldn't keep on their feet. The men at once fell into a dead sleep. Even the sentries couldn't keep awake. The Red camp was like a kingdom of the dead. The Cossacks made preparations for a sudden blow. Their lines crept up till they were almost on top of the Reds. They approached to within a few paces, but were afraid to begin in the impenetrable darkness. They waited for the first faint hint of dawn. Masses of cavalry were thrown out on to the flanks to be ready to give chase to the fleeing, terror-stricken Red Army men. Everything was ready. Death was hovering over the Red units.

The Cossacks' first attack was by way of a trial to see if there would be a panic or not. Would the Red Army men run or would they hold their ground? Just as soon as the thick black September night began to turn to grey, there was a thunderous shout from the Cossack lines: "Hurrah! Hurrah! Hurrah!" The Cossacks began to fire in volleys, and from somewhere in the rear, their guns began to boom.

Sound asleep though they had been, the Red Army men sprang up, seizing their rifles. But there was no order, no organized resistance. The first Cossack bullets had brought down a number of the commanders. Confusion set in. No one knew what to do at once. The men were waiting for orders, and no orders came. Resistance was isolated, haphazard, unsteady. The disorder grew, the confusion increased. A mad, disastrous panic was imminent. Nikolai Khrebtov, commander of the division artillery, he who had done such good work at Krasny Yar, ran up to the guns, but not one of the gunners was in his place. Some had run to the waggons, some were lying flat with their heads pressed close to the ground, trying to save themselves from the enemy's fire. With his shouts, Khrebtov got the men on their feet, and fired a shell, then another and another, and the battery began a fierce devastating bombardment. This was enough to prevent a panic. As soon as the men saw and heard their batteries firing, they took new heart, and now new commanders appeared in place of those that had been killed. A stubborn, bloody battle began. Even the veteran commanders of the Chapayev Division had seen few such battles. From merely resisting, the Red units themselves charged, and then again froze to the ground when the machine-gun fire became unbearable.

Two enemy armoured cars advanced on the Red lines with a roar and crash, one across the plain, in the open, the other along a deep gulley, around their flank. This was nothing new for the men. They pressed themselves tighter to the ground, and lay motionless, waiting. When the first monster approached, Nikolai Khrebtov landed a shell square on the turret, and the machine gave a lurch and stalled where it was! The men again charged and gave the enemy a trouncing. Then they again dug in and waited for the answering charge.

The Cossacks were driven back several versts. Many Red soldiers were killed in the fighting at Yanaisky, but even more Cossacks were left on the field. In places, they lay in rows where whole skirmish lines had been mowed down by the implacable machine-guns.

There were no more battles like that of Yanaisky. Reinforcements soon came up. The Cossacks were driven back through the hamlets and villages where but a few days before, the Red regiments had hurried away before the pursuing Whites. Now the Red regiments again launched an offensive, and they did not stop till they reached Guryev and the shores of the Caspian Sea.

They marched through Lbishchensk, and stood motionless over the common graves; they sang funeral songs, and vowed to fight on to victory, to carry on with the cause of those who with selfless valour had given up their lives along the banks and in the waves of the turbulent Ural.

1923

Printed in the United States
210646BV00001B/10/A